AGAINST THE ODDS

He was a freelance journalist in the Soviet Union. She was an American student, in Moscow for a year of study. When Andrei Frolov and Lois Becker met in Moscow's central Lenin Library, a friendship began that grew into a love affair. In May, 1981, the two married in Moscow.

What started as a personal relationship between two people soon became a complex and dangerous political game. The KGB harassed the Frolovs and the Soviet government denied Andrei his right to emigrate in order to live with his wife in America. The United States Department of State discouraged Lois from taking any political action to secure Andrei's release. Left to their own resources, the Frolovs eventually embarked on a hunger strike, to end either in Andrei's release or in death.

Their ultimate victory was a victory of ordinary citizens over superpower politics, of individual will over the might of the Soviet State.

Against the Odds is the Frolov's account of the love for which they risked everything, and of their long struggle to bridge two cultures and two political systems in order to live together as a family.

The Frolovs pose after their wedding outside the "Palace of Weddings" in Moscow.

AGAINST THE ODDS

A True American-Soviet Love Story

By

Andrei Frolov

and

Lois Becker Frolova

ANDREI FROLOV'S SECTIONS TRANSLATED FROM
THE RUSSIAN BY LOIS BECKER FROLOVA

Chicago Review Press

CHICAGO

Cover photo by Jose More, Chicago Tribune

Copyright © 1983 by Andrei Frolov and Lois Becker Frolova
All rights reserved.
Printed in the United States of America
First Edition
Published by Chicago Review Press, 213 West Institute Place, Chicago, Illinois 60610
ISBN 0-914091-37-9

Library of Congress Cataloging in Publication Data

Frolov, Andrei, 1931-
Against the odds.

"Andrei Frolov's sections translated from the Russian
by Lois Becker Frolova."
1. Frolov, Andrei, 1931-   . 2. Frolova, Lois Becker, 1954-
3. Soviet Union—Biography.
4. United States—Biography.
I. Frolova, Lois Becker, 1954-   II. Title.
CT1218.F75A33   1983   947.085'4'0922 [B]   83-15114
ISBN 0-914091-37-9

TABLE OF CONTENTS

FOREWORD *by Vladimir Bukovsky*   vii

AUTHORS' PREFACE   *xi*

PART I

CHAPTER

1 WE MEET   *3*

The Lenin Library. . .An American in Moscow

2 THE FRIENDSHIP CONTINUES   *21*

The Old Neighborhood. . .Falling in Love. . .Foreigners. . .The First Disturbances. . .The Lubianka. . .Commitment

3 MARRIAGE   *59*

Embassy Reactions. . .Leningrad (Andrei). . .Leningrad (Lois). . .Fate and Lois. . .The Wedding

PART II

4 THE HONEYMOON   *89*

Red Tape and Alla . . . Left Alone

5 SEPARATION   *108*

Life of a Refusenik. . .The Second Refusal. . .Home in Chicago

6 THE HUNGER STRIKE   *136*

Decision to Strike. . .An American Participant. . .To the Death?

7 THE 26 DAYS   *156*

Sleeplessness. . .Court and Washington. . .The Demonstration. . .Recalling My Past

PART III

8 THE LAST ROUND   *227*

An Open Fight. . .Holding Out. . .Exit. . .Reunion

EPILOGUE: PSYCHOLOGY OF AN EMIGRE   *245*

FOREWORD

Why should a superpower take such enormous interest in harassing two people just for being in love with each other? Indeed, after one reads about the twenty-four hour surveillance by specially trained KGB teams, in shifts, with their specially equipped cars and their walkie-talkies, about the twenty-four hour telephone bugging, and the numerous *stukachi* (informers) in the communal apartment, one is left with a feeling of something unreal, almost nightmarish. And all this trouble, this spectacular police operation, is just to prevent two people from getting married? The sheer cost of such an "operation" must be astronomical, to say nothing of the politically damaging international scandal. Why bother?

This question will undoubtedly come to a reader's mind after closing this book. And it is a very good question indeed, particularly for those "sophisticated" people who still call "simplistic" any straightforward condemnation of the communist system. Or, better still, for those who are so sure of the peaceful intentions of the Soviets and who advocate a "dialogue" between our nations. If we are to accept their beliefs, why then are the Soviet people forced by their peace-loving government to treat any foreigner from a non-communist country as an enemy? Why is a marriage between an American and a Russian looked upon as high treason? What kind of a dialogue can we have, if only specially trusted informers are allowed to approach a foreigner?

Simplistic or not, the truth of the matter is that in a totalitarian state a man is a property of the state. And a cheap property to boot. He is just a pawn in a dangerous game played by the rulers. A walking function. It is only naive people of the West who believe that they live in a time of peace. From the day of its creation the Soviet Union has been at war with the West, and the people are forced to be soldiers of this war. In this context, a manifestation of simple human feeling is perceived by the state as a mutiny.

The authors of this book know these answers as well as anybody who once has felt the whole weight of the Soviet machine on his or her shoulders. However, instead of generalizations, they give a detailed account of their ordeal, patiently leading us through the jungles of Soviet life with its Kafka-esque absurdity to an unexpectedly happy ending. They describe only the facts they have witnessed. Yet, their book is a real dialogue, the only one possible between an American and a Russian in our time, a dialogue of partners fighting together against the communist slavery.

For an American it is a painful process of losing naivety, of learning to be a responsible and reliable partner in a situation where, unlike back at home, life is a very serious business and any careless word may prove to be fatal. For a Russian it is a no less painful process of "squeezing the slave out of oneself drop by drop," as Chekhov once put it. What seems to be a purely personal affair at the beginning, at the end becomes a fight for human dignity between two people on one side and the most oppressive regime of modern times on the other. As it happens so often in the Soviet Union, an individual's victory becomes a victory for all serfs of the state. Indeed, the same people who are obliged to condemn the rebel publicly, would secretly congratulate him and express their gratitude. Thus an ordinary Soviet man suddenly becomes a new creature, known in the West under the strange name of "dissident."

Nobody knows what this word really means. Created by the Western press, it was never used by the "dissidents" themselves, who prefer a more modest name: *"pravozashchitniki,"* that is, "defenders of law." In practical terms it simply means that these people appeal to the law as it is written in the Soviet constitution or in an international agreement—hardly a revolutionary idea in any country but the communist one. Because the day when the people learn to demand their rights will be the last day of the communist regime.

Meanwhile, the original meaning of the word "dissident" was somehow lost.

"Oh, no, I was not a dissident," says a ballet dancer to the press after defecting to the West. "I simply could not accept the lack of freedom to create according to my tastes."

"No, we are not dissidents," says a group of workers at a press conference in Moscow. "We simply decided to organize an independent trade union to protect the rights of workers."

"We, the Jews in the Soviet Union, were not dissidents," writes a recent emigrant to Israel in his book. "We were defending the national rights of our people."

Perhaps that is why the Western press has announced the end of the "dissident movement" in the Soviet Union every year during the last decade, while the number of the "non-dissidents" continues to grow quite steadily.

The authors of this book also are quite sure that they are not dissidents. They simply loved each other, and this human feeling appeared to be stronger that the Soviet regime. In the eternal fight of living against dying, of freedom against slavery, they have scored a small victory for everybody. Well, it is a good enough reason for me to call them "*pravozashchit'niki*".

Vladimir Bukovsky
Stanford, California
June, 16, 1983

Ours is a story of two people from different ends of the earth, from opposite worlds, from opposite systems—one, an American graduate student, the other, a Soviet journalist. We met in a library cafeteria in Moscow. The differences in our backgrounds fascinated us, and actually drew us closer together. We fell in love and were married.

Our innocent romance aroused the antagonism of the most powerful police agency in the world. We were followed and harassed by the KGB. Our letters were read, our phone conversations tapped. Finally, the Soviet government denied us the right to live together, either in Moscow or in the United States. Our lives fell into the all too common pattern of divided families and Soviet refuseniks. Andrei, twice denied permission to emigrate, lost his profession and his position in society. Our marriage was "against the interests of the Soviet State." We had no hope for the future.

To claim our internationally guaranteed right to live together, we were forced to announce to world media a hunger strike to the death. We were ordinary citizens, neither one experienced in politics, and we were thrown into an international game between two superpowers. We could hardly even communicate with each other, yet we acted in perfect unison. In Moscow Andrei outwitted KGB agents while in Chicago Lois sued the Soviet Government and forced the United States Government to take steps to support the rights of its citizens. The result: on June 20, 1982, we were reunited in Chicago's O'Hare Airport, ending a long struggle for freedom.

We wrote this book for Americans. Every day Americans read in the newspapers and see on television stories about the Soviet Union, but very few can imagine what life in the Soviet Union is like for an ordinary citizen. Especially for one who has fallen into disfavor for some innocent act. We wanted our story to be known so that Americans might better understand the Soviet Union from the inside and through a simple example. We act on the principle that the world is reflected in a single drop of water.

PART I

CHAPTER 1

WE MEET

A F

I met Lois in the Lenin Library, formerly the Rumiantsev Library. It is the central library of the nation, and is located accordingly in the center of Moscow—in the center of the Soviet Union. My Moscow life from birth was lived in the heart of town on Kropotkin Street. Our flat was not at all far from the library which I began to visit regularly at the age of fourteen. The library became my favorite place in Moscow. For me, it truly was the center of the Soviet Union.

I first started going to the small reading hall, the Hall for Youth. When I became a student I moved to the general hall located in the former house of the nobleman Pashkov. It was constructed on a hill facing the Kremlin according to the plan of the famous Russian architect Bazhenov. Inside the general reading hall the marble bas-relief has been preserved and antique statues still stand along the walls.

After completing my education as an engineer I moved to the new, enormous and stylish building constructed under Soviet rule, with marble on the facade as well as inside. In this library there are different halls for different types of library users. Not everyone is allowed to enter every hall. Hall No. 1, for instance, is for the chosen: for professors and academicians and foreigners. I had permission to use the general reading hall, Hall No.3.

The library has one room of books for open use. That is, a reader may browse through the books and check them out to be read in his or her assigned hall. One does not take books home from the Lenin Library. Books in the basic holdings are issued by order, and not every order for every person is filled. The Lenin Library has an enormous administration with a great many departments among which, as in all Soviet organizations, is "the first department," the secret department under the direct subordination of the KGB. Soviet society preserves this structure everywhere. It is impossible even to read a book without it.

The luxurious internal and external decoration of the new building is supposed to personify the flowering of Soviet culture. The halls of the library are always filled with people, but for a good half of the people the library is above all a place of solitude from work and a refuge from their crowded Moscow apartments, crammed with relatives and neighbors.

For the last ten years, earning a living as a journalist, I went to the library to write my essays and articles. I liked working there. In moments of relaxation I would look through books that I had not yet read, or pace the corridors of oaken parquet, or walk along the gallery of the main staircase with its wide marble steps, bronze chandeliers and high ceilings, several stories high and also bearing decoration.

I worked for many years running as a freelance journalist—"on free bread," in Russian. I worked mainly for *Around the World,* a former geographic magazine, now a youth adventure magazine. I wrote essays of a romantic nature about people with romantic occupations such as geologists, sailors, pilots, etc. The magazine sent me to distant places in Siberia, the Far East, and the North. I also worked for the magazine *Village Youth,* for which I wrote so-called "critical material" about various problems in country life and agriculture. In these articles I was allowed to criticize certain shortcomings of Soviet agriculture but under no circumstances was I allowed to touch upon their basic cause that lay in the social framework. Several of these essays I adapted into scenarios for the Center for Scientific Films, several were reprinted in other magazines, and several were broadcast over the radio.

My life was fairly settled. I lived with a relative degree of independence, having no supervisor or work hours, avoiding assemblies and meetings, sometimes evading the requirement to vote in elections for Soviet official organs, participation in which always struck me as humiliating. I did not read Soviet newspapers which Soviet employees in responsible positions were obligated to read. No one forced me to study at seminars on Marxism-Leninism. I learned of world news through

Western radio broadcasts, and sometimes managed to get my hands on literature forbidden by the Soviet government. I myself wrote for the "desk drawer," a common practice in the Soviet Union where it is impossible to write open and honest material for publication, but where people continue to write as they please, stashing their works away in a desk drawer. And sometimes I managed to slip into a viewing of a film that was closed to the general public. I was alone, lived alone, had no close relatives. But I did not feel lonely for I had enough friends. In the existing conditions of Soviet life I could hardly imagine a life for myself that would have been better.

It was a bright fall day in Moscow. I had just handed in the usual essay to my editor and was spending time in the library reading. If I was going to be in the library I always tried to eat in the cafeteria. The library cafeteria is extremely foul, but most of the cafeterias in Moscow are foul except, of course, those which are closed to the public. I always tried to select a time to eat when there would be the least number of people in the cafeteria so as not to lose time in long lines, twenty minutes, thirty minutes, or more. Frequenting the cafeterias at off hours, it was even possible to eat seated. The majority of tables were designed for standing. There were three tables with chairs along one wall, but only the handicapped and library workers had the right to use them. The space allotted to the cafeteria was so small that to have filled it with tables for seating would have been senseless. There would have been too few tables and the lines would have been even longer.

Thus, one day, not in the slightest suspecting how important this day would be in my life, I descended to the library basement, to the cafeteria. Half of the seats at the three tables were empty and I set my plate down at a vacant table. A bit later a young woman sat down at the same table. She was very small and looked a bit like a little boy. She wore pants and a shirt and a tie. I had to assume she was a foreigner for Moscow women had not yet started to wear ties. The extravagant style made me think she was French. After her two women in blue robes, library employees, sat down at the table. The small woman was Lois. She fished a dictionary out of her purse and started to ask me what the dish she was eating was called. I explained and at once became interested — who was she and from where?

As it turned out she was a graduate student from Stanford Universi-

ty who had come to Moscow on an exchange program. We talked, all
the while consulting the dictionary, I in search of English words and she
of Russian. As we leafed through the dictionary our hands accidentally
met. From a distance one would not have thought that this was a
conversation between two people who had not known each other just
five minutes before. The women in blue robes sitting next to us began
to get upset.

It must be said that the casual acquaintance of a Soviet citizen with
a foreigner is considered reprehensible according to the official morality. However, the official morality does not stipulate that a Soviet citizen
should be rude and uncivilized and, therefore, he should not explain to
the foreigner that he is supposed to break off their burgeoning acquaint-
anceship.

Lois and I continued to converse. The ladies became more upset.
Like many simple people in the Soviet Union who work in places
frequented by foreigners, these women understood the rules of Soviet
morality literally. They were taught at work assemblies that there are
spies among the foreigners who engage in ideological subversion. These
spies bring foreign literature into the Soviet Union, transfer information
to the West that discredits the Soviet Union and, in general, lead honest,
innocent Soviet citizens astray through unauthorized conversations that
serve to spread Western ideology. It is with exactly such words that such
people are instructed at work.

In my youth I worked on a ship that went abroad and my comrades
and I received similar warnings from the political workers that were
assigned to our ship. They tried to drum it into our heads that waiting
for us at every port were people who had prepared various provocations
to try to gain command over our souls. Of course, in reality no such
things ever occurred, but to express disbelief in the words of the First
Assistant to the Captain in the Political Section was simply not done. A
person expressing such disbelief would quickly take final leave of his job.

It is to "protect" foreigners from unplanned friendships with Soviet
people in the library, that the authorities assign them to Reading Hall
No. 1 where only academicians and professors study. It stands to reason
that such people, generally old, highly value their reputations at work
and position in society and would not think of striking up an acquaintance with a young foreign graduate student.

Those for whom such acquaintances are allowed comprise a special category. They are given special instructions on how to conduct themselves and they report back to party organizations on how their friendships are proceeding. Such people are immediately recognizeable by the thin veneer of officialdom in their clothes and in their manners, and they occupy respectable and successful positions in society. They would never dare to be rude to a foreigner and rather remind one of shop clerks, pre-Revolutionary of course, showering false courtesies and flattery on prospective clients.

The women sitting at our table rudely and unceremoniously butted into our conversation. They started to say that the library was not a place for meeting people, the cafeteria even less so, and they discussed with one another "correct" behavior in the Soviet Union, that is, the official morality. These women did not doubt for a moment that I, a Soviet man, was conducting myself poorly by conversing so long with a foreigner. When I politely remarked that they were interfering in our conversation, that we had not asked them about Soviet morality, the uniformed ladies became furious and announced that I was occupying a place that I had no right to occupy. Since there were so few people in the cafeteria at the time I felt that I could sit where I pleased, but I had not the slightest desire to argue with them. I got up from my place, taking my plate with me.

Lois had difficulty understanding what was happening, but it was undoubtedly clear to her that it had something to do with Soviet morals and manners. The women in uniform had by some right interfered in a private conversation and in other people's relations. She followed behind me with her plate. We continued our lunch standing. I was internally grateful to her for the show of solidarity. For her, this was the first lesson in Soviet reality. Two uneducated women decided that next to them something was happening of which the authorities would disapprove, and therefore they could be coarse, impolite, ill-mannered. Lois did not understand by what right these women had scolded me, why I did not become indignant, why it is permissible to sit at some tables and not at others, why she had to study in the hall assigned to her and not, let's say, in the general reading room. In the future she would come to see many people behave in such a fashion: police, customs officials, administrators in hotels — even the neighbors in my communal apartment. She would feel surprise and indignation more and more often, and tire of both as she looked about in quiet amazement. She was born in another country with a completely different regard for the human individual.

LBF

When I met Andrei I had been living a month in the Soviet Union. I was one of eleven American students who had come from all over the United States for a year's worth of research in the archives and libraries of Moscow. Once before, at the age of seventeen, I had traveled to the Soviet Union, but this time around everything was to be different.

The first time I had come with my parents, brother and sister. We spent two weeks in the Soviet Union as tourists, our time split between Moscow and Leningrad. The foreigner who does not know the Russian language and who comes to the Soviet Union for only a short while is given a very limited glimpse into Soviet life. He or she stays at special "Intourist" hotels where only foreigners and special Soviets live. The quality of the rooms and restaurants surpass anything available to the regular Soviet. One must show a pass in order to enter an Intourist hotel. The guards at the doors have an excellent eye for spotting Westerners and Soviets attempting to pass as Westerners. The foreign tourist is shuttled about on special tours in special buses all designed to show the visitor the best view of Soviet life. A common stop on these tours is at a *Beriozka* store—a special store for foreigners. The Soviet officials hope that the foreigner will plunk down some of their "hard" foreign currency—*valuta* in Russian—in exchange for items that are not found in ordinary stores for Soviet citizens. After a busy day of sightseeing and shopping the foreigner will take in an evening at the Bolshoi or the Mariinsky Theaters, tickets for which are impossible for the ordinary Soviet citizen to obtain without using connections and paying exorbitant prices.

Foreign visitors might complain about certain shortcomings in their accomodations, about how the quality and variety of their meals decrease as the tour continues, and about the lack of acceptable souvenirs to choose from. But they have been given the first and best of everything. It clouds their vision. They make judgements about the Soviet Union on the basis of what they have been shown: the closed stores, the closed hotels, the special seats to the theater. They have no idea how distant all that is from everyday Soviet reality. It is a trick like that played on Catherine the Great by one of her ministers and lovers, Commander General Potemkin. When Catherine went on a royal tour to inspect the reforms being undertaken in the countyside, the good General had scores of impromptu villages built along the road that the Empress traveled upon, thus giving her the impression that the Empire's money was well-spent and the conditions of her serfs' lives were improving. Similarly the foreign visitor is treated to a show of "Potemkin villages," as the Russian expression goes.

This time, however, at age twenty-seven, I had come to the Soviet Union for nine months to gather research on my dissertation. I would be living and working amongst Soviet citizens. I was excited at the prospect of seeing the Soviet Union behind the Potemkin villages set up for tourists. Yet, despite close contact with Soviet citizens I was not to be in the mainstream of Soviet life. Over and over again I found that being a foreigner was all-important; it determined my living conditions and my relationships with people. "Foreigner" was my offical status and my social position. In every way we foreigners were privileged and apart from the rest of Soviet society. Some Soviets refer to foreigners as "whites" and to themselves as "blacks." Evoking visions of our own not so distant past in America, they joke about the closed "Intourist" hotels and *Beriozka* shops where entrance is "for whites only." As exchange students we were not given the luxuries reserved for foreign tourists, but nonetheless we received the special treatment that the Soviet Union offers its own most important citizens.

We were given accomodations in the dormitories at Moscow University, for twenty years considered the best that a university student could aspire to. The campus grounds are extensive, but the majority of offices and classes and all of the dormitories are in one monstrosity of a building. Its dimensions are massive with four wings and a main corpus. There certainly are taller and larger buildings in the United States, but this building is of solid stone and its every line emphasizes its significance. It was built in the famous Stalinist "wedding-cake style" with various tiers and ornate carvings leading up to the red star on the top of a spire.

Standing in front of Moscow University one cannot help but feel dwarfed and overcome by its granite might. Its wings stick out from the central corpus like legs on a spider and the individual feels like a fly in its midst.

We Americans lived two to a *blok*: in other words, we shared a toilet, shower and sink and each had our own room. The room was small, long and narrow, perhaps six feet by twelve feet, and the bathroom had long ago been taken over by large, slow-moving cockroaches. It was not paradise but it was assigned to me alone and that constituted its luxury to Soviet students. On the other side of the dormitory and on the floors where there were no foreigners from capitalist countries, Soviet students often lived two, and in some instances as many as four, to a room. Only the cream of the crop and those living in close proximity to foreigners were granted the privilege of their own quarters.

Besides these living arrangements, my income also was provided by the state. As a foreign student from a capitalist country I received a living stipend of 220 rubles a month—almost two and a half times the stipend of a typical Soviet student of my age and training. The 220 rubles was barely adequate for us Westerners. I have no idea how the Soviet student got by on his 90 rubles a month, which is the equivalent of a half a pair of blue jeans, the student uniform in the Soviet Union.

In such a privileged position, I was left only with the problem of obtaining food—the greatest everyday concern of Soviets. They spend an incredible amount of time and energy in the pursuit of nutritious and appealing foods, often taking off from work in order to stand in line. People travel to Moscow and other major cities to acquire the basic foodstuffs that are not available in other parts of the country. We students got by on the regular methods and by taking advantage of a number of sources open to us as foreigners.

Every floor of the dormitory had two kitchens, thirty people to a kitchen. Thirty people cannot share one kitchen. It is difficult to feel a strong sense of responsibility for a facility used by so many people and the kitchen was usually filthy. The alternative was to eat in the student cafeteria which, like all Soviet cafeterias, is a hit or miss proposition. On some days the food was quite nice, hot and filling. On other days it was abysmal, inedible and appetite-depressing.

I took to eating bread and chocolate, both of which are quite delicious in Moscow, if bought fresh. For nourishment I ate at people's homes, a fairly frequent occurrence. Any invitation by a Soviet results in a meal.

It is amazing what people will serve in their homes. Moscow food stores offer so little: cabbage, carrots, potatoes, meat of poor quality, canned fish. And yet in one home after another the foreigner is treated to a feast, from appetizers to dessert. In the beginning I asked: "How is it possible? I didn't see any of these foods in the stores?" Some people smiled in answer, some people laughed. Soviets had long ago formed other outlets. A huge illegal or semilegal market in food exists. People establish their own networks for getting food, food that is skimmed off the top of government stocks and sold at great profit. You can read about it in any political science text but you only understand it when you go to a friend's apartment and sit down to eat *blini* (Russian crepes) with black and red caviar and lingonberry jam for dessert after you have spent the afternoon running after eight mealy apples, a can of sardines and a half-kilo of macaroni.

While I did not use these illegal outlcts I soon received instructions on how to better my diet. I went to the open air market where farmers brought the fresh fruits and vegetables they had raised on their own small land parcels that the state had granted to them for private use. The prices were very high, but I had the money.

I also had the option of using my hard currency at the diplomatic grocery store. In this store the Soviet government itself has skimmed from the top of its stocks in order to provide its foreign guests with edible produce, in exchange for *valuta.* Here the food is expensive, but there are no lines and the variety and quality are vastly better than in the stores for Soviets. For some reason the liquor was cheap, a liter of Stolichnaya vodka, which is not available to Soviet citizens, came to $4.50, so I always brought liquor to greet my hosts who fed me.

We students were feeding only ourselves and not a family. We had money, the diplomatic store and frequent invitations to dine at people's homes. Still, despite our advantages, we experienced the pressure involved in obtaining food. We stood in lines, in crowds with people pushing from all sides, everyone trying to get just that much closer to the counter even though the number of customers ahead in line remained the same. We witnessed fights erupting over places in line. We came to master the system of standing in more than one line at a time.

And finally we came to understand that tense, glum look of Muscovites as they pushed and shoved and bustled down the street, ever-pressured by the problem of providing themselves and their families with the basic necessities and a few touches here and there.

Of course, a country is most keenly experienced through contacts with its people, but again my status as a foreigner determined with whom I had relations and the nature of those relations.

Russians say that Americans think only about money, that Americans use one another and act solely out of self-interest. I found much of this avarice in the Soviet Union, as well as much of its opposite. In every society one gets by on a developed sense, an instinct based on experience about who wants what from whom. In the Soviet Union the rules of the game were so different that in the beginning I had no sense, no instinct to rely on. Like the fly before the spider, at times I felt overwhelmed and helpless.

Dormitory life in Moscow presented an odd mix of people. Our floor was filled with students from capitalist countries—America, England, West Germany, France, Holland and Japan. There were a few Russians on the floor as well but most of the other inhabitants were either from Soviet Central Asia or from Arab countries. There was a veritable platoon of Palestinian Freedom Fighters and their families. For some reason the Palestinian students liked to congregate in the center of the floor. Day or night, as I stepped out of the elevator I was met by a group of Palestinians playing backgammon on the couch next to the floor phone.

Half of the Americans had been placed at one end of the floor where several students from the British Isles had already been living. They seemed quite happy to see us and the first introductions took place a half hour after our arrival. There was a Welshman, an Englishman and a third fellow they called the "Lord." The "Lord" had bright red hair and a striking face, was a bit overweight and spoke in the most beautiful upper crust English. He smiled when his colleagues joked about his aristrocratic heritage, but we had no reason to distrust the truth of what they said.

We stood in the corridor, these three fellows, my roommate, and I, gabbing on and on. We had a myriad questions, technical questions, such as where certain university offices were located, what were the procedures for acquiring all the necessary ID's and passes. We then began to speak in general about conditions in the dorm and in Moscow. They wanted to know what sort of things we had brought with us—if any of them would serve us well in exchange for rubles. The Welshman did most of the talking. He kept poking the Lord in the side and saying: "That's right, isn't it?" The Lord did not respond directly. He spoke about the importance of improving our Russian, how we could best do this, and what cultural events we ought to attend.

The Welshman became more animated. He seemed to be chuckling, enjoying a private joke. Finally he came clean.

"So where do you think the Lord is from? Where did he get his schooling?" he asked.

Judging by his impeccable English I was tempted to say Oxford, but the Welshman broke in.

"Here. He's from here! He's a Sov!"

Sure enough the Lord had received his excellent training in Moscow. I had never heard anyone speak English as a second language that well. I was impressed. But why had we been talking about selling things in front of him? Why had he asked about our friends in Moscow?

The Lord was the only Soviet who lived on our side of the floor. He was always polite and helpful. A week never went by when he did not knock on our door with an offer of tea and a "heart-to-heart" in English. We talked a lot about Soviet theater and film and student life. He was curious about my other acquaintances in Moscow: "Oh really, you went to see that new film on Dostoevsky? With whom?"

Our conversations rarely rolled around to politics. He acted as if politics did not interest him and everything in the political realm had long ago been understood and decided. He casually asked about life in America, as if that did not really interest him, when actually he was bursting to hear about the size of my apartment and my car. Occasionally he would interject a question about the availability and cost of certain items in the United States—items that interest any student of any country: sporting equipment, photographic equipment, motorcycles and cars. I would answer these questions explaining the various models and alternatives that exist, to which he invariably replied, "Yes, you have so much in America, but no one can afford to buy anything."

My first week in Moscow also brought a visit from Vladimir, a "businessman." A knock at my door and he introduced himself.

"Well, hello. So this year's crop of Americans has arrived. I've been waiting for you."

He was in his late twenties, well dressed, with short clipped hair and a breezy, familiar manner of speech. He proceeded to run off a list of names of Americans he knew from previous exchanges. He seemed to know someone from every university that we represented, and it was comforting to hear him speak the names of people we knew. He invited us out, to parties, to restaurants closed to the general public. It seemed that every few nights he was entertaining a group of Americans. He always had lots of money, even dollars.

He was a shady figure, an expression that is identical in Russian and in English although the Soviet context has invested this expression with added meaning. I began to avoid him and none too soon. One night Vladimir arranged a big party at his apartment in one of the new sections of Moscow. Several of the American students went. After they had dined on shrimps and beer the police came to the door and arrested the lot of them for disturbing the peace. It was only 9:30 P.M. Vladimir was furious. He paraded about the police station making indignant speeches and bringing up his father's name at every possible occasion. (As it turned out, Vladimir's father was a major official in Siberia.) After a three hour wait everyone was released. We later learned that the apartment was not Vladimir's —he was not even registered to live in Moscow, but somewhere in Siberia. However, Vladimir was not thrown out of the city. Every now and then he would show up even though everyone now went out of their way to avoid him. He asked a lot of questions and was already in posession of a lot of the answers.

I eventually understood that Vladimir was a *fartsovshchik*—a person who speculates in foreign goods. In the Soviet Union one has to "obtain" almost everything, that is, either buy goods on the black market or through acquaintances. All Soviets live by a system of contacts, from the salesclerk at a store to a famous writer or actress. *Fartsovshchiki* and speculators, those who deal more exclusively in Soviet items, can help in everything; they can obtain all the necessities, depending on their specialties. Some specialize in clothing, others in stereo equipment and recordings, others in books and art, and others in theater tickets or entrance into exclusive reataurants. A large part of their business depends on foreigners, and the items and currency they bring into the country.

If a foreigner does not intend to do anything more illegal than selling a few pairs of blue jeans, then *fartsovshchiki* are harmless. Still, it is often with their help that the Soviet authorities bring foreigners under their control. Many of them cooperate with the police or with the KGB, depending on the category of foreigners and goods with which they deal. As long as they do not work at cross purposes with the government their association with foreigners is not dangerous for them, and the security forces will continue to ignore their illegal activities.

Vladimir was an obvious case of a long-time *fartsovshchik* who enjoyed government sanction of his activities. Less obvious but more disturbing was my friendship with a woman named Nina. Nina was thirty years old and she lived with her ten-year-old son from her first marriage. She was very hospitable, always inviting me over and feeding me well. Her refrigerator was stocked with delicacies. Her son was clever and playful—amused by the fact that an adult could speak Russian no better than he and eager to give me language lessons. Nina and I talked about clothes—she was terribly interested in Western fashions—and about men, another strong interest. It was pleasant to gossip idly in a language I had so long used only for reading the most serious materials. I enjoyed her company and we became friends. I came to confide in her and ask her advice.

Nina was a clothes designer but from what I could tell she went to work only a couple of days a week. She was always on the phone. As soon as she put the receiver down the phone rang again. Nina "arranged things," she brought people together. If she could not get something for you then she would find someone who could. She was a *fartsovshchik* and a speculant. This alone did not bother me, I had already met so many *fartsovshchiki*, dealers in antiques, in rare books, in furniture. Many of them had amassed fortunes and Nina seemed like a small fish next to them. However, as I began to understand my way a bit better I was haunted by the fact that I was only her most recent in a string of "close" foreign friends. She asked a lot of questions, she wanted to know where I had been, and with whom. At first I just wrote this off as her nature, but later I felt that she was not asking out of simple curiosity. Much of what I was to tell Nina came back to me; government officials had information on me and it seemed that she provided it, although I had no positive proof.

The strong distinction in Russian between the words "acquaint-ance" and "friend" became clear to me. In the Soviet context it means a great deal to be a friend. It is a title that must be earned and it means that you are trusted. In my carefree and naive American manner I too quickly accepted Nina as a friend.

Not all of my relationships in the Soviet Union turned out to be so disappointing. Most of all I enjoyed associating with relatives of Soviet emigres that I had met in the United States. I often went to see the relatives of a woman I knew in Chicago. I was very fond of her. She gave me all sorts of gifts for her relatives and friends: records, books, umbrel-las, razors, etc. I contacted them soon after I arrived in Moscow. They greeted me warmly, although they were disconcerted that I had called from a phone on the university grounds. We set up a meeting at a metro station and there we instantly recognized one another as if we ourselves were relatives. Back in their apartment, I told them all the news of my friend, news that they themselves had read in her letters, but it meant so much more to hear it again from someone who had actually seen and talked to her. They knew that they would most likely never again see their relative, and I was the only available substitute, a part of their relative's new life.

There were many other invitations. It is always prestigious to have a foreigner at a party. It is a sign of protest that results in nothing and usually threatens no consequence. I met many young people in Moscow who held their anti-state views just as one might wear eccentric clothing or engage in the newest fad. For such people, association with foreign-ers, especially intellectuals and students, was a great status symbol which, like their anti-Soviet speeches pronounced in small kitchens of small apartments, was not something that the state expressly forbids.

As a foreigner, I could easily have spent my time going from one party to another gracing them all with my presence, but this "movie-star syndrome" held little attraction for me. Except for relatives of friends at home, the people I knew were people who had special vested interests in dealing with foreigners. They associated almost exclu-sively with foreigners. They were fun and entertaining, but they were not the Soviet mainstream I had hoped to be a part of. I did not want to close myself off further, but I did not like playing this game in which I did not know the rules, in which I felt both privileged and taken advantage of. So, I decided to concentrate more time and energy on my research.

I was studying Alexander Herzen, a writer and revolutionary of the mid-1800's, and his relationship with the famous writer Ivan Turgenev. It was a romantic, literary topic. An American professor had once called it "sexy." The Soviets liked it. It was not political and it dealt with two bona fide greats of Russian culture. My Soviet advisor, a world renowned historian, thought it very promising.

I started to attend my Soviet advisor's seminars in order to see how my counterparts were trained, but most of all I was mesmerized by this professor. He was very intelligent and insightful and he treated his students and me with the greatest respect. At Stanford I had been told that this professor spent fifteen years in a labor camp. He had been arrested along with millions of others in the great terror of the Stalinist thirties and forties. Once released he forgave his jailors and reasoned that they had simply made a mistake in his case. I sat there in class and unwittingly stared at him. I had read, even taught Soviet history, but here it was sitting in front of me.

Most of my work I did in the Lenin Library. We foreigners had the privilege of studying in the first hall, which brought two main advantages: first, I could sit by myself and did not have to share a desk with someone as was the case in the rest of the library, and second, the first hall had a reserved coat check so that I did not have to stand in line to hang up my coat before entering the library. At crowded times that might save me a half hour.

Only academicians, professors and foreign students could use the first hall and the result was an odd blend of people. Men and women in their 50's, 60's and 70's, all hunched over from years of study at these very same tables, all dressed in the same brown and gray suits, baggy at the elbows and knees, the women looking much like the men. Interspersed were young students in blue jeans, sweatshirts and bright woolen mufflers wrapped around their necks. The foreigners wore the mufflers because they could not adapt to the habit of "airing the hall." Twice a day the windows that looked out on the golden spires of the Kremlin were flung open and left open for 45 minutes, every season of the year.

One particular day in October the air was crisp—too crisp for my tastes. So, I chose to descend into the depths of the library for a bite to eat. The cafeteria was in the basement. It was flanked by the bathrooms, some of the worst smelling in Moscow, and by the smoking room which consisted of twenty chairs, three tables with platter-size ashtrays on each, and no windows or ventilation. The smoke did not waft out of the room, it simply advanced into the corridor, like Napoleon marching on Moscow. After the freshness of the rapidly chilling reading room, descending to the cafeteria felt like a descent into hell. The food showed a gourmet's sense of the proper complement to the surroundings.

By the time I got down to the cafeteria that day the crowd had already left. Even the few chairs were free and I was pleased at the prospect of eating lunch seated. At the cafeteria counter I grabbed what appeared to be the last plate of marinated mushrooms. I was thrilled with my find. These were the first mushrooms I had seen. To me, Russian cooking meant mushrooms. How could it be that they too were in "deficit," as the Soviet expression goes?

I took my treasure and sat down at the first free chair. There was a middle aged man already sitting at the table. He did not look up; he was engrossed in his borsch. I dove into the mushrooms and let out a gasp. These were not mushrooms. They had the taste of organs. The man looked up and I smiled.

"Excuse me, sir. Could you tell me what dish this is I'm eating?"

"Pochki."

"Ah, uh-huh, yes. And what excellent pochki they are."

I did not have the slightest idea what pochki were. I got out my dictionary and looked up the word "pochki." I winced. I was eating kidneys. Undoubtedly many would find this delightful but I had been brought up on steak and potatoes. The least hint of organ, even the resemblance of meat to the animal from which it came, made me queasy.

The man was now looking me over. He did not understand my outburst. I was embarrassed by my childishness. I smiled and took another piece of kidney.

"What kind of pochki?"

"I don't know. Either cow or sheep."

I chewed. He smiled. It was obvious that I was a foreigner. He continued to look me over. He was probably trying to figure out just how foreign.

"Where are you from?"

"California," I answered, as if California constituted a country all by itself.

"Ah, the United States. And why have you come to Moscow?"

"For the kidneys, of course."

He did not appreciate this joke. I saw that he understood it but he did not see any humor in it. He was a very serious man. He had on heavy brown eyeglasses. The glass was not thick, but then there were only so many frames to choose from in the Soviet Union. The eyes beneath were light brown, the nose sharp, the chin firm. His whole face seemed angular except for his soft brown eyes which were hidden behind the eyeglass frames.

"I'm in Moscow on an academic exchange. I'm doing research for my dissertation in Russian history. What do you do?"

"I'm a journalist. I've been doing some research myself here in the library. My name is Andrei."

Two women sat down at the table. They had on the light blue robes that library employees wore. As soon as they sat down at the table they shot dirty looks at the man.

"What's your name?" he asked.

"Lois."

"I've never heard that name before, Lau·iz. Where do you live in Moscow?"

"At the dormitory at MGU."

The women started to talk very loudly, but I could not make out what they were saying. My Russian was not that good and they spoke in a way I had never heard before, while everything that this man said was as clear as a bell. He kept looking over at the women. It seemed they were talking about him. Something about morality and proper behavior. He tried to ignore them. He asked how long I had been in Moscow, whether this was my first visit, what were my impressions so far. I answered his questions and even managed to get a smile out of him when I said that the university building reminded me of a spider.

The rumblings from the women got louder. It was rude and I was getting irritated. He asked me where I lived in California, at what university I studied. Before I could answer, the women had abandoned all decorum and burst into our conversation. They lambasted Andrei

in a spray of speech that seemed to make no sense and told him that
he had to leave the table because it was reserved for library employees.
They then turned and oh so sweetly smiled at me.

Andrei stood up. I sensed the fury within him but he did not say
a word. He simply gathered up his things and moved to one of the
counters. I did not understand what had happened. I only knew that
these women had been very rude and now they were grinning away at
me, being polite as hell. I knew it was because I was a foreigner and I
felt insulted. Insulted that they could be so rude to a Soviet and then
turn around and smile politely at me. I was supposed to accept this?
Even be pleased by their special attentions?

I got up, too. I went over to the counter where Andrei stood and
placed my plate of kidneys next to his borsch. He looked at me and did
not say a word. For one moment we were in complete understanding.

We continued our lunch standing. He asked questions and I answered. He tried to help me with my Russian, repeatedly pronouncing
the few English words he knew. When we finished lunch he cleared all
the dishes. He then took me by the arm in noble Russian fashion and
led me out of the cafeteria as I gave the women a final sneering glance.
We went up the stairs to the second floor landing where we leaned
against the windows that looked out on the churches of the Kremlin.

He asked to be my guide. To show me Moscow. It was an old line.
One I had already heard and would hear again. But he said it with such
gentility. I needed a guide. I needed someone to explain to me what I
was seeing. I wanted to know why those women scolded him in the
cafeteria. I sensed that in this man was some of the Soviet reality I had
been shielded from.

I said yes to his proposal. We would meet the next day at the
Kropotkinsky metro. It was very close to the library.

CHAPTER 2
THE FRIENDSHIP CONTINUES

A F

In the library Lois suggested that we meet the next day. I joyfully agreed. It was interesting for me to meet an American who studied Russian history and Russian culture. I wanted to hear how the West viewed our history, to hear different views from the ones I had heard my whole life, to listen to "hostile bourgeois ideology." Lois was friendly— not suspicious like Soviet people. She had supported me in an unpleasant moment when two total strangers tried to interfere in my conversation and in my life. Most of all, Lois was a person from a different country where there existed different relations between people, and that fascinated me.

We met at the entrance to the Kropotkin metro station, at the head of Gogol Boulevard. From there it is only a ten minute walk to my home. This old Moscow neighborhood meant a great deal to me. It was my homeland, the village of my birth. I used to stroll along Gogol Boulevard with my mother when I was just learning to walk. Kropotkin Street was Prichistenka Street before the revolution, a religious name connoting the Immaculate Virgin. Opposite the current pavilion of the metro station is a huge open air swimming pool, an enormous bowl filled with green warm water. I had worked as a lifeguard at this pool when I was a student at the Moscow Institute of Cinematography.

I told Lois the history of this pool which had always been a part of my life. Earlier the Church of Christ the Savior had stood in its place. It was torn down in my lifetime, in the 1930's when many treasures of Russian culture were destroyed. At that time the government even wanted to destroy the Church of St. Vasilii, the multi-colored, many cupolaed church that stands on Red Square and that many Westerners consider a symbol of Russia. The Church of Christ the Savior had been built in honor of the victory over Napoleon. Because of its unique construction it took over forty years to build. I think the Soviet authorities wanted to tear it down mainly because its cupolas and cross were seen from all sides of approach to Moscow. They had wanted to construct an enormous "Palace of Soviets" on the site of the church.

The project, like many projects in the Soviet Union, was grandiose and publicized everywhere. I remember as a child being told that the figure of Lenin which was to have crowned this enormous construction would be seen above the clouds even on rainy days. It was suggested that the entire area of residential buildings, the area of Old Moscow, now an architectural landmark area, be razed so as to ease access to the new building. The government's ceremonial processions that celebrate "the triumph of socialism" and always start in Red Square were to move from Red Square along the city streets and pass right through the Palace's interior. And these grandiose plans were being made during the era of mass repression and terror.

By an irony of history this building was never constructed. Underground water was found beneath the building of the former church. Laying the foundation for the future Palace of Soviets demanded an enormous effort. American engineers were even invited to Moscow for consultation. The wet earth mixed with the underground water was frozen by means of special equipment and in this solid state was hauled away. More water seeped in, the earth was again frozen and again hauled away. The walls of the foundation were sealed with concrete and a steel framework was put in place. Many sober-minded engineers had forseen the possibility of such enormous expenditures simply to prepare the area for the foundation. These engineers advised the government to build the Palace in another, more appropriate place, such as the Lenin Hills, formerly Sparrow Hills, where Moscow University now stands. But Stalin, then firmly at the head of government, was adamant. By the time the war began, work on the foundation was finished and the steel skeleton of the first floor was erected. The war effort precluded more work on the building. After the war this spot with its deep basement passages, half-filled with water and piles of rusting metal, became frightening catacombs, a refuge for juvenile criminals. This site, where the church had been, did not give the authorities any peace.

Khrushchev decided to turn it into a new symbol of a change to realistic politics. The foundation designed for the Palace was filled half-way and in its place a swimming pool was constructed. They say it is the largest in the world. Soviet power always wants to astonish the world with something, if not a Palace, then a swimming pool.

The pool on Kropotkin Square, built under Khrushchev, was too deep, and people who did not swim well drowned in its depths. A "legend" was created; representatives of some secret religious sect drowned people to avenge the destruction of the church. This story was of course ridiculous, something thought up by the authorities. It was convenient to discredit religion and excuse their own stupidity.

I was a good swimmer and my work as a lifeguard at the pool for two years convinced me that those who drowned were mainly drunks, people who did not know how to swim, and children. I earned a ruble an hour at the pool. I swam about continuously, mask on my face, scanning the bottom, following after children and kicking out drunks. During my watch no one drowned and I saw no members of religious sects attempting to drown unwitting Soviet citizens.

The legend had its precedents in Soviet life under Khrushchev's predecessors, when such rationalizations of the government's mistakes had more far-reaching consequences. In the first unsuccessful five year plans so-called "saboteurs" were blamed—old regime specialists who were then eliminated without ceremony. Taking their places were poorly educated people whose incompetence resulted not only in personal errors, but in accidents, even catastrophes.

Before I came to work at Khrushchev's pool, Khrushchev himself stopped by one day for a swim. He was then playing at democracy and wanted to take a dip in the pool like any other citizen. I believe he was accompanied by full security, all dressed in bathing suits. Khrushchev's era is famous not only for the exposure of Stalin's crimes, which could no longer be kept hidden in any case, but also for the government's shooting at worker demonstrations, for the occupation of Hungary, and for the "judicial" proceedings against writers. Few believed in his democracy. Students who were at the pool when Khrushchev visited began to shout that they did not need his company, that he had his own pool nicely isolated from the people. The students were arrested, tried for hooliganism and given several years in prison. The "great democrat" Khrushchev did not desire to leave unpunished those who did not care to be in his company.

Today's pool has been rebuilt to be shallow, finally destroying all the work on the foundation that took so much time, effort, and foreign expertise. At its deepest the water reaches only to the chest of a grown man. But the pool, which is called "Moscow," is forever fated to be a symbol of the misdeeds of Soviet power. It turns out that the moisture that results from this enormous body of open water does considerable damage to the invaluable collection of paintings housed in the Pushkin Museum of Fine Arts which is located across the way on Volkhonka Street. Irreversible damage has already been done to this collection, one of the world's greatest, and it is unknown what will happen to it in the future.

The Brezhnev government in my neighborhood is marked by the reconstruction of the Serbsky Institute of Forensic Psychiatry, a block from my home. Here in truth, among the quiet homes and streets, is living history. The Institute of Criminal Psychiatry was transformed into a prison for dissidents. According to information on Western radio, the director of the institute is a colonel in the KGB.

Thus, the various epochs of the "construction of socialism" in the Soviet Union are embodied in the architecture of the neighborhood of my birth and residence. I told Lois the history of my neighborhood although it is forbidden to tell such things to foreigners. According to the official morality such stories qualify as slanderous fabrications, discrediting the Soviet system.

I stopped my talk when we entered the small cafe next to my home. Lois was startled by the sudden shift in my behavior. She did not know that many Soviet citizens are frightened of such places as cafes and restaurants where conversations can be overheard. There are even special people who take seats alongside groups or individual patrons. Soviet waiters have preserved the habit of seating people according to their personal convenience, placing strangers together so that each table is full and thus easier to serve. Therefore, people who have no desire to be together often must sit at one table.

Entering the cafe with Lois I was very careful. I told her that in our country one does not speak about politics in public places. My fears were not unfounded. Open conversations about life in the USSR make the foreigner look suspect to the regime and therefore close off his or her possibility of future visits to the Soviet Union. Meanwhile the Soviet citizen gradually, unnoticeably, loses his position in society, if it was a sufficiently prestigious one.

So we sat in silence.

In the future, when Lois became my wife, we were convinced that the authorities had taken an interest in listening to all our conversations. Every time that we went into a cafe or restaurant, after a certain amount of time had passed, people would sit down at a neighboring table and very casually, as if by accident, place a briefcase practically under our legs. The first time I could not understand why the person next to us had placed his briefcase by our table. Then, each time I noticed a briefcase next to us of the same size and shape, and every time the distance between us and the case was the same. Coincidences do not happen that often in real life. The Soviet system stipulates uniformity in the behavior of its workers and in its standardized equipment; in this instance, there were tape recording devices concealed in the briefcases.

We went back to my home after the cafe. Lois examined the decor of my room in raptures. It was full of old things and makeshift devices, and she said that I was a Russian hippie. I answered that of course I was Russian, but that I hardly thought of myself as a hippie. If in fact I lived the life of a hippie, then so did most of the people who inhabited these old Moscow buildings; although they too never suspected that they were hippies. However, the apartment and my room in it truly were a bit exotic.

In Stalin's time six different families lived in this six room apartment. Every morning there were lines to the bath and to the toilet, and the kitchen was so crowded that one could barely turn around. People pushed one another and fights erupted continuously. When Lois happened into my apartment there were only half as many people living there, but every room still housed a separate family and as before we shared a common bathroom, toilet and kitchen. Fights arose less frequently but they still arose. This was a communal apartment. Twenty years ago such apartments were in the majority in Moscow; now their numbers are much less but more than enough still exist. Almost all of the residences in old Moscow are communal apartments. Before the revolution these apartments were not communal. Communal apartments, just like kolkhozes (large communal farms), are inventions of Soviet power.

I started to tell Lois that I had lived in the same room my whole life. My parents received it on the day I was born. The room is 32 square meters with three windows and high ceilings. When I was born such a room was considered luxurious and even now the entire room for one person is not at all bad. Before my birth my parents lived in the same building but in a much smaller room. We were indeed fortunate to be given the bigger room, and the day I was born I earned the nickname "Lucky". It has followed me as a joke my whole life.

Lois examined the wallpaper that hung on the walls of my room, an old pattern that one rarely sees nowadays. I told her that this wallpaper was as old as I was, fifty years. As proof I showed her a photograph that hung on the wall. In the photo I was a baby in my mother's arms, and behind us was the same wall with the same wallpaper. I told Lois how my grandfather on my mother's side would come to visit us when I was a child. He and my father would split a bottle of vodka at dinner and afterwards they would start to speak in low tones. One had to speak quietly lest the neighbors listen in and write a denunciation (usually without signature.) At that time denunciations were everywhere. My father and grandfather never said anything special: they did not touch on politics in their conversations. My grandfather was simply a man of conservative views. Before the revolution he worked as a technician. He was considered a good engineering specialist and was comparatively well-off, but there was much he did not approve of in the new life and disapproval was sufficient for a denunciation. On rare occasions my father allowed himself to say the kind of things that were punishable by prison, and he said them not only in his room and not only in a quiet voice. One day at work where he served as the chief technical specialist of an engineering project, his supervisor and the secretary of the party organization assigned to his project invited him to join the Communist Party. He responded that he could not do so since he considered himself an honest person. After that we expected the worst: that they would come for my father in the middle of the night. Apparently his supervisor and party official did not inform on him.

Lois listened attentively to my stories. In the beginning she might have been listening as a historian would, taking in data, but by the end of the evening she was listening as a sympathetic person trying to understand a man's life. She then told me about her parents and showed me photographs of home that she had brought with her. The people who looked out at me in these photos seemed unbelievably far away; they lived on another planet. She told me that her father was a business-man but that he spent all the time he could at baseball games. He had many friends among the local fans and was a popular figure in that world. Bursting with pride she told me that her father was a diehard Cubs fan. I had no idea what that meant but it undoubtedly had some significance for Americans. This seemed so strange. I could only read of such things in books; I would never have seen anything similar in my life.

When a man and a woman start to talk about their parents a thread is drawn between them, a thread that in the future can bind them together.

L B F

Andrei and I met at the Kropotkin metro in the late afternoon. I spotted him right away, tall, in a beige trench coat, scanning the crowd for me. I walked right up to him before he noticed that I had arrived. He beamed when he saw me. He led me on to the boulevard and with a grand sweep of his arm proudly proclaimed:

"This is my neighborhood. Old Moscow! My apartment's not far from here, just a few blocks over."

Then he took my arm, gently folded it over his and slipped his hand between the buttons on his chest. We walked like that down the length of Gogol Boulevard, arms entwined at the elbows just like in a nine-teenth century novel. I was charmed.

As we walked, Andrei told me about the history of his neighbor-hood. We started at an old masonry structure that stood opposite the metro station, just beyond a statue of Friedrich Engels. It was a simple structure with a few small, barred windows near the roof, originally white and now dingy from the grime of centuries. There was no plaque commemorating its significance, but Andrei knew the story well enough. It had been the quarters of the *oprichniki,* the secret police of Ivan the Terrible. From here they would ride out in the middle of the night to swoop down on some family suddenly suspected of treason to the state.

On another block he pointed out a small frame house that Turgenev had depicted in his story "Mumu." We went off on a side street and he showed me the home where Herzen had lived and where his literary contemporaries would gather and drink late into the night. We came onto Kropotkin Street with its aristocratic mansions now converted into museums and government offices. Andrei pointed out a building with the most incredible ornate and graceful stone carvings. Leading out from the large center windows was a balcony with intricate grilling like lace on a valentine. Here Isadora Duncan and Sergei Yesenin lived and romanced. After lovemaking Yesenin would come out onto this balcony and, weaving from champagne and vodka, cry out his newest work of poetry to the pedestrians of Moscow.

Andrei's tales were entrancing and he himself was entranced in telling them. The more he talked, the more he had to say. He started to show me locations of more recent history. A block and a half from the site of Yesenin's spontaneous poetry readings was a modern build-ing of attractive white stone, stark in design. It was surrounded by a high electric fence with military vehicles parked all about and sentry boxes at every corner and gate. It was the Serbsky Institute of Forensic Psychiatry.

Andrei started to talk about the misdeeds of Soviet power. Once embarked on this course he could not stop. At first I was suspicious. I thought he might be provoking me, testing my politics to see if I har-bored views antithetical to the official line. Why should he trust to tell me all these stories, stories that could only be labeled anti-Soviet? And then I remembered how he had looked at me in the library cafeteria when I followed him from the table from which he had been "exiled." There had been trust in his eyes, and it gleamed in his eyes now. And he was so wound up in his exposition that he was not giving me a chance to express my own opinions anyway. He breathlessly chattered away, thrilled to be speaking to a representative from the outside world, and not wanting to stop before he could tell me everything. But it was getting dark and we were hungry. We had walked and talked for hours.

Suddenly realizing the hour Andrei hustled me off to a cafe with carved wooden snowflakes hanging in the window.

"I think you will like it here. The food is good and it is not too noisy inside. It's my favorite place in the neighborhood."

He was not alone in his appreciation of the cafe and by the time we got there the "Full" sign was out and the doors were shut. Andrei banged for five minutes before a burly man in a fraying doorman's jacket propped one of the doors open a bit.

"We're full. What do you want?"

"We want to eat. Don't you have a place for two somewhere? We won't be staying the whole night," Andrei pleaded.

"I told you, we are full," the man answered. He continued to stand in the doorway waiting for a certain response from Andrei.

We three stood there a minute. When the doorman realized that no money would be forthcoming he slipped back through the door and bolted it from the inside. I had witnessed such scenes when other Soviets had taken me out to restaurants and cafes. When a doorman insisted that an establishment was full, a two, three or five ruble note always found its way from the hand of my Soviet host to the hand of the doorman and we were promptly seated at one of the numerous vacant tables inside. Andrei would not proffer "the entrance fee" and we continued on to a cafe that was less popular.

On the way to the next spot he kept telling me to be careful, to control myself and not to speak of politics once inside. I thought he was saying this to himself as much as to me, but he had no problem. We entered a cafe that was brightly lit and lightly populated. He helped me take my coat off and then removed his. As he handed it to the old man at the coat check I noticed his face, even his posture, change. He became reserved, sullen. At dinner he asked me matter of fact questions about myself and my family. He changed the topic frequently to avoid anything but surface chatter. At times we sat in silence.

I looked at him very carefully. He was more handsome than I remembered from the library. He had a tall frame and a muscular build that made him look much younger than his years. His skin was weathered, the shadow of the day's beard in clear outline. He was very rugged looking despite the heavy frames of his glasses. He had a strong nose, crooked at the center. He noticed me staring at it. I was embarrased, but he laughed. He explained to me that he had been a boxer as a student and the bend in his nose was one his trophies.

I liked it when he laughed but there was too little laughter as we sat at dinner. The food was greasy, but the cafe had Georgian wine and we contented ourselves with that. I kept hoping that he would spark up again. That he would become animate and lively as he had been earlier that evening when we walked along the streets of old Moscow. So when we finished the bottle of wine and left the cafe and he asked if I wanted to go up to his apartment, I said yes. I had to know who he was.

Andrei lived in a communal apartment on the fifth floor of a building built at the turn of the century. When we got to the door of the apartment he motioned me to be quiet. He opened the door and led me down the corridor to his room and there fumbled for his keys in the darkness. He finally shoved open the heavy wooden door and pulled aside a tapestry that hung at the entrance in traditional Russian style. He switched on the light and I stood there for several minutes taking in the sight. I suddenly felt so close to this man who in culture, age and disposition was so distant from me.

The walls and cabinets of his room were decorated with mementoes of his life. At one desk he had arranged his photographic and developing equipment. Clamps, special lights, scissors and glasses hung from a wire he had extended from one cabinet to another. On the wall behind there were photographs he had taken, mostly of ships, wild animals and old Russian churches, along with several of their reproductions in magazines. His shots were crisp and clear but once printed they had come out fuzzy and oddly green. There was a black target sheet marked up with clusters of rifle shots, along with a certificate pronouncing Andrei Frolov a marksman. A huge poster with several names and a picture of Andrei in bathing trunks announced his participation in the sport of cold water swimming, a member of a sort of Polar Bear Club. On another wall hung a huge map of the Soviet Union with hundreds of small colored pins marking all the places that he had traveled to.

The other desk in the room held his typewriter, pens and an old marble inkwell. A small homemade work bench was laden with heavy, clumsy looking instruments. There were weights strewn on the floor and more weights that had been converted into lamps sat on the desks and bookcase. There were three pictures of his parents and one of himself taken ten years prior, and an icon, on the wall above the bookcase. Everywhere there were wires hooking up one electrical device to another. The rugs and drapes were worn and frayed. The couch doubled as a bed. Another worn rug served as the upholstery.

The confusion struck me as rather childlike. It looked like the room of a fourteen-year-old boy engrossed in all manner of hobbies and adventures. Along with this confusion was an honesty, also almost childlike. A pride and a love of self-expression. I was reminded of my early college days and the nonconformity of "hippie pads" on campus.

The room spoke of a man of fierce independence. All of the things that cluttered the floors and walls were there for a purpose. He preferred to make things rather than buy them. The furniture was old but functional. There was no new Scandinavian bookshelf, nor Western stereo system, nor large television. None of the standard Soviet status symbols. The only Western objects were a photograph of William Faulkner propped up in the bookcase and a copy of Jack London's *The Call of the Wild* that lay next to it.

Andrei brewed some tea on a hot plate that served as his personal kitchen. We sat on the divan, sipped the tea, and talked.

After that first night Andrei and I started to see each other regularly, almost every day. I began to take off from my research to go on excursions with him. First we hit the museum circuit. We took in approximately twenty museums in three weeks. Andrei enjoyed it as much as I did, strolling about, our arms clasped and his hand in his coat like Napoleon, his free hand gesturing as he told me stories about this and that.

We tired of museums as we got to the bottom of the list and were left with such highlights as the Polytechnical Museum and the Museum of the People's Arts and Crafts. We then hit the theater circuit with no less intensity. In the course of six months we saw seventy-nine productions. Andrei helped me pick out the most interesting plays and explained to me the allusions and hidden meanings that were not readily understandable to a foreigner. We were always talking about plays we had seen and about plays we had yet to see. We both felt the deadline of my departure from the beginning of our relationship. Andrei, as much as I, wanted to be sure that I got to see as much as possible in the year I had in Moscow.

Most of all we walked. Andrei loved to take me about Moscow and lecture on Russian literature and Russian history. He told me about the history of old Moscow streets, old houses and buildings. It was all very interesting for me but I would not let an occasion pass without chiding him for telling me the same story the second or third time. He loved Moscow so much that he got carried away.

"Who married in this church? And who lived in that house, what great writer?" I asked him, knowing that he would again begin to tell me all about Pushkin's wedding and Tolstoy's home.

Andrei was very intense. He was motivated by ideas. Everything was a matter of principle, of right and wrong. It did not make life easy, but it stripped it of mediocrity.

We often argued, oh, how often we argued. For example, I told him that in America we fought for equal rights for women—that a woman should be able to enter any profession she desired.

"Any profession?" he asked.

"Any."

"Even become a general in the military?"

"Even a general, if she wants to."

"Nonsense!" he answered.

"Why is that nonsense?"

"It's nonsense because it's nonsense," he said, not even bothering to think about it.

"You have prejudices and old-fashioned ideas," I said.

"Of course. Don't I have the right to have prejudices and old-fashioned ideas?"

We often argued about Russian history and with such conviction that I thought we might come to blows. "Ivan the Terrible" was one of our favorite arguments.

"Ivan the Terrible did a great deal for the independence of the Russian state," Andrei would say.

"You, my dear," I would start off, "like many Russians are attracted to the idea of absolute power."

"Absolute power has played a positive role in the history of many peoples," he responded. "It's just that over time its positive role turned into a negative one, according to the laws of the dialectic."

"You're answering just as they taught you in school."

"I was taught by very good teachers," Andrei contended, "and I agree with many of the theories that they taught us. It's simply that the Soviet authorities have misused these theories and interpreted them at their own discretion. They would never allow anyone to say that theories themselves should develop, that there cannot be an eternally correct theory. In that they contradict the dialectic in the most direct manner, and the dialectic is supposed to be a part of the official ideology."

"That's all very well and good," I answered. "Theory can be a helpful tool, but what about people? Theory is only good in so much as it helps people."

And so it went on. Andrei often said that Americans have too short a history, too short to understand anything as complex as Russian history. Americans have known only one social formation in their short existence. He joked that he as a Russian was 1000 years old and I as an American was only 200. Therefore, he should and did hold within himself far more contradictory influences. I began to think that perhaps that was really so. Certainly the major conflict between Andrei and me was of old versus young; it was a conflict just as much of our worlds as of our actual ages.

Andrei was old in the sense that he had seen it all and therefore doubted everything. He was a cynic of experience. He was very different from the young Soviets I had met who were also very cynical. Cynicism towards the party and government was a popular, even hip attitude among the young. But they never seemed to see themselves caught up in the persecution that they accepted as happening to others. Andrei's cynicism was much deeper. In his fifty years he had seen so much more of Soviet power and he feared it more. He was cynical towards life in general, but he never used this cynicism as an excuse to lower his standards and harm others.

Andrei gave more credence than I to the "big forces," to the force of history. The individual exists, he felt, but is swept along by the forces that make our world. He gave less weight to feelings and emotions. He related to people on the basis of their character which he perceived to be unchanging and unbending. His understanding of personality was so different from our flexible American understanding of psychology.

I, on the other hand, was young, twenty-seven, full of mirth and joie de vivre, piss and vinegar. I believed in progress, justice, innocent pure love. I believed in the individual and his ability to change. I gave more weight to emotions in my understanding of people, showing an American tendency to psychologize everything and thus eliminate good and evil and the responsibility for choosing between them.

I felt that Andrei was right more often than I was (though not about Ivan the Terrible, never about Ivan the Terrible!)—at least I thought that I had a lot to learn from him. But I did not want to concede much to him so I simply said that he was right about being 800 years older than me. To my surprise, he loved it. He paraded about the room majestically, influenced by too much theater. Ceremonially, like an actor from Stanislavsky's Moscow Art Theater he said that today's Russian has to pay for the sins of past generations. I responded in kind. We were in our own little theater, each playing our role. I embraced him and called him "my poor, unfortunate Russian." And he even more solemnly responded in the words of Shakespeare's Othello:

She loved me for the dangers I had passed,
And I loved her that she did pity them.

A F

Before my friendship with Lois I had a very surface notion of foreigners. These notions came first of all from Russian classical literature where I had read about German cobblers and coffin makers in St. Petersburg and about French governesses and tutors on Russian aristocratic estates who in their own land were simple coachmen and cooks.

My first real exposure to foreigners was in my youth when, at the age of nineteen, I worked on a ship that traveled abroad. Those impressions were also very surface. There remain in my memory Italians, storeowners who spoke very fast and tried to trick all their customers; and Englishman and Norwegians, reservedly polite, scrupulously honest. Most of all I bumped into sailors in these foreign ports. Even then I noticed that people from different ends of the earth, of different nationalities and colors of skin reacted the same way to good and evil, similarily showed signs of friendship. Not knowing one another's language they still managed to make themselves understood by a facial expression or a gesture. People everywhere are people: their characters

do not depend on political views or on religion. And all sailors, moreover, are drunks. Among the drunks of various countries differences are
still less noticeable. Mainly, drunks simply want to boast, brawl and sing
the blues about their lives.

My first acquaintance with a foreigner with whom I could speak in
depth was with a Frenchwoman who had what seemed to me a very
romantic name: Francoise. I was then about thirty-five years old and she
was not yet thirty. She had come to Moscow for various conferences of
Slavicists. Thin, elegant Francoise smoked cigarettes with an unfamiliar
aroma and screwed up her lovely eyes with those long lashes and
examined me from head to foot, trying to do so obliquely so that I did
not notice. She started with my tie and ended with my socks. It seemed
to me that she was calculating in her head the level of my prosperity.
She very carefully asked me about my professions, especially about my
engineering work even though she did not understand a thing about it.
My Soviet friends told me that an engineer in the West, unlike a Soviet
engineer, can earn very good money. They hinted to me that Francoise
was not opposed to the idea of getting married in the Soviet Union.

Most of all Francoise loved to talk about how people are followed
in the Soviet Union, how everywhere conversations are overheard. I
think that she exaggerated the level of eavesdropping and even if she
did not exaggerate, why was she especially frightened? She did not
engage in politics or illegal transactions, and she had a French passport.
My all-knowing friends enlightened me on this account. Francoise wanted
to live and work in Moscow for several years in order to save up money
and then spend it once she returned home to France. She felt that
contact with dissident types would injure her financial plans, the realiza-
tion of which depended on her being loyal to the regime.

I did not experience any attraction towards Francoise as a woman
though I did not understand why. She was pretty, elegant, and dressed
with taste. I was told that Francoise loved women.

"Then why does she want to get married?"

They laughed at me: "Love is love, sex is sex, but business is
business."

Francoise's plans came to fruition. She found work in Moscow with
a French firm that sold shoes. She worked there five years and probably
accumulated the money that she wanted in order to have a happy life

in France. Meanwhile she associated with only a limited number of Muscovites. Her constant friend and lover was a woman of Tatar-Bashkir descent. People said that she was an informer for the KGB. This did not worry Francoise: perhaps it even suited her. No doubt the KGB now had good reports on her, and she regularly gave her lover her old dresses and scarves.

Soon she found even more success and prosperity than she had figured on. An old foreign diplomat took an interest in her. Francoise was then just over thirty years old. The diplomat was older than her by some thirty-odd years. She had never manifested any sexual interest towards men and this one was anything but young and robust. I asked my acquaintances abut this. "He's rich!" the answer followed. And happy Francoise left Moscow with her new husband on his next assign-ment to some country of azure blue seas and palm trees. Moscow had brought each of them their own good fortune.

Lois, from the beginning of our acquaintance, joyfully proclaimed me a Russian hippie.

"Go away, get rid of these foreigners," I joked to myself. "For one you have to be dressed in the latest fashion and for another you should be a hippie."

After this Lois persistently asked me:

"What kind of advantage is there for you in associating with an American?"

Again I thought to myself that among these foreigners no one did anything disinterestedly, everything had to be counted out in dollars or francs. But Lois herself did not fit my picture of a capitalist. She did not worry about profits and advantage. She was short, thin and her hair was closely cropped. She reminded me more of a young boy who had skipped out on school and did not listen to his parents. I later learned that back home Lois sometimes smoked marijuana. She often talked about sex. She fought for the rights of women, blacks and homosexuals.

"Oh Boy!" as the Americans say.

Lois told me that in America they fought so that women could engage in professions that were traditionally considered masculine. That women could even be generals! Once she mentioned to me a street in San Francisco where all sorts of odd people hung out, even men who were transformed into women by medical operations. And they wrote books about it and showed them on television! I was fascinated by these strange stories.

"Oh Boy! What marvels are there that don't exist in prosperous America!"

Lois told me that on occasion she and her friends drove to Lake Tahoe and spent the evenings in the casinos there. I myself had read of such cities in the United States that existed purely for entertain-ment—that in America there existed an entire industry of entertain-ment. I read about Las Vegas where for a small price an American could obtain entertainments that in the USSR existed only underground, for big-time black marketeers and for the chosen few who belonged to the circle of the power elite.

"Oh Boy! How well people live in America! They have everything and it's all cheap!"

High placed Soviet bureaucrats on busines trips abroad try to taste the "illicit" on the sly, unnoticed by their Soviet companions, and then once back home in the USSR they brag about these adventures, also on the sly, to their closest friends.

Judging by her behavior in Moscow, it seemed to me that Lois did not think to be frightened of anyone. Often she loudly complained about the behavior of Soviet administrators and bureaucrats, and I tried to convince her that she was wasting her words. First, Soviet bureaucrats had trouble understanding her because of her American accent, and second, for them everything had become clear long ago; they did not doubt in the justice of the world order that surrounded them. They would only smile politely in answer, as they were ordered to be polite with foreigners. But at every occasion that called for it Lois would again express her exasperation loudly. Her indignation sometimes turned on me. She said that in my country everything was bad because we Rus-sians did not know how to rebel. I answered her 'thank you', that with her help we would build a new revolution in Russia, but perhaps it would be better to wait—we still had not settled with the consequences of the last revolution. Lois got angry and said that I did not respect her political views.

"Oh Boy! Political views! For us life would be a bit easier if they simply tossed some good food into our stores."

Lois's most serious interest was in Russian culture. She loved to talk about literature and eagerly listened to my descriptions of Moscow architecture. She very quickly knew the Moscow theaters better than I and her Russian improved at a fast pace. She would go to the theater and sit anywhere in the hall, in the cheapest seats—she would even sit on the stairs if the production was interesting to her.

Everything that I found out about Lois in the first few months of our friendship fully coincided with my bookish notion of an educated American and of the country, enormous and varied like the universe itself. People of my generation and within my circle had a pretty good idea about American society. Each of us knew at least ten American authors very well. My friends and I read the magazine *America* in the Russian language. A by-product of detente, it is printed in the United States and allowed into the USSR in exchange for the Soviet magazine *Soviet Life* available in the United States. It was impossible to buy *America* in kiosks but it was available in central libraries. All of my friends listened to the "Voice of America" broadcasts in the Russian language. Every year several American films appeared in Moscow. The authorities selected and bought those films in which America was shown from her worst side. But the people who went to those films often saw something that the authorities did not intend for them to see. For example, if the films portrayed CIA abuses, they told Soviet viewers that America was a democratic country in which it was possible to criticize, condemn and even limit the activities of that agency, all of which was completely impossible in the Soviet Union in regard to the KGB.

Within my circle of friends, a person's attitude towards the Soviet regime served as a measure of his or her honesty and integrity. All around there were people who feared to say anything against the regime not only at work, but even among friends at home. Fearing that "They" would find out if they did otherwise, these people hypocritically spoke well of the regime so that they might have the opportunity to travel abroad or get a better job. They no longer feared for their freedom or for their life, as they did in Stalin's day. They only feared losing a good piece of the pie. This duplicity, which to my amazement I noticed even among foreign visitors to the Soviet Union, was one of the most disgusting aspects of Soviet life.

One often heard it said of a person that he or she was honest. Honesty meant that they did not play up to the authorities. Some respected honesty, others looked at it with the smile of the cynic.

Lois respected honesty. She was a representative of a free country where the independence of the human personality was one of the moral and political principles of society. Lois's principles were not merely words. They were not simply exhibited in her original behavior, behavior which I could also find in the Soviet life that surrounded me. Lois tried to help people who needed help. This instantaneously made her an enemy of the regime. It made her a person to whose conversations they listened and after whom they followed.

L B F

Andrei was so different from the other Soviets I had met. He was much closer to the literary ideal of a Russian that I had spent so many years reading about in one library or another. He reminded me of a composite of the brothers Karamazov. Like Dmitry he was passionate, sensual, and at times devil-may-care. Like Alyosha he strove to live purely in a corrupt world. And like Ivan he was intelligent, at times morbidly intelligent. He turned his intellect in on himself and would brood and imagine all sorts of plots hanging over his head.

I found myself falling in love with Andrei, but I was not sure how he felt about me. I knew that Andrei was attracted to me, perhaps even strongly, but I did not trust myself to judge a thing—first, because I was so smitten and, second, because my experiences in the Soviet Union had taught me to be suspicious.

When we first started to meet I asked him:

"Why is it interesting for you to meet with an American? What advantage is there for you in our friendship?"

He answered that everything was interesting for him—my views, manners, concerns. But this was no answer to my question.

"I'm asking about a concrete interest, about purposes," I continued. "Perhaps you want to marry an American so that you can leave the Soviet Union?"

"Of course I want to leave," he answered. "What normal person would want all of this that surrounds us? We can't ever speak honestly, always lying, hiding our true feelings. Such a life is disgusting. If you want to deliver me from this abomination, take me with you."

I was not offended by his answer. It was a relief to hear it aloud. It was honest and characteristic of Andrei. But it gnawed at me. I wanted more than honesty from him; I wanted an emotional commitment that most likely he could not give me.

I knew that Andrei had been married twice before. Neither marriage was very happy nor did they last long. His first marriage had ended seventeen years before and had lasted only a year and a half. His second was more a marriage of convenience with a woman from Siberia who wanted to live in Moscow. It had ended five years ago.

As the weeks passed we found ourselves spending more and more time together. We would meet at the library in the late afternoon, have dinner, and then go to the theater. On those occasions when the theater let out late I spent the night at Andrei's. We were becoming inseparable.

One fine day (Russians often say "one fine day" when unexpected trouble comes their way), a horrible scream resounded in the corridor of Andrei's apartment. In the room next to Andrei's lived a woman with an extremely unpleasant face. I had earlier noticed that this woman loved to interest herself in the affairs of others and Andrei and I had a pretty interesting affair going. When we would pass her door in the corridor she always opened it a bit and observed us through the narrow crack. I did not pay her any attention.

On this fine day, Andrei had gone out into the corridor when this woman fell upon him with screams:

"You've always done just what you wanted, Andrei Vladimirovich! You never stop to think about the rest of us in the apartment! You live too easily. You're too damn educated, too literate. But this is too much. You've brought an American into the apartment. Now we're all in trouble! We're all under suspicion! I'm going to tell them all about this—don't think for a moment that I won't."

Andrei returned to the room, restraining himself with great difficulty. He did not want to talk about what had just happened and said only that in order to understand everything it was necessary to live under socialism longer than I had. I had decided that this woman, his neighbor, was simply crazy and we had to forget about it and that was the end. But Andrei did not calm down. He began to listen attentively whenever someone came into the apartment and walked along the corridor, as if he were expecting something.

One night when we returned late from the theater I saw the face of Andrei's neighbor, her glaring eyes, peering out from behind her slightly open door. It seemed odd to me. It was late and she ought to have been sleeping at that hour. Andrei also noticed but said nothing to me. She had actually waited up to see if we would return together from the theater.

Andrei woke up early the next morning and lay in bed as if listening for something. I also awoke and asked him why he wasn't sleeping. He answered that it was nothing, but I sensed something special in his mood. Someone in the corridor picked up the phone receiver. There was one phone for everyone in the apartment and it hung on the wall in the corridor. Someone spoke in a muffled voice, probably holding their hand over the phone so as to speak directly into the receiver. I thought that this person did not want to disturb the others who were sleeping. Andrei sat up in bed.

"What's with you?" I asked.

He was stone silent. I already knew him well enough and if he was silent that meant something very bad. But what could it be? Yesterday everything was fine: we had so enjoyed the play we had seen.

"What's happening to you?" I asked once more.

He did not answer. I got upset. I did not understand anything. Several minutes later the bell rang at the entrance to the apartment, a very short, abrupt ring, and someone immediately rushed to open the door. Heavy steps resounded in the corridor. Several people were coming. They did not concern themselves at all with being quiet.

"What nerve!" I just managed to think. "It's only 7:00 in the morning and there are people barging down the corridor like stormtroopers."

Then there came an even less ceremonious knock at Andrei's door, a loud, urgent knock. Andrei quickly went to the door and opened it, but only halfway. Some people were trying to get into the room. Andrei did not let them in and they said something to him in an undertone. Andrei answered back in the same low voice. There was anger in their tones, even hatred. Andrei held the door, the weight of his body leaned against it.

The people trying to get into the room did not appear to be criminals; in any case their visit and behavior were not unexpected for Andrei. I did not know what to think. Having spoken awhile through the half-opened door these people stopped trying to push their way into the room. Andrei no longer held the door. He slipped out into the corridor and was gone for ten minutes. Again the steps resounded along the corridor. The visitors had left.

"Who was that?" I asked when Andrei returned.

"The police," he answered.

"The police? Why did they come here? Why did they want to come into the room?"

"They wanted to come into the room," Andrei answered, "because almost no one in the Soviet Union knows the laws and they counted on my not knowing."

"What are you talking about?"

"The law declaring the inviolability of my home. I demanded observance of that law. But they said they would come again."

"Fine, but what do they want?"

As I understood from his further explanations, the police wanted to frighten him and upon exiting they had promised that they would not leave him in peace. In such instances the police are ordered by the KGB, and the KGB can arrange their harassments so that they are lawful. If they need to they can invite witnesses who will swear to whatever needs to be said.

Good Lord! I felt that all this was the honest truth. What should I do now? I did not know how to avert the misfortune that hung over Andrei's head.

"You don't have to do anything," Andrei said. "You simply have to sleep at the dormitory where you are officially registered. You can be here at my place only until 11:00 at night and after 7:00 in the morning, just like a visitor at a hotel. That does not change anything, of course. But there is such a law according to which each person must spend the night where they are registered and you are registered at the dormitory of Moscow University."

"What kind of law is that! A law that stipulates where a person should sleep?"

In the Soviet Union there really is such a law and its violation can land a person in jail if he has been warned and does not obey. In this case the violator would be Andrei. I had spent the night at his apartment and he did not report this anywhere, neither to the police nor to the

KGB. Of course, if he had reported it they would have demanded observance of the law and something besides: they would have asked Andrei to keep them informed of my activities.

"OK," I said, "we are violating the law, but in the room opposite where that young woman lives there are always visitors. Young men, always different, sometimes two or three at a time, who drink a lot of wine, make noise, fight, play loud music late at night. Sometimes these carnivals last several days. It's her personal affair, but how is it better than our behavior?"

I had already come to understand that such questions were useless. Andrei could only answer that such was Soviet morality.

When I appeared the next day at Andrei's apartment his neighbors were very surprised to see me but they did not say a word. Besides the woman who yelled at Andrei in the corridor and the young woman whom men often visited at night, there was another old woman who moved along with great difficulty and rarely left her room. She was a former noblewoman. It was her family that had lived in the apartment before it was broken up to serve as a communal apartment. She was frightened of everything and would probably agree to anything she was told.

By the entrance to the apartment lived a couple with two children. The husband was an engineer and his wife also had an education of some sort. They came home from work in the evening after stopping into stores and standing in line to buy food. They showed up rather late and then the two of them spent the rest of the evening in the kitchen preparing dinner and the next day's breakfast and lunch. Their children, a boy and a girl, were very quiet: sometimes it seemed that they did not even exist. At 10:00 each night they all went to sleep. Early in the morning the parents went to work and the children to school. In the evening they returned home and started to cook—the endless cycle.

After these people found out that I was a foreigner, they stopped saying hello to Andrei. They were frightened. The husband had secret work and he was forbidden to associate with foreigners. After the police visit the couple stopped speaking to us completely. Even if we said hello they would not respond. If they were talking between themselves in the kitchen they would stop whenever we passed by and start again in whispers so that we could not hear what they were saying.

The last room stood next to Andrei's on the side opposite from the woman with the evil face. It was empty though registered to someone. One day several people came to this room. They walked along the corridor as if it were their own. They had unpleasant, buttoned-up faces. They said that the registered occupant of the empty room had given them keys so that they might examine it. They were thinking of coming to live here. They spent a while in the room, speaking very softly. We heard them attach something to the wall that divided Andrei's room from this room. They then left never to appear again.

Andrei commented that they certainly did not resemble people looking at a room. People who examine a room do not tamper with it. They definitely would ask the neighbors about something, look about the corridor, inspect the kitchen, the bathroom, etc. Who were these people?

The young woman in the room opposite Andrei's began to behave very differently than she had earlier. She repeatedly tried to enter Andrei's room, often not bothering to knock on the door. Once inside she very quickly and attentively looked about, paying special attention to the books that lay on the table. If she spotted an envelope she would try to read the address. A different type of man began to visit her. These men did not resemble her former friends. They were more serious, intelligent looking, and neatly dressed in suits that looked as if they had just come from the store. They tried to introduce themselves to us, come into Andrei's room. Often they carried expensive wine.

Andrei told me that this woman worked in the courts and that employees of Soviet judicial organs, just like party workers and many governmental employees, had signed and sworn that they were bound to cooperate with the KGB whenever it was required. Therefore we were very wary of this woman and her friends.

Something had happened to the lady with the evil face who lived in the next room. One day we heard her dashing all about the apartment, endlessly going into the kitchen, then back into her room, and back again into the kitchen, as if she could not find a place for herself. She finally stopped Andrei and me in the corridor and began to talk to us. There was fear on her face. Her lips trembled and her eyes shifted from side to side. She asked us to come into her room, and once there she broke into genuine hysterics. She told us that she was often called in to the police but that now they were demanding that she sign some paper on which it was written that I walked naked about the corridor of the apartment, and that Andrei drank a lot, made noise at night and turned on loud music.

We understood from her confused ramblings that she was not worried because she was being forced to sign a false statement against us, but that she herself might someday be punished because of her signature. After all, there would be a trial and she would have to repeat the false statement again, and what if someone managed to prove it was a lie? Then she would be in trouble.

Now the police were yelling at her and demanding still another signature promising that she would never say anything to anybody, and she had already told her daughter-in-law all about it. She begged us not to say anything, she told us that she was extremely frightened, simply an old person, not guilty of a thing. She began to repeat herself like a broken record: she did not know they would force her to sign something, she always tried never to sign anything, it always led to trouble, and she was not guilty of a thing, she simply told them everything that they wanted to hear, she did not know that they would demand her signature. . . .

After this conversation I became very frightened for Andrei. After all, if this woman did not sign her name to lies because of her uneducated fear of signing papers (papers that she could not even properly read), then perhaps someone else would sign their name to these lies. Maybe the neighbor who lived opposite Andrei, or the husband and wife who had ceased speaking to us, or the old woman who always agreed to everything. Maybe they had already signed such papers. My God! What had I done!

When I tried to discuss the situation with Andrei he said that this was a Russian affair and that I had no business getting mixed up in this dirt.

"But what am I do to?" I asked. "These charges are absurd, but I can't wait until they find the necessary signatures and then send you to prison for hooliganism!"

"They don't intend to send me to prison. I'm not a famous dissident or writer who publishes abroad. They simply want to frighten me. They want us to stop meeting."

I thought that Andrei simply wanted to calm me when he said that no one wanted to arrest him. I decided that I could not leave him alone, that my presence provided him some measure of safety. There was little they could do to me, an American, and in my presence they would be too embarrassed to do anything to him.

I knew I was being foolish. There was little I could do to stop the Soviet police. Still, I decided to stay by his side as much as possible. We were together every moment except when it was forbidden by law. Exactly at 11:00 every evening I left his apartment. Andrei saw me to a taxi and I went to the university dormitory. I slept restlessly, frequently awakening, and early in the morning I hurried back to him. I was calm only when I was with him.

A F

When I got a phone call from the KGB in the fifth month of my friendship with Lois I was not surprised. I had expected that sooner or later it would happen.

The headquarters of the KGB are located on Dzerzhinsky Square, by the monument to the "Iron Felix", Felix Dzerzhinsky, founder of the secret police. At one time even this building instilled fear in all the inhabitants of this enormous country. The former name of the square, Lubianka, was a symbol for the Soviet terror that first began under Lenin.

I matured under the terror of Stalinism and there was no small number of jokes about the Lubianka that circulated when I was a young man—jokes that people allowed themselves to pass on only within the small circle of their closest and most trusted friends. Under Khrushchev these jokes came out in the open, for a while at least. One joke about the Lubianka was even in a film of the Khrushchev era. A man is arrested and brought to the Lubianka during Stalin's time. There he asks whether there will be an investigation of his case. They answer him that under investigation are all those citizens who are presently strolling along the streets. Those who wind up here are already considered guilty—all that remains is to determine the extent of the punishment. Such an open attitude towards the Stalinist terror did not last long and such jokes have once again receded back to the private circles where they originated.

In our day the majority of Soviet people think that if a person is summoned to the KGB then that means that there must be something of which he or she is guilty. For them, the KGB is the highest authority in the country. And, if the KGB takes an interest in someone, calls at their work, for example, makes inquiries, then that person automatically loses his reputation in the eyes of his boss and many of his coworkers. I did not know how affairs stood with me: whether they simply had "summoned" me or whether they had taken an "interest" in me as well, that is, called the magazines for which I worked. As it became clear later—both the one and the other.

The man from the KGB with whom I spoke on the phone obviously wanted to seem like a simpleton. He gave me some sort of surname like Karasikov—"Kariskov is my name, yes." (There had been a popular comedy film where the hero had a similar surname.) I did not bother to memorize his name, figuring it was fictitious. Upon meeting, he gave me a different surname that had a more serious sound to it—Mikhailov. I suppose this was also invented, they probably had as many names as they needed, each with a corresponding set of documents. This man who called himself "Karasikov" when we spoke on the phone, kept repeating himself and like a provincial on the streets of Moscow explained to me how to find their office, and at what door I should enter. His manner reminded me of that of Inspector Porfiry from Dostoevsky's *Crime and Punishment*. Inspector Porfiry also was very simple in his bearing, disguising his shrewd intelligence. Either "Comrade Karasikov" had performed the feat of reading Dostoevsky or Dostoevsky's characters continue to exist in real life.

After speaking on the phone to this man from the Lubianka I felt timid and apprehensive. The phone call affected me as it would a mischievous schoolboy who had been called in to the school director. I feared all such calls and summonses since childhood. I inherited this fear from my mother who was frightened of everything and constantly expected "unpleasantries" from all sides. In the Soviet Union there really are many simple things that can bring serious difficulties which follow a person for an entire lifetime.

My mother, having lived through the terror of the first years of Soviet power, was almost always frightened for my father and for myself. She worried that I would be expelled from school, and then she worried that I would be expelled from the institute, and then sent out of Moscow, and so on. And all this worry was not caused by my behavior or performance at school, which were exemplary. It was simply the natural fear of Soviet parents. Repression applied to parents spread to children and vice versa. I thought more often not about what would happen to me if I experienced such difficulties, but about what would become of my mother, that she would fall ill from worry. What would have happened to her now if she were alive and knew that I was being summoned directly to the Lubianka?

Arriving at the Lubianka I waited in the hall and soon a young man, twenty-five years old, maybe more, came out to greet me. I knew by his age that he was not the man with whom I had spoken on the phone. He smiled as if he and I were old friends. I saw him for the first time in my life. He must have been examining the photographs in my dossier. He led me past an armed guard and took me further into the building. We went into a small plain room. It had practically no furniture, the walls were painted gray and there were some sort of pipes in the corner, either for water or for electric cables. An older man was waiting for us. He also was plain, in plain clothes, with a bald skull and a face that gave a frog-like impression. But all in all quite friendly.

"Well, of course, Porfiry," I thought as soon as I saw him.

His appearance reminded me of Dostoevsky's Porfiry just as I had imagined him. "Porfiry" got up, held out his hand for a handshake, introduced himself with some name and patronymic, something like Vladimir Ivanovich, and with a smile got down to business.

"We summoned you, Andrei Vladimirovich, because we need your help." He made a slight pause. "We know that you are an honest, decent person." He again paused, as if awaiting an answer.

"Thank you," I said, "but how do you know about my honesty?"

"We know everything."

"Again thank you for this information, I myself wasn't fully aware of it."

The young man who had met me in the hall and who now was present at our conversation frowned. He obviously did not like my answer very much, but "Porfiry" did not alter the polite expression on his face.

"We also know that you are educated."

"That's not difficult to check."

"Of course it's not difficult. We can check everything that we need to check. You finished two institutes of higher learning, worked on television and now work as a journalist at extremely well respected magazines. Isn't that so?"

I nodded my head and waited for what would follow this outpouring of compliments.

"We need your consultation," "Porfiry" said.

"So," I thought to myself, "there are no longer interrogations, now people are summoned to Lubianka for 'consultations' and spoken to with the utmost courtesy." I looked at him and waited.

"We need some advice concerning one of your acquaintances—a citizen of the United States." "Porfiry" allowed a pregnant pause. "We trust that you know of what we are speaking."

I nodded.

"Fine. We know quite enough about her, but we'd like to have your opinion."

"I was called into Lubianka so that you might 'confer' with me?"

"Porfiry" and the young man attentively followed the expression in my face.

"What do you think," he continued, "is she really a graduate student and historian?"

"Yes, she's a graduate student in history at Stanford University in California. She came to Moscow on the exchange program that—"

"Yes, we all know very well about the program," "Porfiry" interrupted me. "We'd like to know your opinion—is she really an historian and graduate student from some university?"

"I didn't check her documents."

"Documents we ourselves can check if we need to . . . Excuse me, but I must repeat my question from the very beginning. We would like to know your opinion, I emphasize, your personal opinion—is Lois Sydney Becker an historian and a graduate student?"

"I am not a specialist in history."

"Andrei Vladimirovich, I am not asking you what field you specialize in—I already know that. I need to know your opinion. . .if the word opinion bothers you, fine, let's say I'm interested in your impression. Is your acquaintance an historian and a graduate student?"

"I can't give you any impression. I've heard that there is a very big difference between Soviet and American systems of education. I can't judge. You'd do better to invite a specialist for this consultation."

"But we have already invited you and therefore let us continue our conversation with you ... Did your acquaintance tell you how she happened to be one of the graduate students who was sent to Moscow? Was there some sort of competition at her university that she won? Or has she written an outstanding work on Russian history?"

"No, she has said nothing about this."

"Porfiry's" face took on a serious, even anxious expression. The young man instantaneously also became serious and concerned.

"What did she tell you about her university professors?"

"She didn't."

"Nothing?"

"Nothing. I didn't ask her."

"What did she tell you about her friends in America?"

"I didn't ask her about that, either."

"How can that be? You've known each other for almost half a year and yet you haven't asked her about anything?"

"I don't like to ask people about such things. They can talk about themselves if they want to. This is a rule I use in my work as a journalist."

"But you have told her about yourself."

"Yes, quite a bit."

"What exactly?"

"I told her about my work, about my travels, about my friends, about my life."

"That's not good. We Russians, unlike foreigners, are very indiscreet. An American wouldn't tell you about himself, especially about his business. Well, what can you say about her character, about her habits?"

"Is that very necessary for you?"

"Very."

"She loves chocolate, cheese and beer. And she always wants to lose weight."

"That's not a very good way to lose weight," "Porfiry" laughed. After him, like a reflecting wave, laughter spread on the face of the young man.

"What else?"

"She loves animals and plants."

"What kinds of animals?"

"Cats."

"Are there any other 'weaknesses'?"

"Home in America she indulges in marijuana."

"Uh-huh. And are you curious? Would you like to try it?"

"Of course. I'd like to try it very much."

"Don't do that, Andrei Vladimirovich!" blurted out the young man, as if warning me of a danger that threatened me that very moment.

"Nonsense," "Porfiry" stopped him. "It's nothing that terrible. In America they're discussing a project that would permit the smoking of marijuana in Congress."

"You mean that Senators can indulge?" the young man asked.

"Porfiry" didn't answer him. He smiled at me.

"We wouldn't prosecute you for that."

"Thank you, but I can't avail myself of your permission. She has none here in Moscow."

"Maybe some of the other Americans?"

"No, the others also have none."

"Who are her parents?"

"Her father owns a store."

"Big? Successful?"

"I didn't ask."

"What can you say about her Moscow acquaintances?"

"She basically associates with me."

"For whom did she bring letters and parcels from America?"

"I don't know."

"Has she mentioned the names Viktor, Iurii, Vladimir in her conversations?"

"No."

"To whom did she bring books?"

"I don't know."

"What sort of people's company does she prefer in Moscow?"

"She prefers my company."

"What interests her in Moscow most of all?"

"Theater."

"Who does she go to the theater with?"

"With me."

"Who gets the tickets for her?"

"She goes to the theater administrators with letters from the embassy."

"And for whom does she pass letters on to the embassy?"

"She doesn't."

"Which of the Moscow dissidents is she acquainted with?"

"None."

"What does she know about them?"

"Whatever they write in American newspapers."

"What do you know about them?"

"Whatever they broadcast on the foreign radio channels."

"You listen to these broadcasts?"

"I listen."

"How often?"

"Regularly."

"To whom do you relate the contents of these broadcasts?"

"To no one."

"Which of her friends have you met?"

"None."

"Where do you two go?"

"To the theater."

"What had she heard about Moscow theater?"

"Very little."

"From whom?"

"From her American friends who had earlier been in the Soviet Union."

"Who are they?"

"Friends at her university."

"Do you know something about them?"

"Nothing."

"What has she heard about Moscow theater from Muscovites?"

"She's heard nothing."

The "consultation" continued along these lines for a while longer, like a child's game where one of the children is blindfolded and he searches about the room for some object while all the others scream "hot" or "cold" depending on how far he is from his goal. Therefore it was not difficult to guess what "Porfiry" wanted. After repeatedly hinting that Lois was neither an historian nor a graduate student, he then wanted to know her Moscow acquaintances. That was to be expected. I never believed that there was any truth behind these innuendoes; they would hardly search out spies in such a primitive fashion. If there had been something serious they would have been more skillful. In place of my "Porfiry" there would have been a genuine Porfiry like the one who psychologically tortured Raskolnikov and compelled him to confession.

"Thank you," Comrade Karasikov/Mikhailov/"Porfiry" finally said. He apparently had tired a bit.

I, on the other hand, felt a sense of relief. It was over. It seemed that there could be nothing serious; they could not accuse me of a thing.

"Perhaps you need something else?" I said. "She told me about San Francisco. If you'd like, I'll tell you. For example, she told me that there are women prostitutes there who used to be men."

"So, that's what you'd like!" exclaimed the young man. "How can you, Andrei Vladimirovich!?"

I did not even look in his direction.

"That's enough," said "Porifiry" glumly. "I have a sufficient picture of you and I want to give you some good advice. Don't let women lead you by the nose. Your American has had intimate contacts here in Moscow not only with you."

"Would you like me to inform you of some of the savory details?" the young man inserted. "You don't want me to? . . . As you prefer."

"Nevertheless, by the right of seniority, I want to ask you one more question," continued "Porfiry", (he was approximately the same age as I, only shabby and worn). "What are your further plans concerning your acquaintance? Do you intend to marry her?"

"I don't know. I'm thinking about it."

"Think. Think. Think very hard about whom you are intending to marry. What would happen to the two of you? Neither you nor she will ever get work in America."

"And in the Soviet Union?" I asked.

"And in the Soviet Union there might also be problems."

"And where would there be fewer problems?"

My question angered "Porfiry."

"How can you seriously think about this?" the young man was agitated. "After all, you write your essays about the strong Soviet people. Why aren't they planning to marry Americans? Why do they work in Siberia and in the far North, and not in Nevada or Arizona?"

"Fine, I'll think about it," I answered.

"If you'd like, I can discuss this with her," Porfiry said. "I can explain what awaits her in such a situation."

"What! I should tell her that you have also invited her for a 'consultation'?"

"No, you can tell her that you know a lawyer who specializes in international law. . . . Or you can say that employees of the KGB would like to give her some advice. We're no Mafia, we have nothing to hide."

"Fine, I'll pass that on to her."

"I won't hold you any longer. My time is up. Aleksei Vasilievich will continue this conversation with you."

Brusquely, like a military man, he nodded in the direction of the young man. Then having curtly and coldly nodded to me, "Porfiry" left.

Aleksei Vasilievich sat somewhat sourly.

"Well, Andrei Vladimirovich," he said after a moment of sad musings, "let's go. I'll escort you and we'll talk a bit outside. These official surroundings tire me."

The young man named Aleksei Vasilievich walked with me through the center of Moscow, my beloved Moscow, where I had spent my whole life. We went from Dzerzhinsky to Theater Square where the Bolshoi and Maly Theaters are located, theaters well known to me since my school days. This young man aroused in me no respect whatsoever; he carried himself like a bad actor.

"You can't imagine, Andrei Vladimirovich," he said, "how difficult it is for us to work, what a small staff of people we have, so little money . . . You don't believe it? . . . . Well, believe it, it's true. And so many different types come here under the guise of students, tourists, what have you. Yes, it's very difficult to get the job done. . . ."

Letting out a brief sigh he moved on to what seemed to me to be the most important part of the conversation, the reason for which I had been summoned.

"We absolutely must know the telephone numbers or addresses of all the Moscow acquaintances of your American acquaintance."

"You already know everything, even the savory details."

"Yes, of course . . . but among her contacts is someone who directs her activity. We must find him and for this we need all the addresses without exception."

"I can't be useful to you in this affair."

The young man shook his head.

"You consider such work dirty? You don't want to soil your hands? OK, fine respected sir," he said in stern reproach. "Couldn't you, for example, take her to the movies so that she'd leave her purse with her address book in your room?"

"You, it seems, want to get a look at her address book. Who is going to do this? One of my neighbors in my apartment?"

"Oh, Andrei Vladimirovich, you should know whom you are defending!"

"I don't know but I'm beginning to guess . . . What do you hope to find in her address book—the telephone number of the chief American spy in Moscow? Since when have spies started to carry telephone numbers and addresses in books that neighbors can steal?"

"Andrei Vladimirovich! Andrei Vladimirovich! Aren't you ashamed? I can't enlighten you to all the details of the affair. They could be using your acquaintance 'in the dark'—she herself might not know that they are using her."

"All of this, even for me, does not sound like a story involving spies. More to the point, it's psychological pressure on me."

"Andrei Vladimirovich, Andrei Vladimirovich . . . OK. To look in someone's address book is bad, but trading in foreign items is good? Doesn't your acquaintance do this? She does, my dear. I even know to whom she sells her things."

"Again, there's something not right here. Now it appears that you are worried by the fact that American jeans and pantyhose are being illegally sold in Moscow, am I right? Or, are you still interested in spies?"

"No, jeans and pantyhose don't worry us. What does worry us is what is hidden under the guise of simple speculation in clothes."

"I see, so under the disguise of Moscow fartsovshchiki hide American spies?"

"How simply you picture it all. I, by the way, did not use the word 'spy', but imagine, there are people in hiding who are working to

undermine the socialist system, people engaged in ideological subversion on the territory of the Soviet Union."

"I think you would do better to appeal for help to those people that
you already know. To those people who buy and resell the jeans and
pantyhose."

The young man looked at me with a severe expression. He screwed
up his eyes threateningly and knit his brows together.

"I very strongly advise you not to think that way," he said. "Goodbye
for now. If you find that some unpleasantries creep into your life I,
despite everything, am ready to help you. Here is my phone number."

He wrote a phone number in a small notebook, tore out the page
and held it out to me. We gave each other a nod and went off in different
directions.

This page, with a telephone number and nothing else written on it,
I kept for a long time in my desk at home, just in case. In their conversation with me, "Porfiry" and the young man had urgently tried to create
the impression that Lois was involved in something that she ought not
to be involved in. In the Soviet Union, contact with a foreigner who is
involved in any illegal activity is especially dangerous. They could accuse
me of complicity in such an affair.

But Lois had not taken a step away from me for most of her stay
in Moscow. Such a waste of time would have been unallowable for a
person whose specialization was "ideological subversion on the territory
of the Soviet Union." I could not believe what the people from the
Lubianka had told me about Lois. Their intentions became obvious to
me. I tore up the page with the phone number of the young man and
dropped the pieces of paper into the toilet.

I told Lois nothing about my summons to KGB headquarters. The
KGB sternly warns those they have summoned that it is forbidden to
tell anyone about such conversations. I nevertheless warned Lois that
she should be careful, especially with her telephone book.

Lois soon became a witness to the "unpleasantries" that were slated
for me, the "unpleasantries" in regards to which the young man had
offered his "help." One morning a man in a police uniform and another
in civilian clothes came to my apartment and tried to enter my room.
I did not let them. They left, promising that they would not leave me
in peace. The magazines where I had worked for the last ten years no

longer called me in for assignments. When I called the magazines I noticed an odd chill in the voices of my co-workers and superiors. All that was left was to await the results of work I had already done and that had been previously accepted by my editors.

I came to trust Lois more and more. My feelings towards her became even more serious. If at the Lubianka in the section on foreign students they had known psychology better, they would not have bothered to cast a shadow on Lois's reputation. I found in her more and more traits that I liked. Whenever we discussed topics in her field, Russian intellectual history, I listened with great interest to what she told me.

Most of all what astonished me about Lois was her devotion to our relations in conditions that were so difficult for us both. The odds of happiness were very slight. Before me stood a small woman who seemed to love me and wanted to help me, who understood and respected me. She was often nervous, worried about how this "adventure" would turn out. Perhaps there would be years of futile waiting as had occurred with several Americans who married in the Soviet Union. Nevertheless, she forced herself to stand up for what she thought was right. In her outward appearance she seemed so weak, but in fact she was very strong. And who stood against her? The strongest police machine in the world! They spared no expense in following us both in order to create an atmosphere of fear around us, to convince us of the uncertainty of any future we might have together.

My feelings and thoughts were in confusion. I felt that I was not ready to get married. I was too accustomed to the life of a bachelor, to that small freedom that I could possess. And I highly valued my position as a freelance journalist, again with that small portion of freedom that it allowed me. Besides, I clearly understood that a conflict with the authorities was the most likely result of a marriage with an American. And if I ever succeeded in leaving for America I would most likely never be able to return to Russia. I would lose my homeland—the birthplace of my native language, my native culture, my history and the history of my people. I knew that I would have to risk all that I had, but that I could also win a great deal. I could win a life worthy of a human being and I could win happiness. It was worth the risk. "He who does not risk does not drink champagne!" as the Russian saying goes. The Soviet life that stood before me felt like a cold, damp and dark cellar in which I might die never having seen the sun's light, never having breathed fresh air.

Oh, the devil with it all! I wanted to leave with Lois for America and become an American! As for my homeland, I had the faint hope that something might change within my lifetime, that someday it would be possible to return. Futile dreams! These dreams appear with the advent of each new regime and then they fall by the wayside.

LBF

In February of 1981 Andrei and I handed in a petition of marriage to ZAGS, the Moscow Office of Registry on Griboedev Street, where marriages between Soviet citizens and foreigners are performed and registered. We still had to wait three months for the ceremony and registration, three nervous months.

It was my initiative to hand in the petition. I told Andrei that I loved him and that I would take him out of this damned country and then he could do as he liked.

Andrei once told me that people come in two types. There are those who when pushed will yield. And there are those who when pushed push back. I had never had cause to think about it before but I now realized that I was one of those who pushed back.

I decided to marry Andrei because I was angry, because I loved him, and because I did not want him to live like this any longer. Whether or not we would have a future together in America, I was determined to get him out of the Soviet Union. If I had left him the police would have gone away, but Andrei's problem would have remained. He always would want out. I warned Andrei that for a Russian intellectual, life in the United States is difficult. He would be cut off from his culture, his life blood, and American life has demands that are unfamiliar to a Soviet. But these concerns seemed unimportant compared to the insults and fears that he now lived with. At least in America his life would be his own.

I put aside the question of his loving me. He had entrusted me with his freedom, asking nothing. Perhaps in the Soviet Union trust was more of a commitment than love.

MARRIAGE

L B F

When I decided to marry Andrei I was initially quite concerned about the U.S. Embassy's reaction. Being aware of the seriousness of the step and the difficulties that lay ahead I knew it would be important to have the Embassy's support. And I thought it reasonable to expect the sup-port of my government in exercising the rights allowed me by interna-tional accords that the Soviet government had signed and by the Soviet constitution itself. But policy was against me. The Embassy is opposed to binational marriages and was being very vocal about its displeasure the year I was in Moscow.

Embassy officials fear that, more often than not, binational mar-riages are fictitious marriages, that is, marriages in which there is no real feeling and in which an American has agreed to marry a Soviet simply ·to secure his or her passage out of the country. Fictitious marriages are a fairly common occurrence in Soviet life. Often an inhabitant of an outlying area will arrange to marry an inhabitant of a large city in order to secure permission to live and be registered in the city, where the standard of living and the opportunities for advancement are higher. People may marry in order to secure a larger apartment. Often couples remain married long after relations have ceased so as to hold on to apartments granted as a result of marriage. Non-Jewish Soviets some-times marry Soviet Jews so that the spouses can petition to leave the Soviet Union together on an Israeli visa. Last, and certainly least in terms of numbers, are marriages to foreigners in order to leave the country. It is the least common, but is considered the surest way out.

Americans who enter into fictitious marriages with Soviets common-ly do so for one of two reasons. The first is money. A marriage can be arranged in the United States by a relative or friend of the Soviet citizen, or arranged in the Soviet Union. The second is conviction. An American stunned by Soviet reality wants to commit himself to helping one per-son, someone who has risked becoming his friend. The Embassy is steadfastly opposed to marriages on either of these grounds.

Even where the Embassy has evidence of an American's sincere interest in a binational marriage, it has objections. It feels that Ameri-cans agree to such marriages unaware of the problems that lie ahead, such as the possible interference of the Soviet authorities, and the difficul-ties involved in acquiring an exit visa for the Soviet citizen once the marriage has taken place. It feels that most Americans have been hood-winked into marriage, either by some sharpie who simply wants to leave the Soviet Union to come to a better life in America, or, more seriously, by some sharpie who would serve as a Soviet plant in the United States under the guise of marriage vows.

In general, the U.S. Embassy does not relish free contact between its citizens and those of the Soviet Union. It prefers to regulate and control contacts, not as stringently as its KGB counterpart, but with similar sentiments. Ordinary citizens have no place in Soviet-American relations.

The students that arrive each year in Moscow are greeted with a slight air of hostility. Their naive wanderings and forays into Soviet society are a major source of irritation for the Embassy, beneficial only in that they provide new grist for the gossip mill which tires of the continual discussion of who sleeps with whom and how dull and dreary it is in Moscow.

The students are only endured because of the bigger policy picture. The exchange programs were founded years ago when relations were better. They bring a distinct economic advantage to the Soviet govern-ment. Soviet students in the United States study advanced technology. American students in the Soviet union study Russian language, history and literature. These programs continue because the Soviets want them, and the United States government wants to placate the Soviets on this small front in hopes of gaining influence on larger ones. And, the American academic community supports the exchanges because they offer American scholars and professors a rare and vital glimpse into Soviet life.

The year that I was in Moscow quite a few of the younger students who were in Moscow on a four-month exchange program had decided to marry Soviet citizens. It was clear that some of these cases were fictitious. The Embassy decided to put its foot down. It held lectures with the younger students and had our group leader convey the message to us. Fictitious marriages are illegal not only in the USSR but in the United States as well, and since we were in Moscow under the supervision of the Embassy they would take it upon themselves to ship home anyone involved in a marriage of convenience.

I was quite concerned about the Embassy's reaction to my plans to marry Andrei. I realized that eyebrows would be raised when the large differences in our ages became known and most would suspect the worst. I tried to keep my plans a secret, telling only one American friend. I had no reason to suspect that the Embassy knew of my involvement with Andrei or of the problems we had encountered. I prepared all the documents required for the Soviet petition of marriage, obtained the necessary official translations and decided to inform the Embassy supervisor of our exchange program as soon as I handed these papers in to the Soviet authorities.

The man who oversaw our program was like the rest of the Embassy staff in one respect: he hated being in Moscow. Moscow was boring. No good restaurants. No nightlife. No dependable dry cleaners. Miserable food.

This last complaint I never quite understood, as the Embassy people did not subsist on anything approaching the typical Soviet diet. Their produce was shipped in directly from Helsinki. Besides fruit and vegetables, most diplomats boasted a kitchen replete with Twinkies, corn flakes and Swanson TV dinners. In general, they kept to themselves, or associated with the staffs of other Western embassies.

One of our program director's interests was theater, and we often spoke about it together. By his own admission, he did not understand enough Russian to go to Moscow theater much, but he was interested in my impressions. Acquiring tickets was no easy task, and understanding Russian drama, which is often interspersed with poetry and can last up to four hours at a crack, was even harder. My perseverance in the

face of these difficulties seemed to him a valid indication of the stubborn
unreality of my outlook on life.

I did not know what to expect when I went to see him with my news,
and I braced myself for the worst. I had just handed in my documents,
and I wanted it to be clear that there was no turning back. In what
seemed a mocking tone, he asked me how I was doing. "Fine, fine," I
replied. He then asked about my research, if I was getting a lot done,
if I was being given access to all the materials that I needed, how I was
enjoying Moscow. I answered all the questions briefly, perhaps bluntly
out of nervousness, and then I announced that I was here to tell him
that I was marrying a Soviet citizen.

"We know," he replied. "We've been expecting you."

I was baffled as to how they found out. His response produced the
intended effect on me: once again I was made to realize that all was not
as it seemed, that I was involved in a game that had more twists than
I was aware. I was also relieved. It was out in the open. I would not have
to go into any lengthy explanations of my intentions. It appeared that
the Embassy had all the information it required and had formed some
opinion about my case. The program supervisor gave me no hint as to
what that opinion was. He simply asked me if I was aware of possible
difficulties. I said "yes,"and we parted on a friendly note. With a heavy
sigh of resignation he said to me:

"I wish you the best of luck."

The next reaction to my impending wedding was neither solicited,
direct, nor American. It came from the Soviet Ministry of Higher Education and went through the group leader of our exchange.

Soviets do things in groups. It is called "the spirit of the collective."
The idea in theory is that people work together, live together, take care
of one another all in groups. Collective responsibility. The microcosm
of the socialist cooperation of mankind. In reality it means that Soviet
citizens are encouraged to report on one another and criticize the personal lives of others. It means that Soviets travel in threes when going
abroad so that one is there to report on the other two. They send three
and not two because it is easier for two people to collude. In a group
of three everyone suspects one another.

We American students constituted our own collective. We had elected
a group leader and his role was to facilitate certain administrative matters. He, myself and one other student had petitioned to extend our

student visas. The petitions had been filed in December with no re-sponse until March when our group leader was called in by a fairly high-ranking official of the Ministry of Higher Education.

"We have a problem with your visa extensions," the official an-nounced. "It's Lois Becker. I'm afraid that her misconduct will keep you all from receiving extensions."

"What misconduct?"

The official produced a police report. It stated that Lois Becker had moved in to the apartment of Soviet citizen and journalist Andrei Frolov, and had been living there for several months. It was typed on official paper and signed by police authorities. The official continued:

"You understand what a problem this presents for us. She has violated the passport regime by living in Mr. Frolov's apartment. We could kick her out of the country for it."

"Oh, I'm sure it won't come to that," our politic group leader said. "Besides, she's living in the dormitory now, so what's the problem?"

"I've had a phone call," the official said in a menacing manner. "*They* say there is a question of fictitious marriage here. We want you to find out how serious she is, and why."

"But I didn't even know that she was planning to marry. Isn't that her affair?"

"Not if she wants to extend her visa, or for that matter, not if any of you want to extend yours. I think you ought to talk to her, explain things to her. Women are sometimes slow to understand such things. I am thinking of your best interests."

Such is the spirit of the collective.

One week after I got married, five months after I had applied for a visa extension, and three months after our group leader told me about his meeting at the Ministry of Higher Education, I was officially denied a visa extension. My only consolation was that at least the others were granted theirs.

A F

Lois and I lived one life in Moscow; we spent all our time together. I tried to show her everything that I loved: my favorite old streets, museums, theater. But the situation in Moscow had become too tense. When Lois received permission to go to Leningrad and we could go there together I was especially happy. We wanted to get away, spend some time in different surroundings.

Leningrad I love even more than Moscow. I love the Neva, the buildings, the streets, the museums, the parks. I even love Leningrad's weather which many find horrible. Whenever the opportunity arose to spend some time in Leningrad I would go. I looked forward to the night train and then arriving early in the morning at the Moscow station in Leningrad. In a state of nervous excitement I would step out of the station door and immediately come out onto Nevsky Prospect—the center of town. And every time I would walk along Nevsky Prospect enjoying my rendezvous with the city which for me was always more than a city, but an old and best friend.

The first time I was in Leningrad was in the first years after the war. My parents sent me to spend several days at my uncle's, my father's brother. Leningrad still bore the remnants of the war's destruction and those Leningraders who survived the blockade were emaciated, their eyes transparent from exhaustion. It was spring, nature was coming alive, life was returning. In the Leningrad White Nights I wandered about the streets and along the shores of the Neva, gazing at the bridges and at the water. I dreamed of what I might become, and wondered what sort of life there would be now—good or bad? I felt that it would probably be good—the main thing was that it would be new and unknown. People did not talk about politics then: they were hungry, poorly dressed, and lived in horribly crowded conditions.

Two years later I worked on a ship that was based at the Murmansk port and very often I stopped in at Leningrad. Each time I showed up at my uncle's. He lived near the Nikolsky Cathedral, right next to the streets that are described in Dostoevsky's novels. Dostoevsky described them so accurately that it is possible to find the places in which his heroes lived and to retrace their steps.

My uncle spoke with me as with a grown man. It was interesting for me to listen to him. He had been an officer in the First World War, but he did not serve in the Second because of his poor health. My uncle lived in an age that had long ago passed. For him, time had stopped at the moment when he was a lieutenant in the Tsar's army. He viewed the present with open disdain, and he called the government a mob of villains and scoundrels.

My uncle's past as the "acrimonious lieutenant," the fantasies evoked by literary images, the thoughts of my future—all of these were unreal from beginning to end. I spent all my free time wandering about the city that reminded me of a Russia that was young, and full of hope and achievements. Here I had dreamed of becoming a sailor, a traveler and writer. A sailor I already was.

When I was a student at the Institute in Moscow I tried to spend every holiday in Leningrad. A train ticket cost very little, about ten rubles, and I would travel up on the night train. I had heard of people who had their business in Moscow but lived in Leningrad. These were people of the free professions: writers, professors, artists. It was easier to earn money in Moscow but a person who has lived in Leningrad for a while cannot easily part with her. I dreamed of moving from Moscow to Leningrad.

My uncle had become very old by then, and not everyone understood what he had to say. For example, when he spoke about honesty and worth these words had the opposite meaning of that which they had in the Soviet lexicon. I understood my uncle and I still liked to talk with him and listen to his reminiscing. My poor uncle had turned into a reminiscence. They could have dressed him and put him in a museum as an exhibit. He finally left Leningrad to live out his days in Kalinin, formerly Tver, where he and my father spent their childhoods.

I continued to travel to Leningrad on the average of twice a year. Sometimes I stopped on the way to see my uncle, Kalinin being halfway between Moscow and Leningrad. By then I had my own friends in Leningrad and I spent time with them. And just as if in corroboration of my uncle's words that continually railed against Soviet reality, the people of my generation were left with fewer and fewer hopes and illusions. And Leningrad, which in my youth had personified Young Russia, the Russia of Peter the Great, turned another side towards me as I became older. The city represented the power of a different epoch, the age of Tsar Nicholas and the beginning of the reaction. Leningrad continued to hold my youthful dreams which, like my uncle's past, had already become reminiscences. I could not live without this city and I continued to travel to it.

One time I lived six months in Leningrad. I stayed in the empty apartment of a friend and finished up a book that had been approved by a Moscow publishing house. It was again spring and I walked about the streets on those bright Leningrad nights and, well—my dreams, it seemed, had come true. I had been a sailor, I now traveled throughout the Soviet Union as a journalist, and soon my first book would be complete. Perhaps there would be others. I had become a person with a free profession and now I soon might be moving to my beloved Leningrad and on occasion traveling to Moscow on business.

But fate was pleased to make different arrangements. I had returned to Moscow when the publishing firm that had accepted my book unexpectedly informed me that it could not be printed because the role of the Communist Party was not reflected in it. Soon after, a film that was to be shot for television based on a screenplay that I had written was also rejected after having been originally approved. I never knew the reason for my sudden bad luck. Publishers do not want to have dealings with a person who has had two serious misfortunes. They reason that once a person has been refused twice it means that there must be something behind it, some more serious problem. Such a person falls into a series of failures. If fortune turns its back on a Soviet then it is for a very long time.

I again came to Leningrad. Using my former ties and acquaintances I took a room on the top floor, the sixteenth floor, of the hotel "Soviet" which stands on the shore of the Fontanka River. I did not do anything. Whole days I looked out at the city stretching out before me in all its faded pastel tones. It submerged into the fog, its spires shone in the rays of the sun that penetrated through the low clouds. Leningrad was again unreal, inaccessible, unrealizable. Again it had turned into a dream. I consoled myself with the fact that I could still earn a living with a pen as a free-lance journalist.

And then fate sent me Lois. We had put in our petition of marriage to the Moscow ZAGS, and I went to Leningrad again, together with her. A new, perhaps the most serious, turn in my life was about to take place. A vague anxiety filled my soul.

We could not travel together to Leningrad on the same train. Lois went in a car for foreigners and I in an ordinary car for Soviet citizens. Once in Leningrad I quickly noticed that we were under observation.

It was as if they tried to poison everything they could, as if happiness for me in this life ought not to be. I now knew how to pick out people sent to observe me. I knew how they looked, how they spoke, even what sort of morals they had. Oh, how right my uncle had been! If now were the time of his youth I would put on a military uniform and go to fight them, rifle in hand.

At 11:00 each night I saw Lois to the dormitory of Leningrad University where, according to the rules for foreigners, she was obliged to spend the night. I then walked across Vasilievsky Island to my friend's apartment. He was an artist. He gave me his bed in a studio on the top floor of a tall building. A long, seemingly endless back staircase ran up to this top floor. By evening it was in semi-darkness. The entrance to the stairs was off the courtyard, a typical Leningrad well-like courtyard in the cramped space between the stone walls of buildings. The light fell into it from above. From the windows of his studio I looked out on the various streets and roofs of the surrounding buildings, just as I had looked out then from the shore of the Fontanka. The ceiling was slanted with heavy vaults, and the windows peered out of the roof like the eyes of some amphibious creature.

My friend advised me not to find a hotel room. Without papers certifying that I was on an official business trip it would be impossible to get a separate room and in a shared room, the only thing I could hope for, they would probably plant a KGB agent. I did not want to give them the opportunity of rummaging through my pockets while I slept.

The whole time that Lois and I were in Leningrad, about two weeks, I was plagued by the idea that I could be bringing serious harm to my friend. I recalled how they used the registration law against Lois and me. More disturbing was the recent campaign against artists. There were frequent cases of arson in the studios of unorthodox artists. The studio next to my friend's had been burned. Why would burglars break into a studio, gather pictures into a pile on the floor, and burn them? These cases of arson ran simultaneously with a media campaign for "the struggle of the authorities against the contemporary avant garde in painting." No one had any doubt that the arson cases were perpetrated by the KGB against artists that the authorities found objectionable.

Someone had taken an interest in my presence at my friend's studio. On three occasions in the early morning hours someone persistently rang at the door of the studio. I did not answer. It could not have been acquaintances of my friend because they all knew where he was staying while I was living at his home.

Often at night, after saying goodbye to Lois, I could not return straight to the studio and fall asleep. I walked about the city in solitude. I decided not to visit my other friends so as not to throw suspicion on them. It was bad enough with the artist.

There remain in my memory the days Lois and I spent together in Leningrad, how we walked about the city holding each other's hands, as if someone could separate us only when we untwined our fingers. I recall my wanderings through the night city, when rain mixed with snow fell from the clouds. In my memory, the Leningrad of my youthful dreams is full of summer, with green islands and currents of warm air that carry what seem to be happy melodies.

Even now in America I sometimes dream of a beautiful city that resembles Leningrad. In it there are bridges, embankments, arches and colonnades. In my dream I wander about, I cannot recall what city it is. It is empty, there are no people and I cannot find refuge. In Leningrad I left my joy and my pain. The pain comes calling for me more often.

LBF

After handing in our marriage petition to ZAGS, the office where Soviet citizens register births, deaths, marriages and divorces, Andrei and I decided to go to Leningrad for two weeks. Ostensibly I was going there to work in an archive, but it was closed for repairs for the entire year. I would have almost all of my time free to be with Andrei. He was so excited to show me his Leningrad, and I was glad for the break from Moscow.

I had to get an official leave from Moscow University to go to Leningrad. I was obligated to spend every evening in the special dormitory for students from capitalist countries at Leningrad University. Andrei stayed at an artist friend's studio. Just as in Moscow, we could be together only during the day, but at least it would be just the two of us on the streets of Leningrad. Or so we thought.

When Andrei went to buy the tickets to Leningrad he found out that we could not travel together, not in the same compartment, not even on the same train. I had to buy my tickets at a special cashier for foreigners. Here the tickets were a bit more expensive and the security a lot tighter. When I went to buy my ticket I brought every possible document and university clearance. I handed it all in and waited around for half an hour while the cashier ran a check on me and the other foreigners who wanted to travel on Soviet trains the next day. The phone rang, the cashier listened to the instructions on the other end, smiled that sweet smile, and finally issued our tickets.

Andrei traveled on a train for ordinary Soviet citizens, a little bit cheaper, a little bit dirtier. At first we thought we might buy two tickets at the regular cashier and travel together on the ordinary train, but our intuition said no. After the incident with the police we were careful not to give anyone ammunition to use against us.

Our trains left Moscow at approximately the same time, but Andrei's was scheduled to arrive in Leningrad an hour later than mine. On the station platform in Moscow we agreed that when I arrived the next morning I would immediately go to the dormitory and register. Andrei would go straight to his friend's to catch him before he left for the day. Afterwards we were to meet on the bank of the Neva River at the monument known as the Bronze Horseman. I remembered it well from my first trip to Leningrad nine years earlier.

When I got to the Bronze Horseman the next morning I did not find Andrei there. I strolled about. It had been a long time since I first came to Leningrad with my family. The city had left such a strong impression on me. It was so eerily beautiful, the embankments and bridges that adorned the winding rivers—the silvery, slithering snakes of Andrei Bely's *Petersburg*. And here was the monument to the man who built this city. The Bronze Horseman is located on the edge of a romantic park full of lovely old trees and marble statues. The figure of Peter the Great on his mount is encircled by a walkway. He looks out on the Neva as it cuts through the city. That day the Neva was still under ice and a cold, damp wind blew up from the sea, even as the spring sun was shining. The figure on the horse shone in the matte light of the Leningrad sun. It looked as if it were about to jump across the Neva. The ice glistened across the expanse of the river and the sharp spires of the Peter and Paul Fortress sparkled.

After a while Andrei unexpectedly appeared and broke into my meditative mood. He took me by the hand and pulled me behind an old linden tree which had to be at least two hundred years old. It's trunk hid us both. Andrei pointed out a man who was walking about the base of the monument. This man was in no way distinguishable from the rest of the people milling about and, yet, the more I looked at him the more I sensed something unnatural. The man was wearing a shabby old overcoat together with an expensive fur hat. He moved about with self-assurance, threw quick glances to the side as if he were angry at someone or had lost something, and all the while paced back and forth without any obvious goal. Yes, this completely ordinary man did stand out by the incongruity of his dress and behavior.

"Would you like to see that man disappear?" Andrei asked me.

Andrei took me by the hand and in definite, determined steps went right up to the man. I caught just a glimpse of him. He had a sort of nondescript, blank face with colorless eyes. In general he was gray. Andrei later said that this impression is produced by the lacklustre soul that looks out from the gray face. Upon our unexpected appearance something changed on his face; there appeared something like a dull smile that disappeared immediately, replaced by an indifferent expression. Andrei and I began to circle slowly about the base of the monument. For a moment he was right at our heels.

"Now I'll show you some magic," Andrei whispered. He sharply turned with me in tow and headed in the opposite direction. The gray man in the fur hat was nowhere to be seen; he had dissolved into thin air.

"He is somewhere close by," Andrei chuckled. "He's hidden behind other people or perhaps behind a tree as we did earlier. He is observing us. I picked him out by his hat. They give those hats out free to their people, like a uniform. In Stalin's day they wore boots with galoshes. The rest of their clothing might have been as varied as imaginable, but there were always those boots with galoshes. Under Stalin they worked for galoshes and now it's muskrat hats. These people are not paid much, probably no more than 150 rubles a month. To pay them more wouldn't make any sense. They are known as 'the men with the frostbitten ears' since they have to spend so much time outdoors. That's probably why they give them good hats. If we were to disappear again or if he lost us altogether, then he'd be penalized at work, possibly lose his regular bonus. He wouldn't be able to buy something for his family; perhaps he's already promised to buy his son a bicycle."

We hurried to leave, no doubt followed by our friend. I told Andrei not to walk so fast. I said that I did not want this man's son to be stranded all summer without a bicycle. Then I became serious.

"But how did they know that we were to meet at 11:00 A.M. at the Bronze Horseman?"

"Either they overheard our conversation on the platform in Moscow, or simply followed us this morning. The government has the funds to maintain a whole army of such people—maybe that's why we have no unemployment. He's probably not alone—they probably have others in cars and they communicate with each other on the radio. The government doesn't mind spending money on things like that; they don't render an account to anyone. In any case, they certainly don't have to account to the people who pay taxes and are forced to live on such scanty earnings."

All this surveillance shook me. For a moment I wanted to head back to Moscow, but there it was even worse. I had so anxiously anticipated this trip, my "vacation" in Leningrad. Andrei calmed me. He told me to forget about "Them" and try to relax. What's the difference? Let them watch as we enjoyed ourselves. It was not as if we had a choice.

Andrei took me to his favorite places. He wanted me to see everything the very first day. We walked to the grave of Peter the Great in the Peter and Paul Fortress. There were carnations and tulips strewn all about the grave. It is a Soviet custom to show respect to historical figures by placing flowers at their graves or monuments. At the Lenin monuments, which number in the hundreds in Leningrad, flowers are placed by official delegations, but elsewhere this custom is based on individual initiative. Andrei told me that there are always fresh flowers at the grave of Peter. No one knows who places them there, but there they are, every day.

Another place where there are fresh flowers almost every day, winter and summer, is at the monument to Ivan Kruzenshtern, a famous sea captain in the Russian navy who circumnavigated the globe and sailed to Antarctica. His monument stands in an out of the way spot, not far from the port. Behind him are the modern installations—the docks, the hoisting cranes, the moorings. He stands in a gallant pose looking towards the city.

Andrei and I bought red tulips from a gypsy woman at a bazaar on the way to Kruzenshtern. When we got to the statue Andrei jumped the railing, climbed up on the base and placed the tulips in the crook of Kruzenshtern's arm. He jumped back over the railing and hugged and kissed me, just like a student at one of the nearby naval institutes. There is a tradition that when a future sailor gets married he and his bride bring flowers to Kruzenshtern.

I felt young and free, but Andrei was behaving so extravagantly. It was not like him. I asked him if it was due to our meeting with the gray man at the Bronze Horseman. He answered absolutely not. But there was something weighing on him. He talked a great deal in a manic rush, reminiscing about his work on a ship in his youth. The ship often docked in Leningrad and here he would live with his uncle, a former officer in the tsarist army who lived the rest of his days working as an accountant. He had died several years ago. In Leningrad, as in Moscow, Andrei had no remaining relatives.

We walked back along the Neva, back to the Bronze Horseman. The Bronze Horseman is located in Decembrist Square—the site of the famous Decembrist revolt of 1825 against the tsarist government. Troops loyal to the tsar opened fire on the insurgents who had gathered on the square. Many of them escaped over the ice of the Neva River to the other shore, where Leningrad University stands. Several years ago, on the anniversary of the Decembrist revolt against autocracy, students from the university arranged themselves like mutinous soldiers in a square about the Bronze Horseman. The police broke it up and the students, like the Decembrists, ran across the ice to the other side of the Neva. These Soviet students demanded nothing; that would have been impossible. It was enough that they had expressed their discontent with the regime in this symbolic act.

Andrei wanted to make this trip across the ice, which under the spring sun had begun to melt, making it thin in spots. He was very agitated and would not listen to reason. He descended the slippery embankment steps to the ice. From above people shouted out in warning to him. One of Andrei's legs broke through into the water but he continued on. I followed after him and again there were shouts from

above. We made it to the other side. On the granite steps of the embankment Andrei took off his boot and poured out the cold water. Being
much lighter than Andrei I made it across without mishap. Andrei
walked about wet the rest of the day, and when I suggested that he dry
off he simply said that he did not want to discuss it.

We stopped into a bar that was in a nineteenth century wooden
sailing ship anchored alongside the Peter and Paul Fortress. Then we
stopped into a cozy little restaurant, called "Demian's Fish Stew" after
a Russian fable. Everything was simple and wooden; it looked like a
small Siberian meeting hall. There Andrei poured vodka into his dry
boot. He said that the cold water of the Neva had made the one
boot more comfortable and vodka would do the same for the other.
Some vodka also found its way to our stomachs, making us feel more
comfortable.

We walked along the river. St. Isaac's Cathedral always in sight. The
damp wind from the Baltic Sea again forced us inside to another restaurant, also in a ship moored to the embankment. It was late afternoon
and we were the only patrons. There were windows on both sides of
the dining room in the hull of the ship. The setting sun shone right
through and the ice on the Neva glistened. We could see the city and
the port. On the shore were two ancient Egyptian sphinxes that the tsars
had brought to Leningrad. Andrei drank a lot of vodka, an awful lot.
He covered his face with his hands. I saw tears flowing down his cheeks.

"Why are you crying?" I asked. "It's because you won't ever see this
city again, isn't it?"

"No," he answered, "I'm crying because I drank a lot of vodka."

But he was not drunk, he was grieving.

The next day we walked along the river. The ice had been broken
up and was floating out to sea. We were probably the last to have
crossed the Neva that year.

We spent two weeks in Leningrad, wandering about, neither meeting nor associating with anyone else. We had our favorite places. We
always dined at the little restuarant "Demian's Fish Stew." In good
weather we walked along the Neva next to the Peter and Paul Fortress.
From there we looked out on the most beautiful view of the city. We
spent a lot of time on the streets next to Haymarket Square and along
the pea-green "streets" of the Fontanka River that wound their way

through the city. Places that Dostoevsky loved. Places where his heroes lived. These quiet streets were beautiful and sad. They were a remembrance of something that would never return. The evenings we often spent in some restaurant to escape from the cold wind and rain and snow. The people who wound up at our tables saw that something unusual was happening to us. They left us in peace. They did not try to strike up conversations as is customary in Soviet restaurants where the waiters select one's company.

Every night at 11:00 Andrei saw me back to the dormitory and then went to his friend's studio to spend the night. In the morning we would meet and were inseparable the rest of the day. We had nowhere to go but to keep on walking. Andrei had friends in Leningrad but we knew that we were being followed. We did not want the man with the frostbitten ears to become interested in Andrei's friends as well. It was enough that his friend the artist might be in for some "unpleasantries."

In the middle of the afternoon, when we were so tired of being on our feet all day, we would find some quiet spot in a museum or such and there would sit in each others' arms and rest. One day it was very cold and we could not find anywhere to rest. Everywhere there were crowds of schoolchildren on holiday. Finally we went to the lobby of the hotel "Soviet" on the shore of the Fontanka and there we sat for two hours.

When I was seventeen and in Leningrad for the first time my family and I stayed in the hotel "Soviet." I told Andrei and he asked the date. He insisted that he had been in Leningrad that very date and year on a magazine assignment and that his editors had obtained permission for him to stay in the "Soviet." He joked that he had seen me then, that I had caught his eye, but that he had thrown me like a small fish back into the stream to mature.

A F

To believe in fate has always greatly appealed to me. Sometimes it seems that I govern my own life, and sometimes it seems that some higher force has programmed it from beginning to end.

I like to think of the essence of the human spirit in the same terms with which the great Renaissance poet Dante described the essence of art. A work of art, he said, must have several meanings, among which are the literal, the moral, the philosophical and the anagogical—that is, the mystical or mysterious. So, too, must the human soul.

I recall the words of an ancient Greek I once read whose definition of the essence of art could also be understood as the essence of the spiritual existence of man: "Art forces our soul to recall and recognize that which it knew long ago." According to this Greek philosopher our immortal soul knows everything and has already seen everything; during our earthly life it recalls a part of that which is well known to it.

Sometimes I have recurring dreams and I begin to believe in what I see in them. Without fail parts of these dreams appear in real life. For example, when I was young I dreamed of expanses of wilderness covered with snow, and cities standing on the edge of the earth—and fate drew me to the Far North, to Siberia, to the Arctic. I often dreamed of a city, familiar and yet strange, completely void of people. This city was beautiful; in it were parks whose trees were reflected in the water, and tall buildings, light and transparent, their heights reaching the sky. I wandered about the city at night, in total solitude, gazed at its buildings and streets but could not recall where, and in what country, I had seen it before. I was firmly convinced that if I had not yet been in this city it meant that I certainly would be, otherwise my imagination would not have painted its portrait.

On the day that I met Lois—a completely accidental meeting—a light wave passed along my nerves as if sent by a supernatural force. Lois was trusting and she wanted to be my friend. She immediately supported me in the small incident in the library cafeteria. The same things that interested me, interested Lois. We had the same notions about our life's work and about what, in general, makes life interesting. I liked how she related to other people, and I thought that we probably would agree on what a person can call happiness. These feelings were both unexpected and yet familiar. I understood Lois very well, but at the same time she was like a stranger from another planet where there are human beings as on my planet but they walk, speak and breathe completely differently. I sensed in my soul the familiar trepidation in the face of the mysterious. It was fate, impossible to resist—the force that pulled me in the direction of my desires. But perhaps I myself had not given birth to these desires, perhaps someone strong and powerful had placed them in my soul. . . .

After my first few meetings with Lois I naturally had a dream, and of course I believed in it. If I dream about something it is not in vain—it absolutely must have significance. I dreamt that on my chest lay a small dog, soft and warm. A sensation of bliss filled my soul and I was frightened to turn over lest my body crush this small creature nestled on my chest. I spoke about this dream with one of my friends, an old woman, a lover of all things supernatural and an interpreter of dreams. She lived in a small two-room apartment that reminded me of both an antique store and a bookdealer's shop. It was filled with books, pictures, etchings, icons, old dishes, vases and statuettes that she had collected throughout her life. When I told her my dream she said that it was a very good dream, that it signified a new friend in my life. I also did not doubt that it was a very good dream.

Maybe it was easier for me to live on earth because I believed in my fate, believed that no one could disrupt it however much they tried. I always felt that I was not fighting to shape my own life but simply following my fate, and this feeling gave me strength to endure. The real-life circumstances that accompanied my new friendship only helped fate to do its business. The people who tried to keep Lois and me from being together did not understand and could not understand that their efforts led in the opposite direction. In my life a new friend truly had appeared, a closer friend than there had ever been. And I had the feeling that my whole life I had been in need of such a person.

With every day I came to know Lois better and better. My first impression of her was of a very trusting, open, and therefore defense-less, person. In my country it is dangerous to be an honest person. Such a person always loses. He or she is looked upon as not fully normal, even stupid. Later, in the first months of our acquaintance, Lois seemed to me like a spoiled child, her head filled with ideas that struck me as silly. Gradually this impression passed; behind those ideas that seemed silly at first glance I saw something more serious—respect for the human personality. When I knew Lois better I began to understand not only her ideas but the traits of her character, and then my first impression of her returned to me: a person who was open, kind and trusting. I recalled that in my dream I was afraid to turn over so as not to hurt the warm creature on my chest. After my arguments with Lois, when I felt I had hurt her, I experienced remorse and promised myself not to do it again. But the arguments periodically reoccurred. We stopped paying them any attention since they were not serious enough and we both understood that we must hold our relations dear.

In her relation to life, to other people, to success, Lois could be considered strange, at least according to prevailing notions in the Soviet Union. My acquaintances and the people with whom I worked also considered me strange and for the same reasons. Fate was so inclined that one strange person should make a trip to the other end of the planet, to a different system of society, so that there in the stuffy and crowded premises of a cafeteria in the basement of a library she would meet with another person who, in his strangeness, greatly resembled her. Was the explanation supernatural? Or the natural result of pure chance—had the people on earth been mixed and twirled about for so long, like the minute particles in a kaleidoscope, that eventually two of them who needed each other wound up together? Whatever the explanation, natural or supernatural, we both felt that we must cherish our relations since such an instance is very rare in life and in general may not be at all. Lois and I walked about Moscow holding each other's hands, two people who had found one another.

We began to speak of the possibility of marriage fairly early. In the beginning we spoke of it in jest, then seriously, and then anxiously, concerned that we might be kept from doing so.

When I married Lois I understood very well that I could lose everything that I had in the Soviet Union. Now the trouble I had been warned of would begin in earnest. I stood to lose my profession, my position in society, a part of my friends; and as a result I would have to leave my homeland forever. There cannot be a more serious step in the life of any person. I knew of cases of marriages with foreigners when the Soviet citizen did not lose all that I stood to lose. But such cases concerned famous people whose lives could not easily be ruined or people who had come to some compromise with the authorities. I could not imagine what sort of compromise I could make with those who methodically "cut off my oxygen," as the Soviet expression goes. The further the process of suffocation continued the more I hated them. I would prefer to suffocate than get down on my knees and submissively listen to their terms which I am sure would also have been impossible for me to accept. I had the feeling that I myself was not acting, that some threatening and supernatural force was drawing me on, perhaps even to my destruction. But I could not stop or move in another direction. It seemed to me that fate had intended something more significant for me than had thus far happened in my life, and that I ought not display fear or allow faintheartedness to stand in my path. I ought to step straight, gathering all the forces that I possessed. Perhaps Lois had the same feeling, she needed no less strength to walk the path that fate had prepared for us. And if there is a God then it is necessary to thank him for giving us this strength, that neither of us turned back halfway out of fear. I think that we could not have acted otherwise. We would not have been forgiven, neither by Him nor by ourselves.

LBF

We had to wait three agonizing months after we handed in our petition to the Moscow ZAGS. According to Soviet law it is impossible to hold up registration of a marriage for more than three months. In general it is possible to register a marriage immediately after handing in a petition, or several days later, but in marriages with foreigners the personnel at ZAGS always assign the maximum time period of three months in the hope that something will disrupt the wedding plans.

The foreigner's right to marry a Soviet is protected by the Helsinki Convention and other international agreements. Since Soviets are obliged to treat foreigners with more respect for their basic international rights than they do their own citizens, most marriage requests are complied with. However, there are many exceptions where the Soviet authorities have interfered. Because of the binding nature of international accords as pertains to foreigners the Soviet authorities are always careful to construct "legal" reasons for not going through with a marriage request.

Because of the three month wait it is difficult for Soviets to marry foreigners who come to the country as tourists. Tourist trips are short and the tourist must leave the country with the expiration of his or her visa. In order to return when the three month wedding date at ZAGS arrives, the foreigner needs a new visa, and it can easily be denied.

Even foreigners who have a visa to be in the Soviet Union for a sufficiently long period of time can be faced with various artificial obstacles. Simply to get married in the Soviet Union the foreigner has to collect seven different documents. Any of these documents can be questioned. Nothing gets done in the Soviet Union without the proper piece of paper. Usually a warning from ZAGS that something is not right in a couple's file comes at the last moment so that there is little or no time to correct the situation before the assigned wedding date. The burden of proof rests on the couple. They must get new papers and clear their names. This paperwork requires time, which is usually at a premium because of visa restrictions.

After we handed in our documents to ZAGS the local police did not bother us anymore and we were careful not to give them any grounds for interfering in our relationship. The remaining months dragged on. Every day we expected something—some excuse that would keep us from marrying. We tried to anticipate problems.

I knew of another binational couple whose wedding date preceded ours. The Soviet's hometown was in Siberia. A few days before they were to be married ZAGS summoned them in. The marriage could not be performed. A letter had arrived from the local police in his hometown. It had traveled along a fully official route and falsely accused that the groom was already married and about to commit bigamy. The couple needed time to prove his innocence. The groom's parents sent all sorts of documents, none of which were accepted until his mother flew to Moscow and personally pleaded with the ZAGS officials.

We had heard several of these stories and were prepared. Andrei had all of his documents certified and in triplicate. The real problem would be if they said that I was already married. I had my father send me a document from Chicago stating that there was no record of any marriage. Then I had him send me another document from Washington, D.C. It stated that I was not married and was signed by then Secretary of State Alexander Haig. How he knew of my marital status was a mystery to me but his official seal and his name were recognizable and that was all that was important.

The last weeks before the wedding Andrei obsessively checked the mailbox. He expected something at any moment: a call into the reserves, a police summons, an error in our files. We could not sit tight, and went ourselves to ZAGS to find out if there were any problems. The woman in charge looked at us suspiciously. She rummaged through a pile of petitions on her desk but did not find ours. She looked at a list she kept in her drawer. Finally she said:

"As yet we have unearthed no evidence of improprieties in your affair. Why did you come? Did you expect us to find something?"

We were not calmed. She continued to stare at us as we left her office, as if looking for something. We thought, "Now she will surely find some 'improprieties'."

We invited only a few people to our wedding because we worried that we might suddenly have to excuse ourselves before our guests if, for reasons beyond our control, there could be no wedding. I invited several students who, like myself, were studying at Moscow University. They would be our witnesses from the American side. Andrei invited two Soviet acquaintances, a husband and wife that we knew quite well. They would be our witnesses from the Soviet side.

We both categorically rejected the idea of having a reception in a restaurant, an increasingly popular custom in the Soviet Union, especially among the monied set. I had a superstitious feeling about such elaborate and expensive preparations. One Soviet man who was supposed to marry an American woman had reserved an entire hall in a Moscow restaurant in the center of town. Two days before the wedding date ZAGS called to inform them that some irregularities had been found in their files. There was no wedding, much less reception.

Andrei wanted to have a dinner in his room.

"Let these shabby walls be the witness to a new event!" he said ceremoniously.

To my great disappointment he redecorated his room before the wedding. He was looking forward to meeting my American friends and he was embarrassed by his meager living quarters. He did not think that my friends would take delight in his confusion as I had done. He wanted to present a more respectable image. Andrei took down the wires and posters. He stowed away the workbench. He replaced the old wallpaper. (A three day job—two days to stand in line for a choice of four styles and a day to hang it.) He removed the map with all the pins marking his travels in the Soviet Union. He said that he probably would not be going out on assignment any more. It became a more or less normal room. No one would have thought that a Russian hippie lived there anymore.

Andrei and I went for the wedding rings the week before we were to be married. When we handed in our petition we were given a pass to a special closed store called "Spring." There brides and grooms can choose among items usually in short supply, those things they need to make their wedding a happy one. Trousseaus, towels, undergarments and wedding rings. Andrei and I got in line for the rings. Most of the other customers were young, obviously getting married for the first time. The state was going to rebate a substantial amount of the money they spent on their rings. It was very crowded. Everyone pushed and shoved in order to get a good look at the two small display cases that held the rings for sale. We stood in line for forty minutes until it was our turn. The salesclerk was surly. She looked at my small hand and took out two rings. That was all she had in my size. I took the plainer of the two. The sale was consummated in a matter of seconds.

By the morning of the wedding day I was exhausted. My nerves were wrought thinking about not being allowed to get married. And my body was wrought from standing in line the day before to buy all the things we needed for the wedding party. Andrei and I had stayed up late (violating our curfew) preparing the food and laying everything out on lace doilies and metal trays that his mother had stashed away at least ten years ago.

I got out of bed, scattered the cockroaches from their slumber in the dormitory bathroom, showered and dressed. An American woman with whom I had become close helped me to collect my wits. We had met a year and a half before during the orientation for our academic exchange when we shared a room for a weekend in a New York hotel. Each night we discussed our impressions of the day's presentations. On the last day of the orientation one speaker told us that a few of us would get married in the Soviet Union, that it happens every year, and that she herself had married a Soviet. I remember having said to my roommate:

"How could anyone allow themselves to be so carried away as to get married in the Soviet Union? How could anyone make such an important decision while they're living in a foreign country, in the midst of a foreign culture?"

On my wedding day she and I recalled this scene and laughed—a long, hard laugh. Man plans and God decides, as the Russians say.

My girlfriend helped me pack my things into a small case. I intended to stay in Andrei's apartment once we got married. I still would have no right to do so without getting permission from the Ministry of Higher Education which I did not think would be prompt in coming. However, I only had a month left on my visa and it seemed unlikely that they would take any actions now against Andrei for living with his legal wife.

My friend escorted me to the metro. We got out at Andrei's stop where he was waiting for me with a big bouquet of pink roses. We boarded the next train and exited at the next few stops, each time meeting our guests along the way. Finally we got out at Kirovskaya station and our curious company walked along tree-lined Griboedev Boulevard. It was unseasonably warm. I took off my jacket. Andrei was in his shirt sleeves. He wore a light blue shirt and tie that I had bought for him in Estonia. By the time we got to the Palace of Weddings I was flushed.

The Palace of Weddings No. 1 on Griboedev Street is the finest in Moscow. Those who are marrying for the first time have the right to request that their wedding take place here. Those who have been married before do not have this right and must marry at their local ZAGS office. Those marrying foreigners may marry only at the Palace of Weddings No.1.

The outside of the building was not extraordinary in any way, dingy and in need of repair. The sidewalk along the whole street was torn up. The interior, however, was quite nice. Fine carpets from Soviet Central Asia, wood paneling, chandeliers, bay windows that looked out into a garden. The ceremony itself took place in a large well-appointed room that reminded me of a reception hall in an old English manor.

When we entered the Palace we went to the administrator's office to get our place in line. We were asked to wait. We sat for a long time. Other couples were also waiting but they seemed to get ushered in and out much more quickly. Andrei was very nervous. I was exhausted from the uncertainty. For three months we had lived in doubt about whether we would be allowed to marry. Now the final moments stood before us. I was numb.

We were finally received by the same woman whom we had come

to see a few days ago to find out if there were any problems in our case. She glanced at us sternly, took our papers, and then addresed us with that same sickly sweet smile I was becoming accustomed to. She asked to see our witnesses and she carefully checked their identification. They signed some papers. We signed some papers. We were shown up to the second floor landing by a young woman in the Palace uniform of black skirt and white blouse.

She positioned the entire wedding party in front of two enormous oak doors. She showed me how I was to hold my flowers. She told the others the order in which they were to enter and at what distance they were to follow behind. She then said:

"Well, where's the groom?"

"Here," Andrei replied.

"No, this cannot be. The groom is not dressed properly. He has no jacket. I cannot allow him to enter."

Andrei had not worn a jacket because it was so warm that day. We had been worrying about devious schemes, last-minute trumped up charges, and letters from Alexander Haig. Now this small woman in her official blouse and skirt was telling Andrei that he could not marry me for lack of lapel. My friend Bob, a linguist from Indiana, handed Andrei his sportcoat. Bob is about six inches shorter than Andrei, so the jacket did not button and the sleeves were way too short. The escort giggled when she saw Andrei in the jacket, but he had fulfilled his duty to the state and the marriage proceeded.

I could not believe it was finally happening. All these procedures seemed so cold and alien to me. Here I was halfway around the world, so far from my home and my family. It was as if I were a stranger witnessing the scene.

The oaken doors opened and a string trio started to play Mendelssohn's Wedding March. We were greeted by a fat woman in a flowing red robe. From her neck hung a large and ornate government emblem. It reminded me of a first prize award for best steer at a county fair. She lifted her hand and the music stopped. In a very official tone she spoke of the duties of the married couple. They must respect one another, love one another, go through life hand in hand. They should create a strong Soviet family—the living cell of Soviet society. They should bring up their children in the spirit of Communist morality.

Having said this, she gestured to us to sign our names to the document registering our marriage with the Soviet state. The trio started to play. Andrei and I kissed. At last we were officially husband and wife.

We left the Palace of Weddings and for the first time in three months Andrei and I breathed calmly. We stole away from our wedding guests for a few moments. Sitting on a park bench under the hot May sun, we embraced. We were truly husband and wife regardless of the marriage certificate that the Soviet state had finally granted us. We vowed to make a life together. At long last it seemed possible.

We took the metro back to Andrei's for the wedding party. The tension had left me and I was drunk with joy and excitement. There was plenty of champagne. Everyone had brought at least one bottle. In Russian fashion our guests tinkled their glasses at every lull in the laughter and shouted "Gorko! Gorko!"—"Bitter! Bitter!" Andrei and I kissed to make it sweet again.

In order to compensate our guests for the modesty of our wedding reception I used my privileges as a foreigner to get tickets for us all at the Theater on the Taganka to see the stage version of Mikhail Bulgakov's *The Master and Margarita,* the hottest show in town.

Bulgakov was probably the greatest Russian writer of the Soviet era. His novel *The Master and Margarita* is extremely popular in the Soviet Union despite the fact that the Soviet authorities repressed it for over twenty years. Even now Bulgakov's works are only available in the book store for foreigners. Soviet people repurchase these books on the black market at a price ten times the original. *The Master and Margarita* is part religious parable and part satire of everyday life in the Soviet Union. The novel places the Devil in 1940's Moscow where he finds the territory ripe for his tricks.

Only the Theater on the Taganka is allowed to present *The Master and Margarita.* The head director Liubimov is a creative genius and he has been given much leeway to present his own style of theater. The content of many of this theater's plays are *ostrii*—critical, that is, critical of the state. The criticism is never direct. It is always thinly veiled—"a fig in the pocket" in Russian, which, loosely translated, means making an indecent gesture to someone while your hand is still in your pocket. For instance, in Liubimov's presentation of Berthold Brecht's *Princess Turandot* the Emperor of a mythical kingdom has a throne adorned with rolls of toilet paper—an item in very short supply in the Soviet Union. Whenever one of the Emperor's subjects does something he likes, such as praising the regime or informing on a friend or colleague, the Emperor rolls off a certain amount of toilet paper and hands it to the loyal citizen. The allusion to Soviet life, where obedience to the state is often bought by special access to items in short supply, is unmistakable, funny, and yet serious.

Andrei and I saw almost every play in the repertoire at the Theater on the Taganka. We marvelled at Liubimov's creativity and at the freedom he was given to employ it. However, that freedom too can be explained. The number of tickets available for open sale to the Taganka is insignificant, perhaps twenty a performance. The other tickets are set aside for high level Soviet officials, their families and friends, and for foreigners. A ticket to Taganka is the hottest ticket in town and yet I never had trouble getting in to see a show. The audience was usually filled with foreigners. We often joked that the Theater on the Taganka was free art for export. Andrei felt certain that Liubimov was given more or less free rein so that people in the West who came to visit his famed theater would think that free art exists in the Soviet Union—art independent of the state—while the influence of this theater's art on the domestic audience was kept to a minimum.

The play *The Master and Margarita* was marvelous. For some it is a question of prestige to have seen it. For others it is a moving experience to see this work brought to the stage. Our guests were pleased, especially our Soviet friends. The wedding and wedding party had been a great success.

Andrei and I went back to the apartment. It was the first time in three months that I could spend the night. We knew we had little time to sort out our lives. My visa expired in one month and there was still much to do. But we took the next two days to relax.

Andei was elated. A new life was opening out before him. He grabbed me in the shambles of the room. Everywhere there were empty champagne bottles, with three or four unopened bottles that our guests had stashed away for our enjoyment over the next few days. He lifted me up high and then brought me down to his chest. He hugged me close in a great bear hug. He caressed my hair, held my head and looked straight into my eyes.

"My zaichik," he said (he had taken to calling me his bunny rabbit in Russian), "I've lived in this place fifty years, but the last few years it has become unbearable for me. My life is like water running through the same rusted pipe for too long. I've been wanting a change—a complete shift of direction in my life. You've given me this change, more than I hoped for. We will be separated soon and perhaps for a long time. No matter what the future holds, I want you to know that this has been the happiest year of my life."

PART II

CHAPTER 4
THE HONEYMOON

L B F

When Andrei and I married we planned to settle in the United States as soon as possible. We began the application procedure for an exit visa the week after the wedding. This required that we gather a myriad documents, hand them in to the authorities at the Offices of Visas and Permissions—OVIR—and then wait approximately three months for an answer. I went to the U.S. Embassy to obtain one of the documents—a "summons" asking that my husband be allowed to come live with me—and have it signed and notarized by an American official. While there I took the opportunity to discuss Andrei's case with an officer in the consular section who had experience in bi-national marriage cases. The officer said that Andrei's biography did not have any of the characteristics that usually spell trouble in obtaining an exit visa. He had no close family in the Soviet Union. By Soviet law, my parents and I constituted his only close relatives in the world. He had never engaged in political activity nor had trouble with security people until his relationship with me. He had never held a sensitive job and his last ten years' work as a freelance journalist was innocuous. The embassy officer said that she felt reasonably certain that Andrei would have no problems getting out. However, there are always exceptions, cases that are not resolved and in which the Embassy cannot determine the reason why a person is not released, even from the Soviet authorities' point of view.

Andrei was not as optimistic. I told him what the Embassy officer said and he said that it was all very true, but that it was those inexplicable exceptions that trap a Soviet. It is the arbitrariness of Soviet law, more than anything else, that one fears.

Before we were married I thought it would be best if I returned to the United States and there awaited OVIR's decision. I felt that the case for Andrei's need to leave the Soviet Union would be stronger if I were home in the United States. Once Andrei and I were married I could not view my imminent departure in such a sober light. I did not want to leave him and he did not want me to go. At first I thought about staying on in Moscow an extra three or four months. Andrei and I would wait for the exit visa, I would continue to work on my dissertation, and then we would sit together on an airplane leaving for the United States and a new life. But as each day passed and my departure drew nearer I more and more feared that the future would not be so simple. I was willing to stay in Moscow on whatever terms I could arrange.

Andrei and I took our new Soviet marriage certificate to the central Moscow OVIR to inquire about my rights as a wife. I had none. I was told that I must return to the United States in order to apply for a visa that would allow me to come live with my husband in Moscow for a total of three months. The procedure was very complex and demanded a minimum of four months time. When we looked at the forms we were crestfallen. Andrei would have to acquire the consent of his neighbors to allow me to live in the communal apartment and he would have to show ample means of support and bring in good references from work, all of which would be impossible to obtain as soon as it became known that he had married an American. But I still did not lose hope. There were other foreigners with spouses who had managed to stay on in Moscow. I knew an American woman who worked at the Anglo-American school and a Canadian woman who worked as a translator for a Soviet publishing firm. So I decided to look for work in Moscow.

Andrei said that it would be useless, that I would receive refusals everywhere. But I still did not believe that the power of the KGB spread to all spheres of life in Moscow, even to foreign enterprises and embassies. Step by step I became convinced.

For a whole month I walked about Moscow looking for a job. Andrei, downcast and reluctant, often went with me. I went to many foreign firms hoping to find some sort of a job. After all, I knew English and Russian and that alone was sufficient qualification for work in

Moscow. In many places I was told that they wanted to hire me. It did not disturb my prospective employers that I had a Soviet husband. They were glad that they would not have to arrange living quarters for me. They knew that I was quite willing to put up with the rigors of Soviet life and would not be taking a plane out after my first week at work. I was even told that there would be no problem getting an extension on my visa. But then, after several days, when I stopped in again or called a particular firm I found out that the circumstances had changed. They could not hire me. It was impossible to extend my visa.

But after all the Soviet authorities would have to give a visa to someone for this or that job. Why was it impossible to extend my visa? They already knew who I was and why I wanted to be in Moscow; I had a Russian husband. I had married a Russian against the advice of the authorities, and the KGB did not approve.

"They are like the Mafia," Andrei said. "They take revenge and in that way intimidate others who might not want to listen to their advice or understand their hints."

I began to feel that further search for work and further rejections only served as entertainment for those people who had advised me to leave Andrei. I imagined I saw gloating, malicious grins on their faces. But with desperate stubbornness I continued my search.

I then began to offer my services for taking care of the homes and the children of foreigners living in Moscow. The U.S. Embassy, the most likely employer, was out of the question. It had a strict rule about not hiring Americans with Soviet spouses. The Australians and British were likewise wary of such an affiliation. The head of an Indian firm in Moscow went into raptures after hearing my story. He said that by marrying a Soviet I had committed an act that strengthened peace and friendship between peoples and that my problems in obtaining a visa were simply a result of red tape. What a naive fellow! He said he would help me to stay in Moscow. He offered to hire me as an English tutor for his wife and daughter. He received a refusal on my visa in less than the customary five days.

The next serious prospect was at the Venezuelan Embassy. The Ambassador himself received me. His wife needed a helper to look after the house and serve the guests. They were very interested in hiring me, mainly because it would be elegant in front of guests to have a maid who spoke both English and Russian. We spoke together for about an hour. I hoped that the Ambassador, using his influence, could receive permission for an extension on my visa.

Exactly a week later when I called the Embassy a man's voice said to me in native Russian that they could not hire me, that I should not make any more calls to the Ambassador, that there could be "unpleasantries", and that the Ambassador was very busy. In every embassy in Moscow there is a certain percentage of Soviet citizens on staff. It is a Soviet stipulation. Of course in Soviet embassies in other countries no one other than Soviets are employed. I decided that this man's warnings were simply a means of intimidation that I had come across elsewhere. I called the Ambassador at his home using a telephone number that his wife had given me. The Ambassador said that he was very sorry but he could not obtain permission for extending my visa.

As a last resort I went to Progress Publishing House. It is a Soviet organization where all sorts of literature is translated from various languages into Russian and vice versa. They often hired foreigners to do their translations but only under a two year contract. Until such a contract expired there would be little chance of Andrei's receiving an exit visa, but we decided that I ought to apply for the job. As our time grew short we felt more desperate to be together even if it meant two more years in Moscow.

The Canadian woman who worked at Progress told me that several people had just left the English section so I knew that there were open positions. I had an interview with the head of the English section and he told me to call back a week later. When I got back to him he said that there were no job openings at that time. I told him that I had heard otherwise. He sighed and said that he did not know what to do with me, that it was not in his power to hire me.

Andrei told me that such a situation, when a person is refused work everywhere despite the existence of open positions, is known in Soviet jargon as "cutting off the oxygen." It appeared that the decision had been made to cut off the oxygen to Andrei and me. I would not be allowed to stay in Moscow and Andrei's articles and essays would not be printed anywhere, neither by the editorial boards nor by the journals that had used his work for the last ten years.

"It's ironic," Andrei said. "They themselves have left us no choice but to go to the United States."

While I hunted for jobs Andrei gathered the documents that he needed for OVIR. There were quite a few: a certificate from his former job, a certificate from the housing administration office, his parents' death certificates, divorce decrees from his two past marriages, and an application form several pages long, on both sides of the sheets of paper and in quadruplicate. On the application form he had to list all the places he had ever worked in his life, along with their addresses and telephone numbers. He had to list the names and residences of all relatives, including ex-wives. All deceased relatives had to be indicated. The only thing the application did not demand was information about his grade school teachers; everything else was there. Andrei said that such forms had been demanded of him several times in his life. Under Stalin these forms also included the following questions: What did you do before 1918? What did your parents and relatives do before 1918? Do you have any relatives abroad and if so where do they live?

All together the application forms and certificates that Andrei had collected added up to a thick folder. If a person filled out such forms several times in his life and if these forms were filed, then somewhere there must be a whole shelf for Andrei Frolov containing all of his papers. And if all the reports of all the people who had followed him and all the reports of all the informers were also collected and filed, then Andrei's shelf would have to be of impressive size. I began to understand the chronic paper shortages in the Soviet Union. As Lenin once said, "Socialism is like taking inventory."

With this folder ready, containing all the evidence of Andrei's life, we decided to go to OVIR together. The process started at the local OVIR, the division in Andrei's neighborhood. It was located in a very picturesque spot, not far from Novodevichy Monastery which is now a museum. We sat in a small park in front of the monastery waiting for the lunch hour to end at the local police station where the OVIR office was located. It was a warm summer day and we were in a good mood. Andrei felt like a person about to take a very big step in his life.

Actually he had already taken that step, and there was no road back. In all of the certificates he had collected it was written that they were issued for the purpose of applying to leave the Soviet Union for permanent residence in the United States. A person who goes through the first step of the application process automatically announces to everyone along the way that he intends to abandon the country.

For example, Andrei had to get a certificate from the Committee and Union of Literary Workers stating that he held no outstanding debts to this organization. The Committee was in fact Andrei's trade union. His card from the Committee gave him a legal position in society and enabled him to work as a free-lance jounalist. Without his union card Andrei would have no official status. When Andrei went to the Committee to ask for the certificate that OVIR demanded, the president of the Committee told him that since he was planning to leave for America it would be better if he resigned from the Committee. As it was very clear that this suggestion would be followed by official measures if Andrei did not comply, Andrei resigned.

Once embarked on the first stage of the application process a person who wants to leave the Soviet Union is already placed in a position outside of normal society. Each person who takes this step knows that before him or her are months, perhaps years, of waiting. The authorities have consciously set up this deplorable position of uncertainty. There are many people who want to emigrate from the Soviet Union but fear taking the first step. Often they are frightened off simply by the difficulties involved in filling out the forms and gathering the necessary certificates. Moreover, there is the burden of the moral position. According to official Soviet morality the desire to emigrate from the country is qualified as treason. People who have fled the country, if caught, are tried as traitors to the homeland. Under Soviet law this means years in prison, and in some cases execution.

Waiting for the end of the lunch break we walked about the grounds of Novodevichy Monastery. Back in the end of the seventeenth century Peter the Great ordered his sister Sophia cloistered away here for the rest of her life. Alongside the central cathedral are the graves of many famous people. Famous Soviet figures are buried alongside the older graves of famous Russian scientists and musicians. This area is enclosed by a wall, built in the Soviet era, and entrance to it is allowed only with special permission. In the USSR special permissions are in force even where the dead lie, with the concomitant delineations of mortals into the privileged, the semi-privileged and the unprivileged.

Having strolled a bit through the museum part of the monastery, we headed for the office. The local OVIR occupied two small rooms. We were met by a young, polite, I would even say friendly, man in the

uniform of a junior police officer. He courteously asked us to sit down
and immediately set to examining Andrei's application. He made pencil
marks in several spots that demanded clarification. For example, Andrei
had indicated only the address of a former place of employment, the
telephone number was demanded. Time gaps of more than six weeks
between jobs had to be explained. Andrei had to list what he had done
during those six week and longer periods. When the young man, who
was the head of the local OVIR, got down to the column marked
"relatives" his face lit up with a slight smile, as if he had finally found
what he was looking for.

"I cannot accept this application," he said. "You have to obtain
permission from your ex-wives."

"How can that be?!" Andrei was stunned. "I was divorced from one
seventeen years ago and from the other five years ago. There were
never any material claims or disputes and both times I was divorced in
court before a judge. The divorce decrees are there before you!"

"Nothing I can do, you have to have permission."

"How can it be? How can a person with whom I have not lived for
seventeen years either grant or withhold from me permission to leave
the country? It doesn't make any sense. I have no children, you see that
on the application form. The court long ago decided all issues of material claims."

"You have to obtain permission," repeated the official politely but
firmly.

"But what if they don't grant me permission?"

"Then you aren't going anywhere."

There was satisfaction on the face of the police officer. He felt he
had fulfilled his duty and he looked at Andrei with a condescending
smile that also contained a touch of ironic glee. Andrei argued with him
for a few minutes more but without result.

"Nothing I can do to help," said the official. "Those are the rules."
And he transferred us to his aide, a young woman, for further clarification of these rules.

"How can it be?" Andrei continued to ask. "These rules contradict
the law. Where are they written down? I've done everything that was
required in the application forms. I've already lost my job."

"The channels by which you earn money have already been closed to you?!" the lady gaily said and abruptly laughed in Andrei's face. She had practically blurted out "Your oxygen's been cut off!" but had controlled herself.

On the way home Andrei was unbelievably upset. He kept humming a sad melody. He said that it would be very difficult to obtain these permissions. His first wife lived in Moscow and their relations were none too good. Chances were that she would not give her permission. His second wife lived somewhere in Siberia, address unknown. Try searching for someone in Siberia without an address!

Andrei and I decided to go together to see his first ex-wife; we felt it would be more convincing. My presence would assure her of the reality and seriousness of our request. In their dealings with foreigners most Soviets tend to be more polite and calm than in their dealings with fellow Soviets, and we hoped it would be the same with Andrei's ex-wife. Moreover, I was curious to see what she was like.

So off we went. I was going to meet my new husband's first ex-wife to ask for her permission to allow her ex-husband to come live with me. The situation was odd, to say the least. It reminded me of some contrived "I Love Lucy" plot. But the absurdity of the occasion itself far surpassed the absurdity of the situation. What started out as "I Love Lucy" wound up more like a scene from Edward Albee's *Who's Afraid of Virginia Woolf.*

Alla, Andrei's first wife, turned out to be a pretty and slender forty-year-old woman. We explained our situation to her. She congratulated us on our marriage and said that she would absolutely grant us the permission; it was a mere trifle. She suggested that we drink champagne in celebration. It all seemed to be going quite smoothly, but Andrei was not pleased. He apparently knew his ex-wife quite well.

We three, the happy trio, went down to the store on the first floor of her building to buy some champagne. Back in her apartment, after drinking a couple of toasts, Alla fell into a didactic tone. She said that once in America we ought to "sit" quietly, in other words, not say or write anything bad about the Soviet Union lest the KGB take revenge.

"They could make trouble for you at work or at the university," she said. "They could even kill you."

We thanked her for her advice and then Alla suggested that we drink some more champagne. We had already emptied the first bottle so Andrei went down to the store to buy some more. Alla moved her chair close to mine, put her arm around me and repeated her warnings in my ear. She was a little drunk. She asked me to help her prepare something to eat, but first I would have to clean up all the dishes that had piled up from the day before. She made motions to help but only succeeded in knocking things down. She sweetly smiled and handed me a rag to wipe the floor. I knew she was playing with me but I had no choice but to humor her every whim. She sat at the table sipping what was left of the champagne and thought up new household chores for me to do.

"My, you do dishes well, Lisa," she said with a smirk. "You know what you and Andrei ought to do? You ought to open a quaint little Russian restaurant once you are settled in America. There would be Russian music, romantic ballads and gypsy songs. You could serve caviar and stroganoff and pirozhki and Soviet champagne. Lots of champagne!"

Andrei arrived with a fresh bottle right on cue. He listened morosely as his ex-wife painted a detailed picture of our future Russian restaurant. Andrei would be maitre d', greeting people at the door and engaging them in conversation about Russia and the magnificence of the Russian soul.

The more Alla drank the more persistent she became in her advice. She gave us the complete set of official propaganda on Russian language publications, newspapers and radio broadcasts in the West. Andrei listened with a resigned air and nodded his head in time to her words while the skin on his cheekbones crept. I saw he was controlling himself but only with great difficulty. Alla demanded more champagne. Her speech became incoherent. She began to talk about Russia in grandiloquent terms and almost slid out of her chair. She propped herself back up and spoke of the superiority of the Russian soul and the barrenness of America.

"Americans are practical beasts. They think only of business and cannot fathom the depths of the soul as the Russian can," she proclaimed. "You, Andrei, are selling your soul to these creatures."

She was really enjoying herself. Her Soviet soul was getting drunk not only on the champagne, but on the position of power she had over the lives of two people.

Suddenly she leapt up and exclaimed that we had to pray, no doubt for Russia and for her lost soul Andrei. She extracted a prayer book from deep in the cupboard. I could not help but notice how well hidden it had been. Alla leafed through the prayer book which was written in Old Church Slavonic. In vain she tried to read something there.

My curiosity sated, I was getting bored and disgusted with this spectacle. Andrei carefully reminded me that we still needed her permission. Alla overheard us talking. She looked at Andrei suspiciously and said that he would not succeed in deceiving her. Andrei, who I sensed was at the limit of his patience, nevertheless calmly continued:

"What deception? How am I trying to deceive you? All I need is a certificate from you, your permission to leave the country."

"I will not give you such permission!"

"Why not?"

"Because you will go to America and enjoy life there. You haven't earned the good life in America. It would be too good for you."

Andrei restrained himself and remarked that she did not have the moral right to dictate not only his life but mine:

"Lois is not guilty of anything!"

"You will behave the same with her as you did with me! You will act as you please once in America. For you she is simply a means of transportation!"

Andrei and Alla began to go over past injuries. They bickered back and forth about the injustices they had committed against one another. I was no longer the innocent whose Russian was inadequate to the situation as I had been the first day in the library cafeteria. I did not want to hear all this and I resented being involved in such an ugly scene. After awhile they both tired of this squabbling, which strayed further and further from the matter at hand. Andrei, exhausted to the core, said to Alla:

"Perhaps you want money? I have a little in the bank."

"Yes!!" she exclaimed. "I want money. And I want more champagne. Go run for champagne!"

"There will be no more champagne," Andrei answered.

"Then pay me money, all that you have in the bank. Let her pay!" She pointed at me. "Let her pay for you with dollars!"

"I have no money," I answered.

"Let your parents pay!"

"My parents don't have money."

"Then you will never see your husband."

She rushed over to Andrei and threw her arms around him and tried to kiss him. He pried her fingers from his neck and pushed her aside.

"Get out of here!" she screamed. "I'm sick of the sight of both of you."

"Does she really want money?" I asked Andrei once on the street. "If so, we'll just have to pay."

"No!" he answered. "Did you really not understand that?"

I only understood that this situation was absurd. We were in total dependence on this woman and she revelled in it.

"Then why did you offer her money?"

"I thought it would embarrass her."

"We're the ones who are embarrassed, not her. I want to talk to a lawyer, even a Soviet lawyer. This is too ridiculous and humiliating."

"Fine," Andrei answered with a bored look. "Let's go see a lawyer. My American wants to consult with a Soviet lawyer. This should prove to be very interesting."

Then I started to yell at Andrei. I said a lot of insulting things about Russians in general and about Andrei in particular. Andrei nodded his head in time to my words. Every now and then he'd interject:

"Wonderful! . . . A very perceptive observation . . . . You can't argue with that."

I was infuriated. I crossed over to swearing in English which Andrei knew very well; he had learned it from me. Then I burst into tears. Andrei comforted me; he held me close and stroked my hair. We both had finally come to pity one another.

The next day we went to a lawyer. There are small offices in the Soviet Union known as juridical consultations. For a ruble, a lawyer will give Soviet citizens advice and explain laws. There was a line in the consultation office and the lawyer we happened upon was a chubby man in a leather jacket. He looked at us as if we had done something wrong, especially Andrei.

He very diligently explained to us that OVIR had every right to demand from Andrei permission from ex-wives. It was perfectly legal. His former wife could refuse to give him this permission. This also was perfectly legal. There was no regulation which made her obligated to agree to it. Andrei asked him to show us the article of law on the basis of which OVIR demanded such permission. The man irritably answered that Andrei ought to trust official Soviet offices.

"Nevertheless, show me," Andrei demanded.

The lawyer could not cite a concrete article of law. His angry stare followed us as we left the office. Andrei was happy; he kept repeating that I had headed him on the correct path. But I was completely crushed. It seemed to me that we had not been to a lawyer but to a prosecutor who, for the small fee of a ruble, tried to convince us of our guilt.

"Let's go to a notary public," Andrei said. "They are more normal people."

At the notary office, which looked much like the juridical consultation office, an older woman met us with sympathy. She explained that what was at issue here was a certificate, a notarized statement about the lack of material claims. She conceded that three years after any divorce there can be no legal material claims, but OVIR had demanded the certificate and the notary public advised Andrei not to do battle with OVIR. She said it would be significantly easier to persuade his ex-wife; that was what everyone did. She added that his ex-wife could include in her statement that she was opposed to her ex-husband's departure and that she considered him a bad person. Such words had no juridical force.

"But try," she said, "to get this certificate without these comments. You simply need her to sign that she has been made aware that you are petitioning for departure."

Andrei was pleased and said that now the affair was much easier. He called Alla and told her that all he needed from her was a certificate about the lack of material claims. Alla, by now sober, told him that she was a worker on the "ideological front." (She worked at a publishing firm as a junior editor in the section that translated poetry from the languages of small Soviet nationalities into Russian.) She said that she could not give him such a certificate because of the responsibilities that her work imposed. Andrei repeatedly called her. He pleaded and threatened and even said that he was going to kill her. This tense situation dragged on for two weeks and these were our last days together in Moscow.

At my insistence we went to the OVIR of the R.S.F.S.R., the main OVIR for the European part of the Soviet Union. I felt that we ought to take all the legal steps open to us. There another very polite man suggested that we put everything into writing and promised to look into it in the course of a month.

"That's a joke," Andrei said. "They themselves have thought up this trap. Ask permission from your ex-wife! A natural enemy! The only thing that might help is that you, an American, were witness to all this. This is just the side of Soviet life that they want to keep hidden."

We knew that we had to do as much as possible while I was still in Moscow. As long as I was with Andrei people would still talk to him. Once I left they would not be so ceremonious. We had only one possibility left to get the certificate out of Alla. We had to go to the director of the publishing firm where she worked, to the "ideological front." If he told her to give us the certificate then she would have to. Most of all she feared that she would be blamed at work for having helped her husband leave the Soviet Union. This way she would go on record as being vehemently opposed to his departure. I had to go to the director because in the director's eyes Andrei was a person duly subject to condemnation. Perhaps he would listen more attentively to an American.

By all appearances the director was a kind, intelligent man. He was disturbed by the whole story and no doubt a bit concerned about the possibility of further developments, international complications and "unpleasantries" that were of no benefit to his publishing house or to him. I told him that I had already told my parents in America about his employee's refusal to sign a simple statement saying that she had no material claims against Andrei, which the director knew very well she did not have. My parents, I told him, were very upset. I mentioned my parents to him so that he understood that I had spoken of this affair over the international telephone lines which were listened to and recorded. He promised to speak to his employee about expeditiously settling the matter.

The calls to Andrei started. Now Alla was calling him, mostly at night, probably because by night she was drunk. She was hysterical on the phone and yelled at Andrei to get the hell out of Russia. Andrei answered through his teeth that all he needed from her was a certificate, that there were other people who would chase him out of Russia, and that they would do so without her help.

"Since when has Russia become your communal apartment?" he added.

I began to fear that he truly would do something horrible—go to OVIR and attack someone and wind up in a mental institution. After a few more days of this war of nerves Alla informed Andrei that she would give him the certificate. She called me to the phone and with a sad voice said that she was doing this only for my sake, that I was not guilty of anything. She suggested we go together to the notary public's office where the certificate had to be drawn up. She said that her mother, Andrei's ex-mother-in-law, had told her that it was the right thing to do.

We again went over to Alla's apartment. Her mother was also there. She had a kind face, young in appearance. She greeted me politely and sternly looked at Andrei, as if admonishing a naughty schoolboy. She took me into the kitchen, sat me down, served me tea, and there she and I talked while her daughter dressed. She told me that she had always been quite fond of Andrei. She quietly added that in married life a great deal depends on the woman and that Alla, her daughter, had been at fault in much. Alla came into the kitchen and both mother and daughter kept saying that they wished me only happiness and kindness. Alla started to cry. She said she was sorry but she had been told that under no circumstances was she to give Andrei this certificate. Her mother broke in and yelled at her to shut up, that she was again talking too much about things that are forbidden to mention.

Andrei nudged me and whispered in my ear, "We had better go before another scene starts. We have got to get her to the notary public."

Alla calmed down. She stopped crying and suggested that we have some champagne. We three, her mother, Andrei and I, took her by the arm and led her down the stairs and into a taxi that headed straight for the notary office. Alla signed the certificate stating that she had been informed that her husband was petitioning for departure from the Soviet Union to take up permanent residence in the United States and that she had no material claims against him.

When we said goodbye both mother and daughter could not look me in the face. They felt uncomfortable, as did we. This story had left a foulness in all our souls.

A F

Living in the Soviet Union I very often felt as if I were in a gigantic spider web that the government had woven. Once a person begins to move in the web he becomes more and more entangled; invisible threads block him from all sides. Soviet people are enmeshed by dozens of various dependencies.

The neighbors in a communal apartment, for example, can write open and anonymous *donosi*—denunciations—on a whim against other neighbors. The government encourages *donoschiki*, denunciators, calling them honest and useful citizens. Denunciations are euphemistically called "signals"; someone among the "honest" citizens "signals" the government, anonymously more often than not, about the "intolerable" behavior of another citizen. Of course, the signaller himself determines the degree of tolerability or intolerability of the other's behavior, and even if this denunciation is impossible to prove it has nonetheless accomplished its purpose: it throws a shadow on the reputation of another person. Official government denunciators are *stukachi*, KGB informants, and a great deal depends on their reports, such as getting a good job or a business trip abroad.

At work people depend not only on their bosses but on ordinary rank-and-file co-workers, whose opinion constitutes "the opinion of the Soviet collective." It is assumed that such an opinion, once approved or instigated by official organs at a place of employment, cannot be mistaken. Party officials can organize a public meeting of co-workers and draw up a statement of censure in the name of the workers' union against their colleague. Such a censure is not equivalent to a conviction in court but for a person's career and position in society it can be even worse. It is like a set of official instructions on how others ought to relate to this person.

Further, the government tries to place close relatives in dependence on one another and exert control on this dependence. Spouses may write complaining statements against each other and send them to the party and trade union organizations at work. Often a wife, hurt by her husband's unfaithfulness, or only suspecting him of unfaithfulness, may write a statement in which all the details of her spouse's life, few of which have any relation to his work or even his family life, are spelled out. These statements are always eagerly examined and discussed publicly at general meetings. Children write statements on their parents, with the government's encouragement, for this is still one more way to control the lives of its citizens.

In order to leave the country for permanent residence elsewhere one must obtain permission from parents and spouses. My parents were dead and I had been divorced twice. I was divorced from my ex-wives in court where all mutual material claims had been settled. Moreover, this all had been long ago; I had been divorced from one wife seventeen years prior to when I applied to emigrate and from the other five years prior. I had no children and if there had existed any claims, which there did not, they would have been valid for only three years after the date of divorce. My ex-wives had no legal right to block my departure abroad. But for the Soviet government, laws are most of all an instrument of power and they are used whenever it is beneficial for the government to do so. In my case it was very simple: the government could not find official reasons by which they could block my departure abroad and so I was told that I had to have the permission of my ex-wives. Later, when I found out that OVIR had no right to demand such statements of permission and all that was required were certificates confirming the lack of material claims and that my ex-wives had been informed of my possible departure, the officials at OVIR still stubbornly maintained that I had to have in hand papers in which my ex-wives granted me permission to leave for my new wife in the U.S.A. If they did not grant their permission, I would not be let out of the country.

All I wanted was to leave together with Lois. Life for me in my own country now seemed impossible, and it would be even more impossible for Lois. But after the setbacks with the documents that OVIR demanded, I thought that it might not be so bad if Lois lived a while longer in the Soviet Union, during which time my affairs might somehow be settled. Maybe in a year or two it would be easier for me to leave. Lois agreed. It seemed that the authorities were disturbed to a certain degree by the overall picture of marriages between Soviets and foreigners; almost all of the binational couples wanted to leave the Soviet Union and settle in the West. Only a few foreigners agree to live awhile in the

Communist "heaven", either for career considerations or for curiosity's sake. I suggested to Lois the following plan: she would live with me for awhile in Moscow, the authorities would forget about us, and gradually, unnoticeably, we would make plans to resettle in the United States, having soothed the sickly pride of the authorities with our few years residence in Moscow. Several Soviet-American couples had chosen this path, considering it the most reasonable.

In order for Lois to stay in Moscow, in order to get the authorities to extend her visa, she would have to find work. Only work could serve as grounds for an extension or issuance of a new visa. The Soviet authorities will not extend the visa of a wife or husband on the basis that she or he simply wants to remain with a spouse. That is insufficient grounds for the authorities, undesirable grounds which could serve as a dangerous precedent in similar cases in the future.

We spent the last few weeks of Lois's stay in Moscow on visits to OVIR and in search of work for her. There was no other way to get an extension of her visa. There were many places in Moscow where there were vacancies and where Lois could have worked, but every time, when it got down to the issue of her visa, she met with a refusal. We should have guessed how the authorities would conduct themselves. There was only one alternative before us; I had to secure exit from the country. With great difficulty we succeeded in getting permission from my first ex-wife. The demand for such permission had been illegal, and moreover, it was clear that pressure had been applied on her not to sign such a certificate. The scandal around this certificate grew and it apparently became undesirable for the authorities to let it continue. Finally we obtained her permission.

Lois's visa to stay in the USSR had run out and she had to leave. She flew out of Moscow together with the other American students who had been on the exchange. The young Americans were glad to be leaving Moscow. They would soon be home in familiar conditions of life. Only Lois was sad. Her friends wrote down my address and promised to write me. They thought that the authorities who oversaw the correspondence with foreigners would record their letters and that this attention would provide me some support. I knew that in such cases the authorities act very simply; they do not deliver the letters that come from abroad or deliver them at their own discretion. The letters sent from relatives who have emigrated from the Soviet Union to their relatives who have remained behind often take several months to reach their destination, and often are not delivered at all. Relatives in the USSR cannot find out how their relatives are living in the West, how their health is, how they are adjusting. They find out little or they find out late. These letters resemble the light of a dying star. A star in distant space may have already died but the light from its former blaze still travels to another part of the universe.

After Lois's departure I would be faced with a trip to Siberia. I had to find my second ex-wife and get from her the same certificate that I got from my first ex-wife. It would be easier to get her consent but it was difficult to conjecture what influence the authorities would bring to bear on her.

The arbitrary nature of the authorities' rule is far stronger at a distance from the capital—at least in Moscow there are foreign embassies and foreign correspondents. I knew intimately just what an out-of-the-way Soviet province can be like. The authorities could enveigle me in a violation of the law; they could falsify some sort of charge against me. Examples of such things abound.

My forthcoming trip to Siberia would not be without danger. With Lois's departure from the Soviet Union I would be tied to freedom by a thin thread which the authorities could break at will. They could simply not deliver our letters to each another, or not permit us to speak on the phone.

When Lois and I said goodbye I tried to be gay and carefree. I saw how her lips trembled like a child's about to burst into tears. I said that everything would be fine, that I would soon have permission to leave the country. Who am I, after all? The "Lucky" one! My parents received an additional ten square meters of living space on the day I was born. It was a sad joke but I wanted Lois to see that I did not intend to lose heart.

Lois cuddled up to me for the last time, the last time before a long, endlessly long separation. I felt the warmth of a person who was so close to me. She was the only person I had in the world. Finally she moved away from me and, walking alongside the other passengers, turned back and sadly smiled. Her warmth had left me, as life leaves the body. I remained alone in the city in which I was born. Would I see Lois again?

Would I again feel the warmth of a close soul or would everything around me remain eternally cold? I was left with the hope that I would receive letters. There had been a person and now there was none—she had melted into space, no longer real. All that remained was a postal address.

CHAPTER 5

SEPARATION

A F

Lois flew to Chicago, stopping in London where her sister lived. She was to try to call me from there. Lois worried a great deal about whether she would be able to keep in touch with me by phone and whether her letters would reach me. A week before leaving Moscow she had sent a telegram to her sister in London. I wanted to conduct a small experiment though I was almost certain of the result. I suggested that Lois put down my apartment as the return address. Telegrams are not accepted without return addresses according to the law in the USSR. The telegram quickly returned to my flat, as if due to mistakes in the London address. I think the post office simply did not send it anywhere and it probably sat on the desk of one of the supervisors at the post office. Incidentally, administrative work at the post office is considered secret work because it is so closely tied to KGB activities. The next telegram to Lois's sister in London we sent from a different posting station listing the foreign section of Moscow University as the return address. That telegram reached its destination.

My poor wife, having lived with me for only a month after our wedding, now had to think about whether or not they would give me her letters or allow us to speak on the phone. Neither of us knew what to expect when she left. When she flew out of Moscow it was as if she flew to another planet. I waited anxiously for her phone call from London. When the phone rang I was relieved. My application for an exit visa had placed me in isolation in the Soviet Union. When I heard my wife's voice over the telephone I was overjoyed. Despite everything there still existed this line of communication between us. A person feels completely different when he knows he is not alone.

I told Lois that I was leaving for Siberia. I did not know how long I would be gone but I would not return until I got the needed certificate and could take it to OVIR. I could not think about the future until I had that document in my hand. All my problems were now concentrated on obtaining it.

I took the certificate from my first wife and had a copy made and notarized just in case. If I were to have lost this paper somehow I do not know if I would have had the emotional strength to go after it a second time.

My second wife lived in Siberia. Her name was Natasha. I met her when I was in Siberia on one of my journal assignments. She worked with geologists as a laboratory assistant. She often went out on expeditions. Her permanent place of residence was a small town that had only come into existence a decade or two earlier. There people lived not only in modern buildings with modern conveniences, but in wooden barracks and in little vans so small that a person could not stand up straight. The dormitory-barracks were known for extremely foul living conditions. They had one common kitchen for all inhabitants and there the water was kept in a big barrel. The water supply was replenished by a car with a water tank. The bathrooms were outdoors and in a horribly muddy state of neglect filled with frozen blocks of sewage. The rooms were separated by thin plank-board walls. In some rooms families lived together, and in others young single people. When I met Natasha she was living in one of these barracks for single women.

During the day the wooden barracks, constructed fifteen years earlier and now grown dark with time, were comparatively quiet. Towards evening drunk men started to show up. They came to see their girlfriends. Often they got the doors mixed up and burst into the wrong room, sometimes intentionally. Scandals and arguments erupted and these turned into fights. Sometimes the men threatened one another's lives.

The dormitory trembled at night; it shook with all sorts of music from tape recorders and record players. The mix of music and shaking resulted in a wild cacophony. From time to time you could hear drunken screams from one of the rooms, screams accompanied by the sound of breaking plates and overturned furniture. The dormitory gradually quieted down by morning. Then the babies in the rooms of the couples started to cry, one after another, like the roosters in the early morning in the Russian countryside.

The whole town gave the impression of a spontaneous and temporary settling of people. A large section of town was set aside for unjailed prisoners who worked during the day like ordinary people, though at the most difficult and dangerous jobs, and in the evening had to return to the building where they were assigned to live. They could not venture beyond the limits of the town. These people committed a lot of crimes. The town abounded in small hide-outs, dens, where one often saw the hides, heads and innards of dogs thrown from the windows. The prisoners ate dogs because of lack of food in the camps. They killed them, cooked the meat and ate it while they drank spirits or vodka. Then they locked themselves up in one of these dens or in an apartment with a woman or two as drunk and as dirty as themselves. Dog flesh became a symbol signifying the damned life of the prisoner.

Before she wound up in this town, Natasha worked as a teacher in her home village in the Siberian countryside. She had wanted to go to any town to get out of the boredom of the country. She wrote poetry and small articles for the local newspaper, and wanted to live in a big city, in a civilized city. She complained that the town library did not even have the books of famous authors, the authors taught in the local secondary schools. She complained that she could not read, much less write in the dormitory-barracks, without someone or something always disturbing her. She jealously spoke of Moscow, of all the advantages and comforts of life and culture there. I truly sympathized with Natasha, and experienced something like a guilty conscience that she could not enjoy all that I had in Moscow. I lived with her for a month in this Siberian town. I told her that I would bring her to Moscow where she could go to good libraries, even buy books in stores, go to the theater, meet educated and accomplished people. I could only bring her to the capital by marrying her. She could not register to live there any other way. People often conclude fictitious marriages so as to settle in Moscow. Our marriage was not fictitious but neither of us took it very seriously.

Natasha liked life in a Moscow communal apartment even less. Her former Siberian life seemed more romantic; the expeditions in the

company of geologists were more romantic than evenings in close apartments in the company of Muscovites. The staffs of Moscow newspapers
and journals looked on her as an inquisitive provincial. Her poetry and
stories met with no success. In Moscow people more talented than she
could not get their work published, and the city already had its quota
of experts on Siberian life.

Natasha decided to return to Siberia. She did so while I was away
on one of my long journal trips. I was gone from Moscow a month or
two. Natasha probably thought that I had found another "unhappy
woman" who needed my help and therefore I was gone so long. She
left, explaining in a note that life in the capital was not for her. She went
to a construction site of a then popular trans-Siberian rail line. Newspapers, radio and television talked about it all the time so as to raise the
prestige of the project. Working in the difficult conditions of the severe
Siberian climate was compared to a heroic feat. In every way they tried
to romanticize life on this construction site in the midst of the wilderness. Such propaganda is effective on the youth. It produces a general
impression of noise and publicity, as if something is happening, life is
moving forward. And the publicity does bring one real advantage: such
construction sites are usually better provided with food and clothing
than ordinary sites.

Natasha and I divorced by mail, the final decision rendered through
the courts. I did not doubt that Natasha would give me permission to
leave for America, but I had to find her first.

I first searched for her through the address bureau in Moscow. I
started with the city where she had lived before. She could have returned there; they knew her there, and she had friends. Three weeks
after putting in my inquiry I received an answer: she was living there.
Her former address was listed but alongside was a stamp, "No longer
living at address indicated." Nevertheless my task was already far sim-
pler. I at least knew in what town I had to search.

It was impossible to get an airplane ticket there any sooner than in
two weeks so I bought a train ticket, but here too I could not get the
kind of seat I wanted. For the first time since I was a student I was
traveling in a "common car." There are always one and a half times
more passengers in a common car than in a car divided into compart-
ments. The sleeping booths are laid out along the aisles. Lying in bed

you cannot help but overhear the conversations of other people in other parts of the car. It seems to me that such open cars still exist only in the USSR, perhaps also in underdeveloped countries, but in any case not in the U.S.A. and not in Europe. I had to make do—I no longer enjoyed the privileges of a journalist.

I was traveling in the company of people heading to Siberia to earn some money. Some had never been out East before and did not even have a concrete destination. They just headed out and wherever they managed to find something they would settle down. The company of these people put me in a romantic frame of mind.

I had enough money with me so that I could travel for two months. The serious problem was where to find housing, where to spend the night. In many places in the Soviet Union there are no hotels whatso-ever, and where there are it is still difficult to get a room without a special paper or special identification. But it was summertime and warm. My experience as an inveterate traveller told me that somehow I would manage.

My fellow travellers drank vodka the whole way. They kept advising one another about how much money they could expect to earn in various places, at various jobs. They had worked as chauffeurs, bulldozer operators and excavators. For them, finding work in Siberia was not a problem. What was important was finding work with good pay.

Amidst this serious public in the common car was a lone Muscovite alcoholic. His sister had bought him a ticket to the town where I was headed. It was the final station; the railroad ended there. She bought him a bottle of wine, which he started to drink as soon as the train moved out, and gave him a little money for food. He drank that up the next day. Before him stretched four more days of travel, in lightweight clothes, with only a small suitcase to his name, and not a kopeck in his pocket. He traveled not knowing where he would live, where he would work, what he would eat or what he would drink the next day on the train. He had also been a traveller, going about the country with various expeditions. His experience, like mine, told him that he would get set up somewhere. In the meantime our fellow travellers entertained him with vodka and that was the most important thing; long ago he had become accustomed to going without food.

The train arrived in the morning, which was fortunate. I would have a day to find Natasha and then worry about finding a place to sleep. The station, a small shack, was located far from town. Several years ago the railroad did not reach this town. It was accessible only by airplane. Even now there was not enough transportation to deal with demand, especially in the summer when people would stand in line for whole days to get a ticket, several weeks in advance of when their vacations were set to begin. The town had grown since I was last there and now boasted a population of 100,000.

In the station, an enormous crowd of people crammed into the small premises in the hopes of getting tickets out of town. It was very close and difficult to breathe. Underfoot were scraps of paper and leftover, discarded food. A sour smell hung in the air.

The next problem was how to get to town. A bus drove up to the station about once an hour and as soon as it approached a crowd of people threw themselves on. Their numbers far exceeded the space available and some people hung on by the doors all the way back to town. Many people who had arrived on the train tried to get rides from passing cars, making deals with the drivers. I said goodbye to my fellow travellers and we agreed that those of us who did not manage to find a place for the night would head out to the airport. There a body can spend the night sitting up in the waiting area. At least it would be more pleasant to while away the time in the midst of familiar company.

I managed to squeeze into the second bus that had come by the station. It seemed as if the bus would explode into pieces from the crowding within. At times I stood on only one foot. There was no air to breathe and everyone was swearing at everyone else. A gypsy threatened to scratch out the eyes of the woman next to her. The bus shook along the pits and bumps of the dusty road.

I decided that once in town I would search out the places that I remembered. Perhaps I would run into someone I had known back then. I looked for the old weathered barracks that had been Natasha's home. All the inhabitants there were new. No one could tell me anything about Natasha. I asked them to direct me to the office of the organization where my ex-wife had worked six years ago and I went there.

I recognized the office immediately. Like the dormitory it was situated in a building that resembled a barracks. I went to the Personnel section where the workers' files were held. I asked the woman who worked there if they had any knowledge of my ex-wife. I was told that she was currently working there. I rejoiced. But when I asked her to give me Natasha's address she very cautiously looked at me and went into the next room to consult with someone. Returning she took Natasha's folder from the file, again looked at me, and started to dictate the address. Joyfully I ran out, address in hand.

With great difficulty I searched for the address given to me at personnel. I finally found it. I was standing before an empty site. The building had been torn down. The personnel office had lied to me.

I returned to Natasha's old barracks and asked the current occupants what had happened to the former occupants. They said that they had all been relocated to the new project of tall buildings that stood not far from the barracks. One elderly drunk assured me that my wife had to be living in one of the buildings there.

I ran over to the project. It was huge. Every complex of buildings stretched on for a block and there were several complexes. To search for someone in these buildings without an exact address was insane. I went to the housing administration for the project. They told me that not all of the new occupants were yet registered in their office. They looked through their files. Natasha's name was not there.

Just in case, I went to the address bureau at the police station. Their information was even older than that which I had received in Moscow. They still listed her at the old barracks.

I returned to the personnel office where Natasha worked and confronted the woman who had given me the wrong address. She was not in the least embarrassed. She said that her office was not obligated to give out addresses and that I should go to the police. I asked why, then, had she given me a wrong address. The woman looked at me in defiance and said that there had already been such an incident in the town. A former husband came looking for his ex-wife, found her and killed her. I tried to make her understand that all I needed out of my ex-wife was a simple certificate. I did not tell her what the certificate was for lest she think worse of me than she did of the wife-killer.

"I don't know anything," she answered unruffled. "Go to the police."

"The police don't have her new address."

"I don't know anything. We are not obligated to give out address-es."

I went to this woman's supervisor. I tried to reason with him. He answered that they give out such information only in response to official police requests. I asked him simply to tell me whether or not Natasha was in town. The supervisor of the personnel office reiterated, just as his employees had done, that he knew nothing. If I had still had my journalist's identification they would have told me immediately, but I did not and there was nothing that I could do.

I went to the editor of the local newspaper where Natasha had also worked. I was told that Natasha no longer came to them. They only knew that she worked as before, as a lab assistant to geologists. More than that they could not help me. It would appear that Natasha had lost the desire to write for the local newspaper after her short stay in Moscow, after meeting Moscow editors and newspaper people. Perhaps she had completely lost the desire to write.

I went back to the dormitory and to the complex of buildings not far from it. It made no sense but I did not know where to turn next. I saw a car drive up to one of the entranceways at the new building site. It was a van of camouflage green, the kind of van that geologists use. Most of the people who piled out carrying their things dispersed to various entrances on their way to their apartments. Only two young women remained talking to one another, their backpacks on the ground next to them.

I asked them if they knew a certain Natasha. One of them did. She began to tell me how to find her apartment. She said that Natasha was not on expedition now so she ought to be home.

I ran over to the building where her apartment was and flew up the stairs. No one was home. I continued to ring the bell, as if that would help. I finally went back down the stairs. I was happy. I knew her address, she was in town. I would see her soon.

At the bottom of the stairs I met a man whose face was familiar to me and I asked him if we had met several years ago. He remembered me and said that he had just seen Natasha and she was nearby. Her girlfriend's husband had "chased off the geese," that is, he had drunk himself to delirium, and Natasha was helping to calm him. I hurried to the new address.

A van stood next to some sort of dwelling that might have served well as a garage for automobiles but not as a residence for people, especially in the wintertime in the severe Siberian frost. The howls of a drunk rang out from the van.

I approached and saw Natasha in the open window. She looked at me as if she had seen me yesterday or just an hour ago. In fact we had not seen one another for quite a few years. She turned away from the window.

I entered the van. There a man about twenty years old was pretending that he was about to break up the furniture. Seeing me, an unfamiliar face, he calmed down for a moment. His delirium was obviously not genuine. The youth probably thought that chasing out the geese was prestigious for someone so young. It showed that he was a person on the edge, a desperate character, which seemed romantic to him. He asked me if I had a bottle. Seeing that his ravings ceased with my appearance everyone stopped paying attention to him, to his great chagrin.

In a businesslike tone Natasha said that she could now leave with me. She quickly bid farewell to her girlfriend, threateningly shook her fist at the young man and said that she would come again later that evening after she settled matters with her ex-husband. Natasha very often behaved like a school teacher, taking it upon herself to look after and instruct the people around her.

"Well, tell me, what have you gone and done?" she asked me once outside.

"Why weren't you surprised?" I asked her.

"I saw you yesterday in a dream, besides, that's not important. Tell me about you."

While we walked towards her apartment I told her everything and I again noticed that she wasn't surprised. As if every third acquaintance of hers, including her ex-husband, had married an American.

"I'll give you the statement tomorrow morning. It's too late today. The notary public office is closed."

It suddenly dawned on me. "How did you know that I needed a statement from you?"

"Why, you don't need one?"

"How did you know?" I repeated.

"One of my girlfriends married a foreigner," she said with hesita-
tion.

"Oh, sure. Her American husband probably lived for a while in your
dormitory, fighting with the other drunks. And she also had to get a
statement from her ex-husband who lived somewhere in Siberia without
registration?"

"Anything's possible," Natasha answered seriously, as if she didn't
notice my ironic tone. "We'll go tomorrow at 9:00 in the morning."

I could not get anything else out of her. Why wasn't she surprised
by my arrival? How did she know that I needed a statement? Why did
she insist that the statement be drawn up as soon as possible? I could
only assume that if someone had approached her, had tried to convince
her that she should not give me this statement, they had achieved the
opposite result. Natasha had an independent character. Only people she
respected could influence her.

I asked Natasha about her life. She would only talk about a tragic
accident that had recently occurred at a campsite outside of town. A
helicopter crash with people aboard. Along with the passengers the
helicopter was transporting barrels of fuel oil for expeditions, which
was, of course, against all rules. The helicopter fell from a low height
upon landing but the barrels exploded and all the people were burned
alive. The Second Secretary of the local committee of the Communist
Party flew to the site of the accident, together with her retinue. That
evening at a bonfire, having drunk a little of the local committee's stock
of cognac, she allowed herself to say that there was no reason to grieve
especially for the deceased. They had all been alcoholics. Natasha was
standing next to her when she said this and she slapped the Second
Secretary. There was general confusion for a moment and then the
retinue carried off the victimized party official. They flew back to town
early in the morning of the next day. Everyone waited to see what
would happen next. The incident was hushed up and everyone pretend-
ed that nothing had happened. Natasha was saved by the fact that she
was a mere laboratory assistant. If she had been someone with a higher
position it would have turned out badly.

We entered her apartment. She had only one room with very little
furniture. Natasha had worked her whole life and all she had to show
for it were the basic necessities, just like me. She said that I could say

whatever I liked in her room. I could get drunk and swear and curse at Soviet power and no one would know. I could live here as long as I dared, so as to rest from the strain. She would go live at her girlfriend's.

But she did not go anywhere; we stayed up talking all night. My ex-wife told me that I was doing the right thing. Someone ought to knock against this wall of serfdom. She thought my new marriage and desire to leave for America was a lofty affair, undertaken for the sake of principle. She recalled in detail how difficult it was for her to move from the countryside to the city—that she could only move to Moscow by marrying me, as if a Moscow registration and the right to live there was something like the inheritance of nobility. But then she started to worry. She said that I would not like it in America. No, I absolutely would not like it. After all, there people count money from morning till night and we Russians are not used to this materialism; we are all idealists. Then again she said that I had to go.

"Your American wife shouldn't live amongst our Russian drunks, shouldn't have to stand in our lines for a piece of sausage. Only we can endure it."

In the morning we went to the notary public and I got the second statement. Now I had to get back to Moscow. Several of the certificates that I had obtained earlier were valid for only one month. A month from the day that I received them they would become invalid and I would have to go after them all over again. By then the certificates that I had just obtained might become invalid. I would fall into a vicious circle and there spin about until the end of the century.

I tried to get a ticket out of town, on a plane, on a train. I even said that I had been in the town as a journalist, that I was writing about its inhabitants. It did not help. Too many people wanted to head out for the European part of the USSR. Summer is vacation time and most of the people who worked here were not deeply rooted Siberians. They wanted to spend their vacations in their original homes. The lines stretched out to incredible proportions for tickets valid only two or three weeks in the future.

I figured out a route back to Moscow. I would go by boat along the river far up into the North, to a quiet place where there were no construction projects. From there I would catch a plane to Moscow. The plan worked. I sailed north for a day on a speed launch along a river, arriving in a town located practically at the Polar Circle. There were few travellers here. That night I took a plane to Sverdlovsk in the Ural Mountains. The plane was assigned to an expedition. The chief took me on board semilegally. Since I myself had traveled on all sorts of expeditions it was not difficult for me to find a common language with these people.

In Sverdlovsk I hopped on a train traveling from Vladivostok to Moscow. Fortunately there were a few empty seats and in a couple of days I was back in Moscow. It took me only a week to get the statement from Siberia, including the trip there and back. It had taken twice as long to get the same paper in Moscow.

Back in Moscow a postcard was waiting for me at my apartment. It invited me to come into my local OVIR. I appeared there the next morning holding close to my body the documents I had obtained with such difficulty.

I was met by the familiar young man in the uniform of a police officer. He was alone. He asked me to wait a moment and went into the next room. He returned with a paper in his hand. I recognized it as the petition which Lois and I had left at the OVIR office of the R.S.F.S.R.— the office for the main European republic of the Soviet Union. We had gone there to complain that OVIR's demand for permission from ex-wives was not legal. The official with whom we spoke said that we should draw up a petition and that his office would look into it in the course of a month. I did not seriously expect anything to come of it. After all, it was OVIR that had thought up this ruse. We nevertheless brought in a petition hoping that Lois's signature on it would have some impact. Now the month had passed. It appeared that they had read it. The uniformed young man looked at me politely and said that the statements from my ex-wives were no longer necessary.

I wanted to curse. I wanted to complain. I wanted to write about it. After all, I had been a journalist. But I kept silent. I hoped that now everything would go smoother. Perhaps now they would let me out.

I settled in to wait patiently. Every morning I ran along the shore of the Moscow River opposite from Gorky Park. I studied English, and finished writing a play I had started long ago. I tried to save as much money as possible since it would be needed upon departure. Every day I increased the distance of my run and when I talked to Lois by telephone I joked that if they allowed me to run in the direction that I wanted I would make it to Chicago in good time.

They did not block correspondence between Lois and me, but it was not without restrictions. Even in ordinary circumstances when individuals call abroad from the Soviet Union, or are called from abroad, Soviet operators have been known to say that no one is home, that no one is answering the telephone, while at that very moment someone is sitting next to the phone waiting for it to ring. This happened to Lois and me many times.

In a word, the authorities try to limit as much as possible the correspondence and telephone conversations of Soviet people with the West. In some cases they read all the letters which a Soviet receives from abroad, and in other cases they only check periodically. The KGB can read unopened letters with the aid of X-rays and special equipment for the texts of folded pages. Letters several pages long and photographs are held up for a long time, six weeks or more, obviously because it is more difficult to become acquainted with their content. They probably have to send these letters to another place in order to unseal them. For this additional effort time is needed.

I knew one woman who carried on a constant correspondence with relatives abroad. Both the woman and her relatives were well-known in the Soviet Union and their mail was closely checked. She was sure that her letters were examined by the same person all the time. She could even tell when this person was on vacation because her letters were held up longer than usual, and then a whole package of several tens of letters would arrive when vacation ended.

The same thing happened to our letters. Sometimes they were held up for a while, a month or six weeks, and then they would all come at once. After a year of corresponding I knew which letters would take ten days to two weeks, and which would be held up for over a month. Sometimes I would purposely compose a text that I thought might interest the KGB. Without exception these letters took a month or six weeks to reach Lois. I came to the conclusion that the KGB checked all of our correspondence, and likewise our phone conversations. When a phone conversation began to revolve around a topic unpleasant for the KGB, then we would immediately be cut off.

Lois called every week. We had decided that she would call me, for to phone in the opposite direction, from the USSR to America, was several times more expensive, and my sources of income had dried up. It was easier and more certain for her, an American, to get a line into Moscow than for me to get one out.

Every time she told me that she loved me; she wrote the same in all her letters. Besides sincere feelings in these words of love I also saw an attempt to stir the pity of the KGB, which was listening to our conversations and reading our letters.

Problems with my work ran the predictable course. When I went to my union to collect a document that OVIR had demanded, it was suggested that I resign from the union. I was given no new assignments. All that remained was to wait for the publication of an article that I had written several months prior. This assignment had been exhausting. I spent a few weeks in Siberia at the construction of a trunk line of a railroad into the wilderness. We traveled as a group of six men in three cars. We fought our way through snow drifts and over and around the mountains of ice that form above rivers. It was forty degrees below zero on the Celsius scale. We slept next to bonfires. The settlement from which we began our journey was overrun with the flu. All six members of our small expedition came down with the flu. We took aspirins, washing them down with alcohol. It was difficult to endure.

When I finished this assignment and returned home I felt as if I had returned from the grave. I needed a month just to set myself straight. I wrote an essay about the trip and the magazine liked it. But when they found out that I wanted to leave the Soviet Union for my wife in the United States they destroyed the already composed typeset. As compensation for this assignment they finally agreed to pay me forty-seven rubles—one-fifth of the money due me. At the film studio that I had been working for I was treated even worse. They did not release a completed film that had been shot according to my scenario and refused to pay me anything. I did not doubt that in the other places where I earned money with my pen the same thing would happen.

Two months after I had handed in my documents, OVIR called me in and presented me with a refusal to my request for an exit visa. They told me that the commission that examined petitions considered my departure to my wife in the USA to be impossible at the moment because of bad relations between our countries. They expressed their sympathy and said that in accordance with existing laws I could apply again in six months.

When I told Lois that I had received a refusal she could not hold back the tears. She repeated that she loved me, that she could not live without me, that if she had to she would wait her whole life for me. These words were not spoken for the KGB. She was truly broken-hearted. All we could do was wait six more months for the new decision, which more likely than not would be another refusal.

I could no longer study English. I stopped running. I had staked all that I had on a new life with Lois and now I had lost everything—my former life and Lois.

I was refused on the basis of bad relations between the USA and the USSR. What if these relations were to remain bad for several years? The war in Afghanistan and the state of affairs in Poland left me with little hope. Then the Reagan administration cancelled direct airplane flights between our countries. Our letters started to come more irregularly than usual and I did not know where they were held up, in the United States waiting to be sent or at the KGB waiting to be read.

I did not know how I was going to live further, what kind of work to look for. I could no longer work as a journalist. Whatever job I applied for, I would have to show my "work book." There my education and former positions were listed. If I applied for a menial job the supervisor would immediately suspect that I had had trouble with the authorities; why else would I be looking for a simple job? It would take a liberal-minded supervisor to hire me.

Lois called me every Sunday morning and repeated her love and urged patience and prudence. How often we had argued about patience when we were not yet husband and wife. Lois would say to me that a people should not be as patient as the Russians are. Now she, an American, was urging me to patience. The poorly masked metaphors and the "between the lines" cursing of the regime in my letters frightened her. Lois wrote that she would ask the help of her government, of her senators and her fellow citizens. She wrote that a famous and influential Senator was writing letters to the Soviet Ambassador in Washington. OVIR summoned me to tell me that they had received a letter from Lois's mother, requesting that I be released. These statements of outside concern gave my American wife hope. But I, having lived under Soviet rule for fifty years, felt that the reaction could just as well be contrary. The authorities in the USSR do not like it when someone tries to exert pressure on them. And "statements," letters that they receive, are used at their own discretion. They could have shelved the letters of support and set in motion the letters written under duress by my neighbors, in which they asked that I be kicked out of the apartment for disturbing the peace. The KGB could still have me evicted. And my neighbors acted as if they might, treating me very rudely, demanding that I do everyone's share of the communal work.

In December, five months after Lois had left Moscow, I received an invitation from the American Embassy to come to a reception with the Ambassador. The invitation took twenty days to arrive by mail from one district of Moscow to another. A usual letter would take two to three days to traverse this distance. The envelope had obviously been opened and resealed. It was done too obviously, the glued edges resealed with tape. The Soviet authorities were not ashamed. They undoubtedly were irritated that simple Soviet people received invitations to the Embassy without their knowledge and consent.

In a very detailed letter written by Mr. Curt Struble, the assistant chief of the Consular section, I was informed that Ambassador Arthur Hartman was concerned about the fate of approximately twenty divided American-Soviet families including Lois and me. We members of these divided families were invited to visit him at his home.

I was not prepared for such an honor. On the eve of the reception I spent the whole night letting down the sleeves of a jacket I had borrowed from a friend for the occasion. I had such trouble finding clothes that fit that I had no suit jacket. I always wore jeans, cowboy shirts and sweaters.

On the day of the reception Mr. Struble stood before the entrance to the Ambassador's residence. With my appearance at the gate he notified the Soviet police standing there that I was one of the officially invited guests. This assurance did not stop one of the policeman from demanding my passport and taking it from me into his sentry box. He zealously leafed through the passport, made a phone call and five minutes later returned my passport saying to Mr. Struble that he was only concerned about the security of the Americans inside the embassy compound.

Of those invited only seven or eight people came to the Ambassador's home. Among these were people who had not been allowed to leave for their husbands and wives for several years. With one woman this story had already dragged on for seven years. And there were a few like myself who had received only one refusal. The American officials—the Ambassador himself, his first assistant, his first advisor, the Consul, the Ambassador's wife—tried to speak with each one of us at length. The very fact that we had been invited to the Ambassador's was at the same time both a challenge to the Soviet authorities and a guarantee of our security. It would be uncomfortable for the authorities to inflict their repressive measures on us after we were received by the Ambassador himself. On the other hand, the authorities very often do try to demonstrate their strength, to show that they are not concerned about how they look.

At the end of the conversations each of us was asked if we would like to receive similar invitations in the future, whether we would like to come to the Embassy for concerts or to see movies. We all answered yes. Once such an invitation was sent to my apartment by special messenger. He asked if he could speak to Mr. Frolov. Such treatment sent my neighbors into utter confusion. After all, they took every opportunity to yell down the hall at this Mr. Frolov. For a long time they could not calm down. They expected the sky to fall in on me for having the utter audacity to refer to myself as a "Mister" with all the respect due that title.

As soon as we all stepped out of the Ambassador's residence we immediately broke up into two or three groups which then both secretly and openly quarreled with one another. Such, as is well known, is the custom among Russian people. Our disagreements centered around our tactics in the future.

At the head of one of these groups was Iurii Balovlenkov. He had a wife and daughter in Baltimore to whom he had been trying to leave for three years. Balovlenkov had been searching for members of divided families to unite them for common action. He already knew several people who had wives and husbands in other countries, in France and West Germany.

My meetings with Iurii became frequent. Iurii looked like a student; he wore a beard, jeans, threadbare sweaters and jackets. However, he had graduated from the Bauman Technological Institute in Moscow, one of the most prestigious technical institutes in the USSR, and was a computer specialist. After marrying an American of Ukrainian descent while she was in Moscow as a tourist, he naturally was not allowed to work in the computer field. He took odd jobs, sometimes working as a tour guide for Soviet citizens, for instance.

He was very nervous in manner, and I started to think that this trait was the natural result of the uncertain position of the refusenik. Iurii usually talked a great deal. He would start out speaking in a smooth unobtrusive voice, but as people started to listen to him his formerly unobsessed speech would start to stream out like flowing water. Sometimes he did not have enough air to finish a thought. He would take a short but deep breath like a man under water who surfaces for a moment, fill his lungs with air, and again submerges for as long as he can.

Balovlenkov knew a lot of foreign students and graduate students who wrote various letters and appeals for him that they then sent to different organizations, including the United Nations. His pockets were always stuffed with projects for letter writing campaigns, and his address book was filled with names of people, mostly foreigners, who might prove useful.

Iurii insisted to the small group that had formed around him that it must become an "organization." He often used the words "organization" and "movement." It seemed to me that these words used by revolutionaries at the turn of the century and still popular among dissident circles, hardly applied to this small company which had before it only one goal: to leave the USSR to be with their wives and husbands.

However it must be said that the word "organization" is the word the authorities hate most of all. They recognize only organizations created under their own control. They try to immediately disperse not only any organization that has goals inimical to the government, but simply any organization that they have not approved. Or they will infiltrate an organization with their own informers, keep its members under close surveillance, and later, at the necessary moment, break it up after having learned all the acquaintances and ties of the group. Therefore, any "organization," if its existence is not approved by the authorities, surrounds itself with a halo of secrecy, danger and romance.

"We have to embrace different countries in our organization," Balov-lenkov said. By this Iurii meant France, where Tatiana Vlasova Azure had a husband, and West Germany, where Iosif Kiblitsky had a wife. Balovlenkov and Tatiana Lozanskaya had American spouses. All togeth-er there were four people and they called themselves The Divided Families Group.

Iosif Kiblitsky was an artist and he prepared a large poster on which the continents of Europe and Asia were pictured. From Western Europe a woman's hand stretched out. Coming out to meet it, roughly from Siberia, was a man's hand. The poster was furnished with an inscription in English: "Divided Families—Unite!" This inscription is a paraphrase of the famous Marxist saying "Proletariat of all Countries—Unite!" I do not know which there was more of in this paraphrase, irony or serious thought. Balovlenkov and Kiblitsky suggested that it contained a subtle political approach, as if they were protected by its Marxist allusions. At the same time they felt that these allusions enhanced the significance of the group's efforts. Using photographic means Kiblitsky prepared but-tons from this poster. He and Balovlenkov bought a large quantity of children's buttons that were sold on the streets in kiosks and replaced their messages about the revolution and Soviet sports with the miniature images of the poster Kiblitsky had created.

In order to attract the attention of Western journalists and therefore of Western public opinion, the four members of the Divided Families Group conducted a ten day hunger strike in April of 1982. I did not participate. I was to receive my second answer from OVIR at the end of April and I had not excluded the possibility of permission to emigrate. Balovlenkov called this hunger strike a warning. He wanted to know what the authorities would do, how they would react.

The group was encouraged by the success of Andrei Sakharov's hunger strike which resulted in the departure to America of his adopted son's fiancee, and by the success of Ina Lavrova who, after a thirty-seven day fast, left for her husband in Paris. They were also encouraged by the fact that two other spouses that had earlier received refusals from OVIR suddenly received permission to leave. They had been close to the members of the group and had planned to join in the hunger strike. They spoke of their plans everywhere, including on the telephone, and Balovlenkov explained their sudden permission exclusively by their desire to join his group. He said that the authorities feared the expansion of his organization.

Others did not assume easy success. The experiences of Sakharov and Lavrova made many think that the authorities would not let another hunger strike succeed lest hunger-striking become a system. Many would go this route. One need only fast a little, make a little scandal about it, and, poof! an exit visa.

The group was to gather in Lozanskaya's apartment. Her father was a general, the head of civil defense for the city of Moscow. In responsibility and rank he was practically a marshal. He had acquaintances in government circles and rubbed shoulders with the powerful of that world. Tatiana's husband, Edward Lozansky, had left the country six years ago on a visa to Israel. He lived in Washington where he worked as a professor of physics. Edward and Tatiana had a ten-year-old daughter who lived with her mother in Moscow.

The group hoped that as long as Lozanskaya was with them no serious repressive measures would be taken against them, and that if her high-placed papa wanted to, he could get exit visas for the whole group. Lozanskaya's father had supposedly sent to the West all those who were closely associated with his daughter and who wanted to leave. The father was probably trying to save his daughter from this "bad" influence, but the people who wanted to leave among Tatiana's acquaintances did not diminish, they increased. Tatiana herself had been unsuccessfully trying to leave for several years. Her departure depended on her father's will.

She, like so many refuseniks (people who applied to leave the Soviet Union and were refused permission), lost a prestigious job as a chemist. Her father was unable to make an exception for his daughter. They say that Lozanskaya's parents were not bad people. The father, for example, often went to the store without his general's uniform on and there stood in the lines as all Soviet people do. The majority of Soviet officials have fenced themselves off from the people with their privileges, which they consider normal and legal. But there still exist those who experience a moral discomfort seeing that the people are without the most basic goods, that they do not have adequate food, clothes or apartments. In Tatiana's desire to emigrate there was a special relation to the authorities. If her father had wanted to grant her permission she probably could have emigrated. But in this case the reputation of her father, his official position and his place in society, would be at stake.

Tatiana lived in the Lefortovo district, far from the center of town, in a big though somewhat empty apartment. The furniture that was there had a bureaucratic look about it. Most of the other residents were military people, and the building was considered departmental, that is, it belonged to the Ministry of Defense. The insufficiently cozy apartment was sufficiently spacious and it had a piano in one of the rooms. Here a large number of people could gather and even hold concerts. Tatiana had many acquaintances, among them actors and dissidents. To have friendships with such people is considered quite prestigious in Moscow.

The ten-day hunger strike ended with no result. The group did not manage to pull off a press conference in Lozanskaya's apartment. On the appointed day the KGB did not allow the press into the apartment. On the stairs, on the street, everywhere, there were plainclothes officers. Outside the apartment Balovlenkov gave a small interview for Voice of America and there was some information about it on these Western radio broadcasts which, on the whole, are listened to by people within the Soviet Union, even though the authorities jam the airways, making listening close to impossible.

Kiblitsky did not have a Moscow registration and was registered in a small town, Podolsk, not far from Moscow. They grabbed him up and took him back to his apartment in Podolsk. His parents had lived there several years ago. His father had been the director of a large factory—a "numbered" factory, which means secret. His rank was similar to that of a general in the army. Kiblitsky's parents had left several years before on an Israeli visa and lived there still. The authorities did not touch Tatiana Azure, but then she did not step out of Lozanskaya's apartment. Balovlenkov did venture out and was chased by the police back to his parents' apartment on Smolensk Square. They either wanted to hold him for awhile or simply scare him. The foreign radio reported in Russian that the hunger strike had ended unsuccessfully.

Several days later, on the Russian Easter, a great many guests gathered at Lozanskaya's apartment. I was among them. On the walls hung photographs of the participants of the hunger strike along with pictures of various episodes from their married lives. This had been done for the foreign television cameras that never made it into the apartment.

In a prominent spot hung the poster "Divided Families—Unite!" and in the most prominent place was an enormous portrait of Brezhnev that Kiblitsky had prepared. Brezhnev looked tortured and exhausted, his hand stretched forward as if giving benediction. In the original photograph he was probably greeting an assemblage from a platform. Before the image of Brezhnev stood a traditional Russian Easter cake with a red flower stuck in it. All this, like the slogan "Divided Families—Unite!" was unmistakably ironic.

The topic of conversation among the guests was, of course, the hunger strike. They discussed all the possible conditions that might make the next hunger strike successful. The four hunger strikers had visibly lost weight; the women had big shining eyes in their pale faces. Naturally they talked of OVIR, the KGB, and of *stukachi.* I said that they should keep in mind that the KGB might be listening to all of this—in fact, they had to be.

The KGB can listen from the street in cars using special microphones directed at the window glass. They can listen through the telephone apparatus. They can put microphones in the ventilation pipes and finally in the walls. Taking into account that Lozanskaya's apartment had already enjoyed a particular type of reputation for several years and that the building was within the Ministry of War, then it seemed certain that full surveillance had long ago been established.

Kiblitsky objected, saying that the KGB should know everything about us. The group had nothing to hide. Iurii also held to this opinion. He tried hard, too hard, for them to be fully informed.

The next hunger strike was set for May 10. It was to be without limit. They invited me to join the group. I wanted to be with these people, I found them likeable. But I answered evasively, saying that I might join if I received a second refusal. I was not convinced that it would be smart to join them even if I did receive another refusal. The whole enterprise seemed a bit frivolous.

Balovlenkov, hoping to attract me to the group, kept reminding me of the two refuseniks who had suddenly received permission to leave. He explained their good fortune by the influence of the group. I was hoping that he was right and because of my known association with the group the authorities would approve my new application and release me too.

On April 24, approximately one year after Lois and I were married, I received my second refusal. When I told Lois on the phone, she repeated how she loved me and would wait for me as long as need be. I calmed her and said that they might possibly allow her to come live with me for three months.

I was informed of the refusal by the deputy chief of the Moscow OVIR. He had been promoted to this position not long before. There had been extensive shake-ups at OVIR in connection with revelations of wide-scale bribery there. The deputy chief was dressed in everything new: a new suit, a new shirt and tie—even the watch on his wrist looked fresh out of the store. He told me that the decision of the commission remained unchanged; I was refused exit. To my questions about the reasons for the refusal he answered that my departure was not deemed to be in the interest of the government. I demanded a more detailed answer and he said that his office did not give out more detailed answers.

"Fine," I said. "Could my position change in half a year, or might the interests of the government change in half a year?"

"It's completely possible," he answered.

"Could my wife be permitted to come visit me for a short while?"

The little eyes on his fleshy physiognomy took on a mocking expression.

"Of course not," he answered.

"Could my wife come to live with me, say for the allowed three months?"

"Try it. Hand in your documents."

"Fine. I'll try."

To continue this conversation was useless. This OVIR bureaucrat himself knew nothing. All was decided above him by the KGB.

Iurii phoned very often urging me to join the group in their limitless hunger strike scheduled to begin May 10. He lost his patience with me and said that I had not yet matured. He said that I still believed in illusions, in the promises of OVIR, and that usually people come to lose their illusions after they have waited two or three years thinking after each new refusal that the next time they would get permission. OVIR feeds these illusions so that refuseniks do not commit acts in opposition to the government that keeps them locked up. I, in turn, got angry and asked Iurii not to teach me how to live.

In order for my wife to come visit for three months I again had to fill out forms for the local OVIR where I had brought all my documents the first time. The local OVIR accepts the forms and passes them on to the city OVIR where they make the decision, or, more accurately, where they pass on the decision of the KGB.

Going into the local OVIR with the new forms I saw the same people. I immediately recalled the whole story with the certificates from my ex-wives. I now understood that these certificates were merely one of the obstacles set up in this giant application process to trip us mortal souls. It is constructed in such a way that a stumbling block is found for every person. Ideal people with perfectly clean biographies are very few on this earth. By the time a person is fifty years old he will have someone in his past, and if not he has to have permission from his parents no matter his age.

It seemed to me that I read derision, mockery, in the eyes of the staff at the local OVIR. It was as if they were saying:

"Well, now, he ran after certificates, waited almost a year, and now he's still running, still waiting."

Then I recalled all the advice I had received from various acquaintances about my wife's plan to visit for three months. Few thought it a possibility. I would have to show support for those three months and I did not have a job. I lived in a communal apartment, and my neighbors had already "expressed their displeasure" with my wife's stay a year ago.

Among my acquaintances was one woman that I suspected did some informing for the KGB. This *stukach* was very dissatisfied with me because I had not sold her all the things that Lois had left behind with me when she left Moscow. She was angry at me, and she envied me, as practically all Soviet people envy one another.

When I told her that I was going to petition for Lois to visit she laughed and said:

"Go ahead. Try. Put in your documents."

I feared that this *stukach,* knowing about our plans to have Lois come be with me for three months, would report to the KGB that Lois intended to bring in something illegal or that I was planning to send something out with her.

I instinctively sensed that the authorities would not give Lois a visa.

They would only dangle this petition in front of us. And when they finally did refuse us we would be given no explanation.

Standing in the threshold of the local OVIR office, the mockery I saw in the eyes of the bureaucrats, and the fact that my wife's visit depended to some degree on *stukachi* and to a large degree on my neighbors, all together brought me to a state of impotent fury. I turned around, not saying a word, and left.

LBF

I had returned to the United States and my parents' home in Chicago on July 3, 1981. We celebrated the Fourth of July together with a new sense of admiration for this holiday. I was still very nervous from the stress of the last month in Moscow. New-found habits died hard. I jumped when someone unexpectedly knocked at the door. I preferred to speak about Andrei while we were out on the street. I turned the radio up loud whenever we did discuss something sensitive in the house. And I was averse to using the telephone. My parents found all these "paranoic" tendencies quite amusing and after several weeks so did I.

The plan was to stay in Chicago for the rest of the summer. I would live with my parents, work as a waitress and save my money so that when Andrei arrived we would be ready to travel out to California by the time the fall quarter started at Stanford.

On September 7, 1981, Andrei received his first refusal. I was shattered. The weeks of waiting would now be months. Maybe even years.

I arranged to continue my work on my dissertation in Chicago and made some progress over the next months, but the work went very slowly. I would sit down at the desk every morning and write Andrei. I took my time over this, the most pleasant part of the day.

The reason given for Andrei's first refusal was "bad relations with the United States." I knew these words meant nothing; the real reason for his refusal was and always will remain a mystery. Still, I became intensely interested in anything concerning Soviet-United States relations. I pored over every newspaper sold here, reading everything I could find about the Soviet Union. I read journal articles. Went to lectures. I followed the course of every proposed international business deal with the Eastern bloc. I had become a pathological Kremlinologist. Every up and down movement in our governments' relations was registered in my mood. The imposition of martial law in Poland and our government's adoption of sanctions in protest was a personal blow for me.

During the year I talked regularly with the people at the Soviet Desk of the State Department. I thought they knew what they were doing, and I took their advice. They said that they could see no reason why my husband should be held; he had no "security clearance" problems, no financial indebtedness and no family obligations. Thus, if there was no reason for the Soviets to hold Andrei, they would eventually release him so long as I waited carefully and did not stir up any trouble. "Can I ask my representatives in Congress to write letters for me?" Certainly, replied the man at the Soviet Desk. A letter is okay so long as I did not "go public" with Andrei's case.

My representatives in Congress all wrote letters on my behalf to Soviet Ambassador Dobrynin. After several months had passed with no replies, and right after the imposition of martial law in Poland, I asked my Congressman and Senators to write a second letter for me to Dobrynin. When I mentioned this to the man at the Soviet Desk, he told me I had blundered. "This is no time to push the Soviets on anything," he said. I called an aide to an Illinois Senator and relayed this conversation to him. The aide replied that a polite letter from a Senator expressing concern over Andrei's case certainly did not strike him as "going too far."

When I confronted the State Department with the fact that the letters that were being written for me were the only things that the United States was doing in my behalf, the man at the Soviet Desk said that there was a "system" for dealing with cases such as mine. He could not go into details, but I should trust him that the system was in place and had worked in the past.

One glimpse of this "system" came prior to the Haig-Gromyko talks in the spring of 1982. I called the Soviet Desk and asked if my case might be brought up at this meeting. I was told that my case would be mentioned. "We like to mention these cases at summits. They are always good for propaganda purposes."

These words sent shivers through me. Now my husband was a pawn in a propaganda war. Yet maybe—maybe the pawn would prove to be an embarrassment to the Soviets. Maybe they would tire of hearing his name and simply send him out of the country. Or maybe the Soviet Desk at the State Department was simply telling me what I wanted to hear, and they would not bother the Soviets at the summit with insignificant cases such as mine. How was I to know? I was contending with a bureaucracy in Washington made up of administrators, while thousands of miles away Andrei was contending with a bureaucracy in Moscow made up of administrators.

I phoned Andrei once a week. We would speak for about ten minutes. Sometimes I would sit on the phone for two hours trying to get the call through. On New Year's Eve all phone communications with the Soviet Union were cut off for about five hours. The international operators, who by then had come to know my voice, did not know what to make of it. In my panic I feared that this silence was the prelude to World War III. I would never see Andrei again and he would be shipped off to prison as a suspect citizen.

I bought a shortwave radio. I spent hours trying to tune into Russian language broadcasts on Voice of America, the BBC, and Radio Canada because they gave more coverage of Soviet news, including news on Soviet human rights. Moreover, I knew that Andrei listened to these Western radio broadcasts and I felt closer to him knowing that we both were listening to the same words at the same time. Or perhaps I was quietly going berserk.

I found out about the second refusal on one of our regular phone calls. We knew approximately when to expect an answer from OVIR but as usual we had no definite date. When my husband told me, I could not hold back the tears. I had cried too many times this last year.

I feared for my husband. I feared that he would do something that would make our situation worse, even irretrievable. It would be better simply to wait some more. I told Andrei that we should wait and endure this calmly. I told him that next time we would absolutely receive permission. I was comforting myself more than him with these words, for I knew, just as he did, that if they refused him twice without a reason, they would refuse him a third time, a fourth time, and a tenth time. They hold refuseniks intentionally so that others will be frightened— frightened to marry foreigners, frightened to put their documents into

OVIR with a request to leave. They need fear. Without fear their system cannot exist. I hated them with every bone in my body, with my soul. I, an American, was in their power along with my Russian husband.

I kept repeating to Andrei that everything would be fine, that we just had to wait a little more, and that life did not end with this refusal. We should be grateful that they still let us talk on the phone; even that might not have been. I started to call Moscow more often. I was frightened when my husband, following my lead, started to talk of being cautious, even submissive. I knew after that that something was bound to happen. I feared that the spring which held him in submission would break.

CHAPTER 6

THE HUNGER STRIKE

A F

I decided to join the hunger strike that the Divided Families Group planned to start on May 10. I would stand together with Tatiana Azure, Tatiana Lozanskaya, Iurii Balovlenkov and Iosif Kiblitsky in defiance of the Soviet government. Although I had originally scorned Iurii's idea of "organization," I had to admit that it made sense. I knew that what the Soviet government feared most of all was organized activity, since under a totalitarian system, any group is considered competition for the allegiance of the populace. In the attempt to achieve a political goal a group has more chance of success than an individual does. Its actions are more significant. After all, Lenin spoke of organization as the most important political principle, even more important than class. In a group a person feels stronger. Group members offer each other support, emotional and tactical. Group members share information, and tell each other their experiences with Soviet governmental organs. In the Soviet Union it is only through the grapevine that people acquire information about the workings of the Soviet government. A group may also provide the individual with some protection. The authorities can do whatever they like with a lone individual; it is more difficult to do so with a group.

Obeying the instinct that I had cultivated throughout my lifetime in the USSR, I carefully hid this decision once it was made. In the presence of two people who I suspected were *stukachi* (my suspicions were later proven right), I zealously spoke about how I had come to terms with my fate, that one should not hope for too much, that perhaps my wife would be allowed to live with me for a while. I had to be patient and prudent. The *stukachi* believed me mainly because it seemed to them that there was nothing else that I could have thought.

Three days before the hunger strike was set to begin I announced to Iurii Balovlenkov and his friends that I would join them. They accepted me into their company with joy. The group had grown by one. Iurii told me that he admired how carefully I had kept my intentions hidden all that time, misleading the authorities. Iurii and I both sensed that it was to our advantage that the authorities did not know my real intentions. I did not tell Iurii that my decision was practically spontaneous; my patience had suddenly worn out.

I met with Iurii and the rest of the hunger strikers at the apartment of a married couple who were also waiting for permission to leave the Soviet Union. As time passes a refusenik becomes more and more isolated, and is eventually left to associate only with other refuseniks. It is a close-knit world—a world in which the KGB takes an active interest. This couple very graciously offered us the use of their apartment for the press conference with foreign journalists at which we would announce our hunger strike to the world. We replied that we had not yet decided where we would hold the press conference but that we were very grateful for their brave offer. A day later a high placed foreigner warned us that this husband and wife were informers, that is, *stukachi*. Several months back other people had almost caught them red-handed. When we found out that this couple reported back to the KGB we were greatly disturbed; I had hidden my intentions so carefully only to have ruined everything at the last moment by announcing all to these two people.

We decided to hold the first press conference with foreign journalists in my room in the communal apartment. We felt that the authorities would consider this the least likely alternative. Still, now that I had announced my participation in front of informers, the authorities might consider my room a possible site. We were shaken by this negligence and as a result we became as careful as possible. We agreed upon our plans while on the street, away from possible listening ears. Our error had motivated us to become deadly serious.

Perhaps their *stukachi* did not inform in time, or perhaps these subordinate KGB workers took too long in reporting to their superiors, and the superiors took too long handing out instructions to their subordinates in the field. Maybe we were lucky because I had announced my intentions on a Friday while the press conference was set for Monday. It is possible that the KGB also rests on Saturdays and Sundays. What really happened is not known, but for the two days before the hunger strike Iurii and I observed the utmost caution. On the phone we said that all measures in conjunction with the hunger strike would take place in Lozanskaya's apartment and that the apartment of the husband and wife about whom we had been warned would serve as our second alternative. Just in case, we spoke of some other apartment on the outskirts of town as the third alternative. The KGB workers were already accustomed to Balovlenkov's and Kiblitsky's principle of discussing everything openly, hiding nothing, and therefore it probably did not even occur to them that we would misinform them.

A rule that my father often repeated to me came in handy. He often told me that Talleyrand, the great diplomat in the era of Napoleon, said that the tongue was given man in order to hide his thoughts. My father, an open and straightforward person, could not hide his thoughts, and neither could I—usually. At the necessary moment the words of Talleyrand, which my father had taught me, proved very useful.

Relying on the KGB system of eavesdropping we group members continued to pursue our naive campaign of misinformation. Nevertheless, we knew that my residence was now most likely under surveillance. It would cost them nothing. What is another couple of agents when they had multitudes at their disposal? The scale of the surveillance that the authorities had placed on us became clear later on during the hunger strike. A few of the people remaining in the human rights monitoring groups came to visit us. They were met by plainclothes officers at the metro station and were accompanied the whole way up to the door of my apartment.

We tried to take everything into account, to think of all possible contingencies. In this game without rules fortune was on our side; we were helped by one instance of dumb luck after another. After the game had ended someone in the KGB probably paid for it with his service-issue easy chair, as we say.

We gave foreign correspondents slips of paper listing my address and telephone number and we strictly told them that they were not to call me until the press conference had begun on Monday morning. We asked them to call Lozanskaya's apartment frequently over the week-end. But, according to the laws of probability, one of the correspondents got mixed up and started to call me on the eve of the hunger strike. He kept asking me about the "approaching action." I told him that I knew nothing and that he should call Lozanskaya. He found out nothing worthwhile at Lozanskaya's and failed to show up at my apartment the next morning for the press conference. He did everything backwards.

At first Kiblitsky, Azure, and Balovlenkov hid out in an apartment in an outling area of Moscow. Balovlenkov soon noticed that their movements had been observed and this apartment was now under surveillance. Most of all he worried that we would not pull off the press conference on the first day, the most important day. If the KGB did not manage to stop the press conference, if in the beginning our hunger strike was announced to the whole world, then it would be more difficult to disturb us in the future. Foreign journalists and the staffs of foreign embassies would be following our fate.

It was decided that on the eve of the hunger strike Kiblitsky would be in Lozanskaya's apartment and they would use the telephone heavily to create the impression that the others were going to join them there later. Balovlenkov and Tatiana Azure hid themselves in the apartment of an old woman who lived a few streets from me. Just to be safe we assumed that the KGB agents knew where they were. They were to arrive at my apartment in the wee small hours of the tenth of May. Before they came I was to go down on the street to check if all was in order.

Iurii and I agreed to meet, just the two of us, without Azure, late at night on the corner of my street. We had set a time of meeting: anywhere from 1:30 A.M. until 2:00 A.M. Amidst all the tension Iurii got a bit mixed up. He thought we were to meet at 2:00 A.M. This mistake helped us, as it turned out. All of our mistakes worked to our advantage.

At exactly 1:30 I left my apartment and went out on to the street as if to get a breath of fresh air, to calm my nerves. This behavior was not unusual—I often went out late at night. My irregular style of life as a free-lance journalist got me into this habit.

I knew my neighborhood well. All the courtyards, lanes and alleys in this area of old Moscow were familiar to me since childhood. I knew the entranceways to each building. I knew which entrances could be passed through, how to go up and down stairs and then come out on the other side of the building into another courtyard or alleyway. I knew which courtyards led from one street to the next without falling into a lighted area. All the buildings were different in this part of Moscow. The gaps, courtyards and passageways between them, where they met and where they didn't—they all varied, but I knew them all.

I passed through the courtyard behind my building. I went down the next street to the north of my home and came back two streets over, one street to the south of my home. There wasn't a soul to be seen. I found myself on a dark corner in one of the courtyards and stood there awhile. Then I left through the arched passageway of one building and came out on the main street near the corner that meets with the narrow street on which my building is located. I stood under the arch of the entrance to a courtyard and from there examined the street. Very few cars passed by. There was no one on the sidewalk. After awhile, as I looked down the street again, I noticed a young couple strolling arm in arm down the sidewalk. At first I paid them no mind and continued to stand in the darkness under the arch.

It began to drizzle. The rain drops became heavier and more frequent. The drizzle would soon turn into a downpour. I again saw the young couple, still walking down the street, arms about each other in the same embrace, only now they were strolling in the opposite direction. They looked about as if admiring the scenery. There is nothing in particular to admire on this street, especially where my little lane meets the main thouroughfare, and especially when it is about to pour, and especially not for ten minutes walking back and forth in one and the same embrace, arms around shoulders without the slightest change in position. I looked at them more carefully and noticed that the lad had a diminutive figure, while his companion had an equine face, and a figure that was quite masculine. The pair looked unnatural, even from behind. I noticed that they had on the exact same jeans, as if bought in the same store and even of the same size; they fit the young man loosely and the young woman tightly. I laughed to myself—again, clothes on the public account. Thirty years ago it was boots with galoshes at the public's expense; nowadays, it is muskrat fur hats, blue jeans and briefcases with taperecorders that show up on the floor next to your table in some quiet cafe.

I had to confirm my suspicions. I waited until the pair turned the corner at my street. I left the main street through the courtyard of the building on the corner where the pair had turned. I stood in the darkness and was not seen. The couple stood at the corner of the building. Their pose had changed completely; they were no longer in embrace. The young man carefully looked down the street from which they had just turned and where I had just been standing, only now I stood in the narrow cross street watching them from behind. I was enjoying my experiment. I started in their direction, as if I too was simply strolling while the young man kept looking down the other street. When I had already approached fairly close to them they finally noticed me and were surprised that I had come from the other side. They could not hide their irritation but grabbed each other again by the shoulders and started to stroll. It was more than funny—the rain was really coming down.

I walked away from them into the center of the courtyard. I started to think about what I should do next. These undoubtedly were people sent to follow me. Iurii was supposed to arrive any moment; it was almost 2:00 A.M. I had walked about a half hour waiting for him and, as it had turned out, not in vain, for I had discovered the pair surveilling me. Maybe they had been following me since I left my home, or maybe they had been assigned to one end of my narrow street and on the other end different people waited for me. I did not know and did not want to know. Somehow I had to intercept Iurii before he got here. I knew which direction he would come from. I moved away from the darkness back toward where the couple had stood on the corner. In one of the cars parked close by I again spotted them. They were inside the car, settled way down in the seat so that they would not be visible from the street. It was truly difficult to spot them; the light from the street lamps did not reach their faces. I walked up to the car and peered directly in at them. There was not a shadow of a doubt as to why this couple was here.

I saw Iurii walking down the main street towards the narrow cross street where I lived. Fortunately, he also saw me. I made signs to him that he should go away. He understood, turned back and ducked into a dark, narrow street a couple of blocks away. I hurried through the courtyards and passageways of my neighborhood. I met Iurii and told him about the couple that was watching me—there were probably others.

We decided to meet again with Tatiana Azure at 5:30 in the morning and then go up to my apartment. I told Iurii that I could lead them through the back entrance of my builing. It had not been used for years. One could get to the back stairs that went up to my floor only by going through the basement which also had not been used for years.

Iurii liked this idea. We split up in the darkness, each going our own way along the alleys and courtyards. Iurii went back to the apartment of the old woman who lived a couple of streets away. There Tatiana Azure awaited his return. I went back to my building. Going up the front stairs to my apartment I saw a homely, middle-aged woman on one of the landings. She stood there leaning her elbows on the railing like a person waiting for something. Seeing me she became slightly animated, but then with an indifferent air she turned away. This was the customary behavior of agents that I had already become too familiar with. As soon as they spot their target they involuntarily liven. They are no doubt shown photographs of the person they have been assigned to follow, and finally meeting them face to face their normal human reaction is one of mild excitation. Immediately afterwards they diligently pretend that they are not in the slightest interested in the object of their surveillance, while following him all the time out of the corners of their eyes.

"How good it is," I thought, "that Iurii and I are taking this extremely seriously."

Many people would laugh at us and say that we were playing cops and robbers. But we had to achieve our goal and if we were not going to be deadly serious about it, then why even start the whole affair? On the other hand, our adversaries had not taken us seriously enough. Their organization has all types of agents and all sorts of technical equipment. They could have arranged the surveillance so that we did not notice a thing.

Going up two more flights of stairs I discovered another woman on this higher landing. It was a mystery what she, as well as the first woman, could be doing there on the stairs of my building late at night. Their presence and the uniformity of their behavior left me with no doubt. KGB agents very often work in pairs.

"My goodness," I reflected, "their agents come in all shapes and sizes. How noticeably this business has improved since Stalin's day."

I could not sleep a wink until 5:30. It poured all night. That's also to our advantage, I thought. Agents of the KGB are ordinary people. Those who were out on the street were chased away by the rain to some sort of dry spot. The agents probably saw Iurii and me and how we split up. They undoubtedly saw that I had returned alone to my apartment and then the hardest rains came. Perhaps the agents decided that watching my apartment was less interesting. In any case they lessened their attention. Whoever commanded them probably decided that they had to concentrate all their attention on Lozanskaya's apartment where we were all supposed to gather by nine the next morning.

Therefore, everything went well for us. At 5:30 A.M., in all probability not noticed by anyone, I made my way out of my apartment by way of the back entrance and went through the courtyards to the place where Iurii, Tatiana Azure, and I were to meet.

I awaited them, peering out from a gate in a courtyard. Very soon I heard them walking along the side street. Tatiana was fretting, something about a puddle, about the rain. Iurii dragged her by the arm and growled through his teeth. Tatiana told him that if he was going to be rude she would not go any further. It seemed so funny to be fretting about such things at a time like that, but then our nerves were raw.

We walked back through the courtyards to my building. We went down to the basement where we had to thread our way through to the back stairs that went up to my apartment. The basement had flooded with sewage not long ago when the pipes burst. By the time we happened upon the basement it had dried out a bit. Still, not every person could have made their way through—only one who knew the premises well. My building was fairly large and the basement was labyrinthine. As a child I had played here with the other little boys in our neighborhood. Now that the boilers were no longer being used, the basement was just abandoned catacombs, and very few people knew how to get through it to the back staircase. If KGB agents had taken an interest in the back staircase they too would have to get into the dark flooded basement first. Not knowing the way they could only have crawled on their knees through the sewage. I seriously doubt if anyone, besides us, had this route in mind.

Lighting matches and swearing at one another, we walked along unsteady, rickety boards that lay over the flooded mush. Tatiana practically cried at having to be in such a horrible place. Iurii was indignant. He swore and told her that only this way could she wind up with her husband. For Tatiana the path to Paris lay through the fetid basement of an old Moscow house.

Once up in my room Tatiana started to chat. Iurii made a horrible face at her, lifted his finger to his lips, and let out a hissing warning noise. It was quite reasonable to assume that the microphones of the KGB were already eavesdropping on my room. Tatiana calmed down and drifted off to sleep on the divan. Iurii and I sat in the armchairs, once in a great while explaining something to one another in gestures or getting up and whispering in each other's ears.

At exactly 9:00 in the morning the bell to the entrance of my apartment started to ring. Every minute I jumped up and ran down the corridor to open the door. Each time as I met and led to my room the next correspondent the door to the room of my nearest neighbor opened up a crack and each time I saw her evil, dumb-struck eyes. Something unbelievable was happening in my room. In this apartment, the residents of which feared the very word "foreigner," about fifteen foreign news correspondents had gathered. They had all kept the secret that they would meet at my place at 9:00 A.M. Monday morning. Only the one German confused everything and did not show up.

Iurii explained to those who had gathered why there were only three of us, why Kiblitsky and Lozanskaya were absent. We three were enough for a press conference.

We announced that we had begun a limitless hunger strike, a hunger strike that would end either in victory or in death.

LBF

When they called me from the *Chicago Tribune* and said that my husband had announced a hunger strike in Moscow, I immediately understood that this was the misfortune I had foreseen. The conditions under which Andrei and I had lived together made me sensitive to the slightest intonation in his voice. When he had started to talk about patience over the phone, I had felt that his patience was nearing its end. Perhaps he himself had not known it, but I had.

It was morning in Chicago when the newspaper called me with the news of the hunger strike. I had just sat down to breakfast. As soon as I heard I lost my appetite. What had Andrei done? Would the authorities arrest him or would they let him starve to death? Or was there any chance that it could work?

In half a minute I was negotiating with the international operator to put me through to Andrei's apartment. Miraculously the call went through, but it was not Andrei who answered. Andrei's neighbor, the old woman who lived next to him, said that Andrei was not home but his young lady friend was there, and moreover she had spent the night there. I was surprised she did not add that the young lady was beautiful and walked down the corridor naked. And she in turn was surprised when I asked, calmly, to speak with the young lady. It turned out to be Tatiana Azure. Tatiana said that Andrei and Iurii had gone out on business and would be back in an hour.

Well, at least I could still get through to his apartment, and he had not been arrested. I began to take stock of the situation. Andrei had chosen to go the public route—to take his case to world public opinion and no longer sit idly by. I thought it dangerous, perhaps even foolhardy, but I understood the sense of desperation that had led him to this decision. And now I was faced with a decision. Should I try to get as much media coverage as I could about his hunger strike in an effort to get him out of the USSR? Or should I be the Soviet model of an unassuming and patient wife, who quietly waits in the hope that the Soviet State will throw her a favor?

I decided to call the brain trust of the United States, the office which, in such affairs, was supposed to serve as a safeguard for the legitimate interests of citizens all over the country. I called the United States Department of State and asked to speak with the officer at the Soviet Desk. Here was a man who surely had inside information.

The man from the Soviet Desk listened to my brief story though he apparently already knew the details. He asked me whether my husband was naive. There were incredibly complex questions of *politics* here, he said. Big, Large questions. What questions?, I asked. Extraordinarily sensitive questions, he replied, questions that Andrei undoubtedly could not understand.

So, I decided, I had wasted a phone call. I made a few calls to various people in some of the emigre organizations. Maybe they had inside information. Their replies scared me. They said that the venture was hopeless. They predicted that my husband would wind up in a psychiatric hospital. They said that he was in a very dangerous position. They cautioned me to advise him not to leave his room and step out into the street.

What did these people really know? I could see from their answers that they were speculating on the basis of no information, that the idea of a hunger strike was new to them. In fact, as I learned later, most of the organizations that are concerned with Soviet emigration are totally bereft of ideas except one: write letters. Whatever the situation, they advise writing lots of letters. Write to everyone: Congressmen, assemblymen, aldermen, Vice Presidents, ambassadors, mayors, corporate CEO's, Soviet representatives in Washington, Soviet officials in Moscow, plus letters to friends who will in turn write letters for you to all the previously mentioned persons. Why all the letter writing? Because sometimes "it works." But how do they *know* it works? The more I thought about it, the more I realized that tons of letter writing is a kind of superstitious behavior. It is like savages doing a rain dance; every once in a while, it rains! Then the medicine men say to the people: "See, I told you, if you keep doing the rain dances, they will *work.*"

An hour had passed and I called Moscow again. I got through to Andrei. I suggested that he renounce the hunger strike, that everyone had advised me that it was senseless. I told him that the State Department felt that he was too small a person to take on such a complex affair, that he was no Sakharov, and that he did not understand the politics involved. The more I spoke, the more anxious I became. I was simply trying to convince myself against my own judgement. I said to Andrei that if he did not stop, all would be ruined, that I would never again be allowed to see him, that he might end up in a state psychiatric institute on the ground that he was insane to go on a hunger strike to the death.

Andrei told me to get hold of myself. He said that if he retreated now, a horrible fate would await him. He could not go halfway. His name would be on the blackest of lists, and all roads would be closed. Nothing but failure awaits those who hesitate. Even if we talked for a whole hour, there would be nothing new to say.

The conversation ended. Maybe Andrei was right. But the more I pondered it, the more it seemed irrelevant whether Andrei was right or wrong. The only thing that mattered is that what he had done was a fact. A fact I had to live with. I reproached myself for being too emotional over the phone. That was no way to deal with the situation. I needed calm logic.

I had reached a resolution by nighttime. In fact, my body decided the question for me. I could not eat as long as my husband was on a hunger strike. I reached Andrei over the phone, and informed him that I had decided to join him on the hunger strike—and also "to the end." He joked that it was healthy to fast a little. I said I was serious. Why? Was it not enough that he was fasting? He advised me to get a doctor to monitor my condition. With this our conversation ended.

As it turned out, my hunger strike was of great significance in garnering support and attention for Andrei's case. But the decision was not made in terms of calculating its effect on the media. I confess that I simply could not stand the idea of eating food while my husband was starving in a Moscow flat for the sole purpose of getting an exit visa to come here and live with me.

A F

It was an extremely serious thing that we five had done when we announced the hunger strike in Moscow. What is a hunger strike but a slow suicide, lasting a month or more during which the people to whom the protest is directed have time to think and take some sort of action? This question of suicide troubled me a great deal. One often hears of unsuccessful attempts where the party in question never in-tended to end his or her life, but only wanted to throw a scare into those around them. Their intentions sooner or later became obvious and they became objects of mockery. Then there were those who truly attempted suicide but at the most decisive moment stopped, and everyone around them saw that they hesitated in the face of danger, and they also earned no respect. I did not want to be a laughing stock or behave like a second-rate actor about anything so serious.

Sakharov was in the hospital on the sixteenth day of his hunger strike. Ina Lavrova, after a month. These were the hunger strikes that preceded ours. Ina Lavrova was granted permission to leave only on the thirty-seventh day of her hunger strike after having suffered permanent damage to her health. The Soviet authorities decided to release her in the face of a very vigorous campaign in the Western press. Still, her case would not have been favorably decided without the intervention of the top levels of the French government.

My comrades in the hunger strike had sent a collective letter to the Supreme Soviet of the USSR, the highest organ of power in the Soviet Union. They wrote that they sought departure from the Soviet Union to be with their families or their hunger strike would end with their deaths. It was written in the most dramatic language and included references to the rights of man. My signature did not appear on this group letter to the Supreme Soviet. I would send my own letter to the Soviet government when I had decided exactly what I wanted to say.

My comrades hoped that before they died they would go to the hospital, and once there they would not be allowed to die. Being in the hospital would certify their dangerous condition and increase the indignation in the West. Most of the participants of the hunger strike suggested that it was possible to get into the hospital by simply calling an ambulance and once there they could continue to refuse food and medical help while keeping up communications with foreign correspondents, as had been the case with Ina Lavrova.

I was not certain that I had enough emotional and physical strength to fast for so long. I did not know how my body and my psyche would react to a total fast. I did not want to go to a hospital since I was not sure that the doctors would offer their help, and on our terms. They could refuse to accept us saying that we were taking the places of others who truly needed medical help.

Because medical treatment, including hospitalization, is free in the Soviet Union, there are never empty beds in the hospitals. Still, they will take in anyone truly needing medical aid. In some instances, due to the lack of space, patients lie in the corridors.

Kiblitsky and Balovlenkov insisted on the hospital. They also wanted each of us to send a last will and testament to our spouses abroad so that it would fall into the hands of the KGB. One of their friends even suggested that once we were in the hospital, and our health began to fail, we should send for a priest.

I was against the hospital idea but I agreed to go along with the will of the majority when the time came. Tatiana Azure, who was a doctor, was categorically opposed to the hospital. She felt it would constitute a violation of her professional ethics, and that she would lose her standing as a doctor.

Another important question was whether doctors could certify the condition of total fasting. Tatiana assured us that it could be established without difficulty, that the condition of a total fast has many signs obvious to doctors. More dangerous than a total fast was the condition of emaciation resulting from a partial fast. Tatiana said that it could quickly lead to dystrophia with irreversible effects, which does not occur under a total fast that may last as long as 30 to 40 days. A healthy person can gradually go off a total fast without any damage to his health, and in some cases it may even prove beneficial. But all of these facts assume an absolutely healthy person who fasts under a doctor's supervision. Not all of us were absolutely healthy. Not all of us could inflict extreme emaciation on our bodies.

In the name of the group Balovlenkov appealed to the American Embassy to have their doctor establish some kind of medical control over us. The Embassy turned down his request. They felt that such a step might qualify as American interference in the internal affairs of the Soviet Union. They said that the Embassy doctor did not have the right to give medical aid to citizens of the USSR. Fortunately, the doctor at the French Embassy agreed to render us unofficial help during the hunger strike.

At the first press conference, to the correspondents' question: "How long will the hunger strike last?" the others had answered, "Until the end, until victory or until death." I had to answer that I did not know how long my resolve would hold out. I said that my hunger strike was a form of protest against the actions of the authorities in refusing me permission to leave.

That day, after the press conference and my conversation over the telephone with Lois, I decided for myself that I would fast "until the end." Let whatever might happen to me happen, but I would not retreat or surrender.

I wrote a letter to the Presidium of the Supreme Soviet of the USSR. It read:

I am notifying the government of the USSR that I am on a hunger strike which began on May 10, 1982. At the same time my wife, Lois Frolova, a citizen of the USA, is on a hunger strike in Chicago. Our fast has the purpose of attracting attention to the actions of the Moscow OVIR which prevents the reunion of our family. The hunger strike is without end.

With respect,
Andrei Frolov

Of course I signed with respect. After all I was addressing the top echelon of the Soviet government. My complaint was ostensibly with the operations of OVIR and it was only in this manner that I could broach the issue with the leaders of the Soviet state. In fact my complaint was with the state itself, a state that does not allow its citizens the right to live where they want, does not provide explanations for its capricious behavior, and does not provide any relief from administrative injustice. The state itself forces such extreme measures as hunger strikes on its citizens.

After taking leave of the correspondents on the first day of the hunger strike, Iurii and I went off to visit one of our acquaintances who was involved in human rights activities. He rendered us all sorts of help, translating things from Russian into English. We sought his advice on our line of behavior throughout the whole ordeal.

After the success of the first day we were so excited—we experienced such joy! It was no small thing we had done. We had deceived a mighty organization, probably the most powerful organization in the country, which had at its disposal an enormous staff of permanent agents, as well as "part-time" agents, *stukachi*, various listening devices, and the capability to tape our telephone conversations and read our letters. That they used this arsenal against us was beyond any doubt. They use everything and do not regret the money spent even in the least significant cases. We managed to put together a press conference under their very noses, using all of their own tools against them. Now that Western radio stations had spoken of our hunger strike and newspapers had written about us in at least three countries (the U.S., France and Germany), "They" did not seem so frightening.

To make short work of us on the sly would be very difficult and to do so openly was almost impossible—the whole world would know about it. Of course, the Soviet government does not always shrink before world public opinion, but in this case reprisals against us would be very undesirable against the inauspicious background of the occupation of Afghanistan and the imposition of martial law in Poland. Still, it seemed to me that perhaps this whole story could be convenient for the authorities. Perhaps they were giving us the opportunity to stir up Western public opinion in order to inflate our importance and then release us in exchange for some sort of concessions from the other side, or to demonstrate to the world how kind and good they were. After all, the world still remembers how the Irish died of a hunger strike in a British jail. We, of course, had nothing in common with the Irish, but I think that for the Soviet authorities our story could have served as a basis for a deceitful demonstration of their humanitarian principles. Anyone could have made this supposition or any other.

The motives of the KGB in this and in others of its decisions are held in secret so that neither inside the government nor outside can anyone understand the logic of their actions. Perhaps no logic at all exists, but only the arbitrary tyranny of big and small bosses who are concerned with their personal positions, with their own "easy chairs." Such conditions exist in all spheres of the Soviet governmental system. Secrecy engenders them. Secrecy is the source and the cloak for arbitrariness. The authorities do everything hidden from their own citizens, citizens who they consider ought to spend less time discussing the issues and more time expressing their approval of the decisions of the authorities.

That first day Iurii and I were in a hopeful, happy mood. We felt that we were in a position of relative, though temporary security, and we gloated over the "poor uncle," the KGB official to whom "we had given an enema," perhaps even ruining his career. For Iurii, this was his first success in his many years of effort to make a breach in the wall that stood before him. For me, it was the first serious protest of my life. Until now I had only protested passively, refusing to participate in elections, for example. Now I had succeeded in protesting to the whole world. It inspired me. I felt that I was now ready to go the whole way. I was ready to place my freedom and my life at stake. After all, now my sacrifice, if it came to that, would not vanish into the thin Soviet air. It would not fall into obscurity; it would not be in vain. My back straightened up. I was openly expressing my disgust with the Soviet system. After a year of cowering, my fate in the hands of others, *I* was now acting. I had found my human dignity.

Iurii's head also spun from the consciousness that he was leading an open struggle with the KGB, that threatening spectre that had hung over our whole lives. He said that now he was going to bury the KGB in a torrent of letters, letters to academicians, letters to factories, letters to editors of magazines and newspapers, even letters to party organizations, officials and bureaucrats, knowing that all the letters would wind up in one place—the KGB. Let them work a little! Let them read, sort and file those letters! Let them run to their bosses with reports! That was, in general, the role Iurii wanted to play. He wanted to raise as much noise as possible. He wanted the authorities to tire of him all the more so that finally they would want to run away from him.

Once in the West after my hunger strike, I immediately used my freedom to read a book of Vladimir Bukovsky's recollections and Aleksandr Solzhenitsyn's *The Oak and the Calf.* Iurii had read these two books and tried to emulate their authors; he even took to using several of their expressions. I think that in his struggle with the authorities he overrated his own strength and possibilities. In the end, Iurii's role would turn out to be almost tragic.

To me fell the role of devil's advocate, the person who doubted everything. In the future I would also be christened the pessimist of the group. Tatiana Azure gave me that name. Tatiana was the weakest physically, and as the days passed this weakened her emotionally. Kiblitsky, on the other hand, was excited by danger and difficulty, and seemed to seek out trouble. He continually went to the German Embassy, where he had conflicts with the Soviet police at the entrance. He talked about these run-ins everywhere, knowing full well that association with diplomats was at the same time a defense and a danger to him. Tatiana Lozanskaya frequently invited foreign correspondents to her apartment and thus regularly sustained blockades by KGB workers. The high position of her father allowed her to act more freely than the rest of us.

When Iurii and I returned to my apartment that first day, we had already forgotten about our being watched. We continued to talk excitedly to one another with that joyous glint in our eyes. With every passing day this glint took on more of the glaze of insanity. As we walked from the courtyard into my narrow street we saw Tatiana standing at the window of my apartment. She was making warning gestures with

her arms. Iurii and I doubled back into the courtyard and there discussed what her signal could mean and what we should do. We decided
that no matter what it meant it was now impossible to hide and perhaps
it made no sense to do so. We moved into the street peering about us
but we discovered nothing. It became clear later when we were up in
the apartment.

Tatiana, alone in the room, after speaking to my wife, had been left
with nothing to do but await our return. She had gone over to the
window and gazed out. My God! The street was literally covered with
plainclothes officers. Besides them, there were two details of voluntary
police, *druzhniki*, with their red armbands, and yardkeepers who from
time to time whispered rumors to the police. They all paced up and back
on my narrow street. At first Iurii and I marvelled at how we managed
to jump through all these people but then realized that "our audience"
had so far been assigned simply to watch us. Obviously all Soviet organs
charged with keeping the peace were called into action by the KGB, but
too late. At 9:00 that morning the entire street had been filled with
automobiles bearing diplomatic license plates. Now, in the middle of the
day, there was no one left.

After a while I had my conversation with my wife, one of the last
of our phone conversations in Moscow. I told her that I would fast to
the end.

The day after the first press conference another one was held in my
room with the correspondents of two television companies, one American and one French. Our entire group was in attendance. Kiblitsky and
Lozanskaya were now with us after spending the first day acting as
decoys at Lozanskaya's apartment. Now we gathered openly. The correspondents together with their apparatus passed into the apartment
without obstruction. Radio stations had already reported our story
worldwide: The Voice of America, BBC, The German Wave, and Radio
Liberty. The KGB certainly did not want to add to the texts of these
broadcasts that their agents kept foreign correspondents from doing
their work in Moscow by not allowing them into private apartments and
keeping them from speaking to Soviet citizens.

The other four of our group took seats on the divan on which I had
slept for at least twenty years of my life. I was left to perch on a chair
placed next to it. While the television cameras stared at us we felt as

though we were in front of the whole of Europe, as well as America. And before the cameras, as before the window of humanity, the French commentator again asked each of us in turn whether we were ready to fast to the end. He wanted to hear how serious our intentions were. Obviously this question was of the most interest to foreign viewers. The first press conference had ended with the same question.

My Moscow acquaintances that I met in the next several days were interested in the same thing. They also wanted to know if we were really fasting. They asked if perhaps we were eating a little bit on the side. To all of these questions I answered in the same way. It was easy to discover any deception with a medical examination, and besides, "to eat a little bit on the side" was more dangerous to one's health than a total fast, physically as well as politically. I advised people to read special medical books on the subject. Eventually we got very fed up with these naive questions. To explain to each person what a fast meant from a medical point of view was impossible, and that certainly was not our purpose.

At this second press conference we all felt more confident and more resolute. The publicity had given us strength. And now we understood what the world wanted to know—whether or not we were bluffing. How were we to prove ourselves? In the meantime, only with words.

And thus the commentator from French television, a handsome, well-wishing Frenchman, asked:

"How long are you prepared to fast? A week, two weeks, three weeks, or to the end?"

The fatal question was addressed to each of us in a row as we sat on the divan. The first to answer was Iurii. He had the face of a man possessed:

"To the end! To the end!"

Kiblitsky was next. He was sitting comfortably sprawled on the divan. When the commentator turned to him he sat forward and clenched one knee between his clasped hands like a man prepared for an important matter. He held his hands fast, hung his head and looked up from under his brow. Kiblitsky was a person firmly set, impossible to budge, and this resoluteness showed when he answered the commentator's question:

"To the end!"

Next in turn was Tatiana Azure. Tatiana's chin rose in defiance. Her brows also rose a bit from the tension and then broke and fell as if not bearing up:

"To the end!"

"To the end!" said Lozanskaya, as if she were speaking these words directly into her father's face.

It was my turn. I looked at the camera while thinking to myself, "And what if I don't hold out, what if I leave the circle in a week? After all, my comrades have already had experience fasting and I have not." The pause after the commentator's question dragged on. I began to nod my head in assent and said:

"I, also, to the end."

It came off unconvincing. The commentator was silent, the camera continued to stare at me.

"Yes," I added. It was a bit raspy and not too loud. The commentator seemed disappointed with my answer. The crew began to gather up the equipment and the lights. Everyone in the room started to speak at once.

Lozanskaya said to me, "You didn't have to say 'to the end.' You could have said 'I don't know,' and that's all."

Kiblitsky also said to me that I could have said that I had not definitely decided.

"What do you mean, not decided? Who hasn't decided?" I answered.

I had decided, but I had other doubts; unexpected consequences of the hunger strike threatened me in the first week.

CHAPTER 7

THE 26 DAYS

A F

In the corridor of my communal apartment the heartrending cry of my neighbor rang out, while in the bathroom, sitting on chairs carried out from my room, were the Chief Consul of the French Embassy and the head of the Consular Division of the American Embassy. In my room the doctor from the French Embassy was examining Tatiana Azure and therefore the rest of us had to leave and wait in the bathroom. There was no other place. The corridor was dark, while the bathroom was spacious and had a large window. The toilet of our apartment was located in another room, or more precisely, in a closet with barely enough room for a grown man to sit comfortably.

My old neighbor took to screaming periodically. No one knew when the next scream would come but it always did. One of her last screaming fits was conducted in Lois's presence. Several days later, in hysterics, she confessed to us that the police had demanded her signature on a statement against us. Being uneducated she feared anything requiring a signature. Now she was again emboldened. According to her view of things it was not only possible now to yell at me, it was even necessary; perhaps the police would praise her for it. So at first she took to screaming that it was forbidden to sit in the bathroom. Then she complained that she had to use it at that very moment even though usually she used it only once a month. We then left the bathroom and stood in the corridor. Her shrieks continued with unremitting force. At first provoked by the bathroom situation, her complaints had now become totally unrelated to our presence in the corridor. With rabid eyes, like a howling dog almost exploding in anger (but nonetheless not yet resolved to bite), she screamed in abrupt, jerky phrases that I had sold myself to the foreigners, that police followed me on the street five-thick, and that they would soon send me off to prison.

The Consul from the French Embassy and the American were familiar not only with the Russian language but with life in the Soviet Union. Therefore they patiently waited and I waited together with them. After awhile the medical exam finished and we went back into the room, while in the corridor the howls still resounded, their repetitive message being that I did not have much time left to canter about in freedom.

These howls, like much else in the communal apartment, personified my repugnant Moscow life. Here yelling at me was a woman that Moscow communal life had tossed me together with and who hated me for my education, for my occupation, for my acquaintances. And I could do nothing. I could not summon the police for they would have found the means to turn this incident against me. I could not respond to my neighbor even if I had wanted to. I, and not she, would have been accused of abuse. I could only endure it silently. How much longer? Years? The whole rest of my life? No! Only to the end of the hunger strike which might last for another month. In a month something in my life would change.

When my neighbor yelled about the police following me five-thick she had in mind plainclothes officers. If the old folk and invalids of our little street, who often hung about with nothing to do, had begun to notice that I was being watched by police five at a time, then too many agents had been sent to look after me. I myself had already stopped looking from side to side to discover when and how many people were watching me. Now it was all the same to me—one or ten, if they succeeded in seeming indifferent or not. But all this surveillance was apparently not enough for the KGB.

One day uniformed police came to my room and demanded that I go with them. When I asked them why, they simply answered that their chief had demanded it. I refused to go and suggested that if they really needed me then they could return with an order for my arrest, signed by a judge. They called their chief right there in the corridor of my apartment. The chief asked to speak to me and I told him the same thing I told his subordinates. The police left empty-handed. Their boss had spoken with me in a very polite manner, addressing me by my first name, patronymic, and last name. I was told that they would call and come again. I repeated that I would accompany them only if I was summoned on the basis of concrete business with the judge, and until then they should not bother me.

The next visit was made by a threesome, for some reason all dressed in leather coats or jackets. The one with the longest leather coat, pudgy-faced wth whiskers, was obviously the senior officer. He said that they were from Criminal Investigation, and showed me his identification card in its special red jacket, also leather. They had come to check the apartment, ostensibly for criminals, and to check the passports of all the residents. And they truly did go about the whole apartment, peering into corners and checking everyone's passport.

Only one officer came into my room and by my invitation. Criminals obviously did not interest him greatly. He took my passport, turned it about in his hands, and asked me how old I was. All this, a search for criminals, just to ask me this question! He did not know what else to say. He told me that I did not take very good care of my passport. It really was a bit tattered. With that, he left.

These visits only increased my confidence. I saw that they could not do anything to me—they could only try to exert psychological pressure. That was why they followed me five-thick, but I had stopped paying attention.

When the doctor from the French Embassy finished his examination of Tatiana Azure he said that it was dangerous for her to fast any longer. Her legs had begun to swell and the blue splotches on them were moving higher and higher, threatening to spread over her whole body. Tatiana herself understood the danger perfectly well. She knew she had kidney problems when she decided to go on the hunger strike.

It was my turn. The doctor took my blood pressure, once, twice, and raised his eyebrows in surprise. My pressure was not only low, as it should be after a week of fasting, but it was uneven besides. Speaking in French, the doctor told me through Tatiana's interpreting that I was very nervous. Outwardly I held myself calmer than the rest. I made light of it and said that of course you get nervous when you are shrieked at in the corridor in the presence of diplomats. Through Tatiana the doctor asked me what complaints I had.

"The government and my neighbor," I answered.

They both laughed.

"What else?" the doctor asked.

"Well, I don't sleep."

"How long has this been?"

"Since the beginning of the hunger strike, a week ago."

"You haven't slept at all?"

"Not at all."

"Adrenalin," Tatiana said to her colleague in French.

I knew that adrenalin was coursing through my blood like in an athlete at the moment of competition. Upon fasting the same thing occurs—adrenalin is produced in excess. The medical instructions we had read warned of the disruptive effect this outpouring of adrenalin might have on sleep. But I had not slept at all. It seemed that my adrenalin was even higher than the level of that of an athlete in a sporting competition.

"Looks like I'll run to the finish first," I joked with the French doctor. But he was very serious. He did not want to joke anymore.

"Is there a chance that I will die but not by starvation?"

He very seriously nodded his head in answer.

"How long can a person go without sleep?" I implored.

"It depends on the conditions."

Yes, and my conditions, I thought, were not the very best; there was still the hunger strike. Then I thought, what if the KGB was listening to this conversation? Of course they were listening! My God, how convenient for them! They would know my weak spot, and it would be very easy to drag me off to a psychiatric ward and pronounce me insane.

"How much weight have you lost?" the doctor asked.

I had lost 8 kilos, close to 18 pounds, in the first week without food and sleep. The doctor became very serious.

"If it continues like this you could perish in a week. You must sleep at any cost."

"Is there some medication I can take?" I asked.

"Under no circumstances!" he answered. "Any medicine would act like a poison on your system in its present state."

After seeing off the diplomats, the doctor, Tatiana Azure, Balovlenkov, Kiblitsky and Lozanskaya, who had come by later, I was left alone in the room. I started to think about what I should do. The doctor told me that I had to sleep whatever the cost. And now the KGB knew that I was not sleeping. Perhaps now they were waiting for me to lose my balance. I would do something rash. Maybe I would pounce on someone and in the presence of witnesses. Then it would be very easy to send me to the crazy house.

Balovlenkov had already been charged with not working. According to Soviet law he could be exiled from Moscow for a year or more. Kiblitsky lived in Moscow illegally, as did Tatiana Azure, both violating the passport regime. A woman from Lithuania whose husband had defected to the West came to live at Lozanskaya's. The police had already accused Lozanskaya with a violation of the passport regime for failing to register her guest. Therefore it was already clear how the authorities were going to deal with each of us.

I stepped out into the corridor and at that moment my neighbor, the screamer, popped out of her room and flitted across the corridor into the kitchen.

"I'm going to kill you," I told her. "I'm going to club you to death, just like Raskolnikov killed the old pawnbroker!"

My neighbor stood there, her eyes agog, not moving from the spot. Talking to her about Raskolnikov was silly. Where would she have read Dostoevsky? It was not worthwhile talking to her anymore. Enough— the fright I put her through calmed me; it was retribution for the pain she had caused Lois and me.

I went out for a stroll, feeling a little easier; maybe the adrenalin in my blood had eased. I sat down on a bench on Gogol Boulevard. One person not far from me was busy trying to look indifferent.

"Come on. Come after me, you dogs . . . I won't be your loony, I'll think up something more interesting for you . . ." I thought to myself out on the bench. "The most important thing is to lead you away from the usual plot. In order to act according to a new plot you on the bottom have to report to your bosses higher up. The bosses higher up have to relay their decisions downward, and only then do you get to execute your orders. Oh, I'll make a wonderful report for you through one of your *stukachi.*"

I went to visit a speculator-acquaintance of mine. In need of money over the past year, I had planted trees, dug earth and done some carpentry at his dacha. I gradually came to understand that he was a *stukach*. He was very interested in foreigners, had many foreign friends and was always trying to increase his contacts among them. He obviously had sent back no small amount of information to the KGB. In the beginning I thought he was simply a speculator, a black marketeer. But I could not understand how he was able to have plied his craft for so long, acquired so much money while not working anywhere, built a home outside of town and collected in his Moscow apartment more antiques than in a government consignment store. Now, having come to understand something about the ways of *stukachi* and KGB methods of operation, I had no doubts about this man.

One day he had not wanted to pay me all the money I had earned working on his dacha. I flared up. I threatened to administer "physical justice." After that incident I always received my money in full and with it respect in his eyes as a person capable of decisive action.

Now, visiting his apartment, I started to say that I intended to go off this earth in no simple manner, but "with music." In the language of the criminal world, to go out "with music" means to manage to do something to your enemies, even kill one of them.

"You know," I said, "my music will be like this—I will set myself ablaze on Dzerzhinsky Square, at the foot of the Iron Felix."

He was listening to me very carefully. He was a very serious person and he considered me no less serious than himself. Moreover, he felt that I still trusted him.

"When do you intend to do this?" he asked.

Ha, ha! I laughed to myself. His report must include the time of the event as well!

"I myself don't know yet," I told him. "I won't notify anyone, no correspondents, no one, so that they can't stop me."

Of course, I knew that they could stop me at any moment, that they were following me all the time!

"But I'm still not sure if that's enough," I continued. "Perhaps I'll take down one of their people beforehand."

"What is their person guilty of? He's just following orders."

"He's guilty of working for boots with galoshes, for muskrat fur hats ..." I stroked my chin. "Perhaps I won't finish off one of those simple ones—I'll go after someone a little fatter, if I can manage it."

"Where does that get you?"

"It's for the show trial! After all, show trials do exist."

"No, no one will know about what you intend to do, except the office," he countered. The "office" is slang for KGB.

"I'll try to do it so that people find out. I'll do it publicly, on the street. And if they explain it by insanity, well, after that it wouldn't be so offensive to sit in the crazy ward."

On that we parted. I left a calm man. I had let off steam. On the way home I thought to myself:

"Now there will be a report. Absolutely. It will state that this man, who knows me well, thinks that I am really capable of such actions. Now they'll have to think up a new move, a new variant for me. Perhaps they'll hurry up with the insane variant but nothing will come of it, for tonight I will sleep, without fail, I will sleep. They will strengthen their surveillance—let them! I'm not going anywhere. It will only cost them more money every day."

That night I truly did sleep, for the first time in eight days. My dangerous crisis had passed. My sleep returned to normal. Now the fast alone was left.

People from the American Embassy began to visit us regularly. They had apparently received their instructions. Their presence every day safeguarded us while at the same time they tried to determine for themselves the seriousness of our intentions.

In the presence of diplomats Iurii was a fish in water. He wrote innumerable proclamations, translated them into English, made copies and passed them out to whomever he could. In these proclamations he appealed to humanity, to justice, and reminded his readers of the legality of our actions. I refused to place my signature on these papers. I felt that our business, after our story had been handed over to worldwide publicity, was to fast and place ourselves on the edge of life and death, and I considered letters to representatives and presidents unnecessary. I quarreled with Iurii. The other members of the group quarreled with him, too. He considered his form of action to be the only correct way. When he spoke with someone he heard only his own voice.

We all became very weak and irritable from the fast. We were in an extremely excitable state that coincided in every detail with the medical descriptions we had read. When we all gathered together the most furious arguments arose about the tactics we should employ. These arguments were senseless. What kind of tactic could we talk of if the game is played with blindfolded eyes? Our advisor was not reason but animal instinct.

I categorically refused to participate in any of the bustle that Iurii insisted upon. In addition to our general nervousness and our fruitless arguments people started to call me frequently late at night thinking my apartment was our headquarters. For instance, some sort of women from Paris who spoke Russian called me. In Paris it was evening, in Moscow night. They spoke for ten minutes and I still couldn't figure out why they called. All the news about us they already knew. Perhaps they wanted to lend us moral support, which was welcome, but more than that I needed sleep.

My neighbors began to crawl the walls again from the midnight peals of the telephone. I was afraid they would write a collective letter to the police complaining about the continuous nighttime disturbances— and now it was all true. I myself could not live with these constant telephone calls.

Lozanskaya's husband, Edward, called from Washington. He was in a safe, comfortable place, during the day, while I stood barefooted in the corridor, nervous as I heard my neighbor begin to bump about her room having been awakened by his call.

The phone often rang in the evening, too. These were calls from within Moscow. The rings would repeat at intervals of five minutes. The neighbors stopped answering the phone. They knew the calls were for me.

All of a sudden, day and night, all the people that I had suspected were *stukachi* started to call me and invite me over. I answered rudely so as to stop these sorts of calls in the future. Most of my friends were frightened to call me. They knew that in such situations all telephone conversations are recorded. Two of my closest friends called and said: "Stand firm!" They called at different times, probably from phones on the street, and said very little, but although they did not know one another they both said the same thing, as if by arrangement.

One day, late in the evening, when I had just begun to fall asleep, the phone rang. I didn't bother to get out of bed. Five minutes later it rang again and for a long time. The next apartment must have gotten upset, not just ours. I felt the adrenalin again rise in my blood—I would not fall asleep tonight. I got up and went to the telephone and lifted the receiver. . . . I found myself on the floor while the phone receiver was dangling from the wire along the wall and an insistent female voice was saying:

"Allo! Allo! Where did you go?"

I hadn't gone anywhere. I was sprawled on the floor. I had lost consciousness for a short while. I got up slowly. One must get out of bed and up from a chair slowly during a fast or else one's head starts to spin.

"What do you need?" I said coarsely into the phone.

"Could you call Iurii to the telephone?"

"Iurii doesn't live here. Have you tried calling him at home?"

"No one answers the phone there."

"Well, of course, it's late." With that the other end of the line went quiet. A long pause.

"Excuse me, I didn't know."

"What do you mean, you didn't know it was late?!"

"I didn't know it was difficult for you to come to the phone."

"Yes, it's difficult, very difficult. And what exactly do you want?"

"I wanted to give Iurii a book."

I knew quite well that if it had been something important they would not be calling on the telephone. Several other young women called on every silly pretext. They were simply curious, and asked for Iurii, saying that Lozanskaya had given them my number. Truly many people were calling Lozanskaya. I had to tell her not to give my phone number out to anyone else, not to people in Paris, nor in Washington, nor to Iurii's friends. To leave me alone, like a beast in his burrow.

Lois could not call me anymore. Our telephone calls were simply cut off. We would just manage to say two words, sometimes only one. She tried calling again and again, at various times, but they invariably cut us off. They let whomever wanted to call me get through, even from Washington and Paris, but they did not let me speak with my wife. I hated and despised them. A foul system, based on foulness. They search for a person's weak spot and then hit them there. My wife was truly brokenhearted from grief. She heard my voice but could not manage to say one word back.

L B F

I had decided to support Andrei in a "parallel" hunger strike. It was not enough simply not to eat. I had to act as effectively as I could. The power of publicity is crucial to any hunger strike. It is the pressure of public opinion which influences a government to relent and correct its own injustice. There was no coverage of my husband's actions in the Soviet press and no possibility of "internal pressure." Any pressure had to come from outside of the Soviet Union where the Soviet government is concerned about its public image. The Soviet Union spends a great deal of time and money on propaganda throughout the world. Its efforts are mainly directed towards the Third World where the nature of their image is still in question, and towards Europe where they are currently seeking large-scale political and economic gains. The United States is somewhat barren territory for Soviet propaganda due to our hostile relations, to American awareness of the abysmal record of the Soviet Union on human rights issues, and to our own massive internal propaganda effort against the Soviets. Still in all, the story of a husband and wife who are willing to starve themselves to death in protest of the Soviet Union's refusal to allow them to live together does not help Soviet public relations efforts.

More importantly, publicity provides protection. Without public knowledge of the existence of an Andrei Frolov my husband might very well have vanished in the night only to turn up in prison on charges of "having threatened the Soviet state," or in a mental institution under the pretext that he was a danger to himself and therefore had to be committed and treated. Andrei's vulnerability was my main fear from the outset of the hunger strike. World attention was his only protection.

Finally, publicity might influence the United States government to take a more active stance in support of our case.

But I had reservations about "going public." It was not something I looked forward to: displaying my life before strangers. And, I worried that publicity on my end might somehow backfire and hurt Andrei. This enterprise had to be handled delicately and responsibly.

I called my friend Susan Keegan for advice. We had been friends and rivals since our first day in college. Due to the healthy competition between us, we studied hard and emerged at the top of our class. Susan went on to become a top attorney at an excellent Chicago law firm, and I went on to study Russian history and marry a tall, nineteenth century-looking figure straight out of my doctoral dissertation. Despite our differing fates, Susan and I were very close and I valued her opinion.

Susan was positive and supportive. She said that Andrei's press conference on Divided Families had gotten worldwide attention; now it was our responsibility to keep this attention going. The question was how to get publicity. How to arrange a press conference? And how to convey the seriousness and sincerity of my intentions? Susan said that she would help in every way. She suggested that we call a friend of hers who had been her professor at Northwestern Law School. He probably would have some ideas about how to hold a press conference.

That evening Susan called Professor Tony D'Amato. Although a professor at one of the more staid legal institutions in the country, Tony had a reputation for being unorthodox and tough. Susan told me that he had argued many cases against the United States government at the time of the Vietnam War, contending that the war was illegal because there had been no declaration of war as required by the Constitution. In one Chicago case involving four students who had poured blood on the files of a local draft office, Tony got their felony convictions reversed in the Court of Appeals by arguing successfully that the statute under which they were prosecuted was unconstitutionally void because it could have been used to suppress free speech. This had been a ground-breaking case. I eagerly wanted him on my side.

Susan and Tony spoke for a while. Later I got on an extension phone and we continued the conversation. Tony had to be told the facts of the case, and whether I was really sincere (he was cautious that it might be some kind of publicity stunt.) The more I listened the more it became clear that the voice on the other end of the phone had gotten enthusiastic. Tony asked me why I wanted to hold a press conference. I replied that maybe I did not—maybe it was in some way dangerous for Andrei. He said that it probably would only help Andrei, since if there was anything the Soviets decided to do to him they would be less likely to carry it out if he were in the limelight. (Tony later informed me that my question to him—about whether or not I should have a press conference—clinched for him the fact that I was sincere about the whole business. Anyone intent on just a publicity stunt, he explained, would not have been willing to scrap the idea.)

Susan and Tony decided between them that the best place for the press conference would be in the faculty lounge at Northwestern University School of Law, a campus in downtown Chicago. It would give the conference the serious tone that was necessary to convince skeptical members of the press that my hunger strike in support of Andrei's was genuine. Tony said that there might be a problem in getting permission to hold the conference there, and that Susan, being an alumna of the law school, might have some "weight" with the Dean. When she called, the Dean was out and she left the request on his answering machine. It was probably fortunate that she did not talk with the Dean directly, because he might have turned her down. Weeks later, Tony got something of a reprimand from the Trustees of Northwestern University for holding press conferences on school grounds; they did not like the use of university property for "radical causes."

The press conference the next morning was well attended. Susan and I had stayed up the night before calling the appropriate news agencies and preparing a statement. Tony had advised me that members of the press are apt to be very cautious; they do not want to be victimized by fraudulent publicity stunts. The night before the conference we also went over any tough questions that the reporters might ask. But the press was very gentle with me. Tony said that they were obviously convinced of my sincerity and of my urgent concern for my husband.

My prepared statement to the press said in part:

"Yesterday I learned that my husband had made the difficult decision to begin a hunger strike in protest of the Soviet Union's refusal to allow him to leave that country to live with me, his wife and only close relative in the world. I firmly support my husband and his actions. This clear denial of his human rights is in violation of the Helsinki Accords and of the Soviet Constitution's stated support of the family. The Soviet authorities have placed us in this desperate situation. Upon learning of my husband's hunger strike, I began a fast yesterday. I stand by my husband's side regardless of the intervention of great forces which deny us the right to live our lives peacefully together and instead force us to live a world apart. My most immediate concern is my husband's health and safety. I am going on this fast to show solidarity with my husband and demonstrate the seriousness of our plight."

The press conference was a success. The story was covered well in the Chicago newspapers, on radio and on television. Newspaper and radio reports went out to other cities. This publicity helped with the second part of our emerging plan for securing Andrei's release. I called, and in turn was contacted by, a variety of human rights organizations. Their support, if we could secure it, would increase public awareness and provide us with further contacts in government and in the media. Most of the people I spoke to were very sympathetic but felt that there was little they could do. They would not even announce their support. I was particularly disappointed with the reactions of several Jewish organizations. I assumed solidarity because I am Jewish (although Andrei is not) and because of their efforts on behalf of freeing Soviet Jewry. It seemed to me that my case was such a clear violation of the Helsinki Accords and the Soviet Constitution that public awareness of it would serve to demonstrate the illegality and tremendous obstacles that Jewish emigration faces. One local organization tried to persuade me to quit, repeating the State Department's admonitions almost word for word. Another organization, after long deliberations, denied me public support, explaining, "we are having problems with your hunger strike and that aspect of the case. Some of the Orthodox members are upset since the Talmud does not condone suicide." No mention was made of Andrei's hunger strike; that did not seem to concern them. One or two Jewish organizations understood the precedence of our case, but most of the organizations could not get deeper than the most superficial analysis of the situation.

The day after the papers announced my hunger strike I called the Soviet Desk at the State Department and asked to speak to the person who was in charge of the binational marriage cases. I had spoken with this man, a Mr. Goodman, many times in the course of the past year. Our dealings left a taste of insincerity in my mouth. He spoke with a sort of feigned lightheartedness as if to demonstrate the Department's composure and mastery of the very serious and complex problems that arise in United States–Soviet relations. Whenever I had tried to reach him in the past he was either out or busy. This time my call was immediately put through.

"Hello, Lois. You've had quite a day. So you've announced your own hunger strike. Interesting strategy. Sets Andrei apart from the rest of the group. You realize, don't you, that it looks as if you're doing this as much against us as against them?"

"What do you mean?" I asked indignantly.

"That's alright," he said, avoiding my question. "We can handle it."

My hunger strike was perceived as a protest of some sort against the American government. I suppose this perception was not farfetched; after all, my hunger strike was here in the United States. There was nothing the Soviet Union could do about it directly; they could not force-feed me, for instance. Yet the Soviet Union could end my hunger strike by releasing Andrei. So why was my hunger strike against the United States?

Later, I could see that the State Department's reaction fit a pattern. The State Department did not want anyone to do anything that might make a problem for them. Because my action could create a publicity problem for the State Department, my action was "against the United States."

I asked Mr. Goodman what steps had been taken in my case over the course of the last year. He sputtered a bit. I repeated my question and he then answered:

"We presented your husband's name to the Soviet Ambassador on a list of divided family cases but it was probably done too late to have had any effect on his last petition to leave."

"Why was it presented too late?" I asked.

"Well, it was on the general list that we present every year."

My husband's and my case was one of approximately twenty such cases of divided husbands and wives. In the course of almost one year of separation the State Department had managed to place my husband's name on one representation list containing all the names of all the relatives—sisters, brothers, cousins, aunts and uncles—separated by Soviet borders. So this was the "system" my friend at the Soviet Desk had asssured me with for the past year.

I called other government agencies, but the response was not encouraging. Public interest organizations urged me to call the Office of Human Rights and Humanitarian Affairs in the State Department, assuring me that it was the proper agency for my appeals. I called several times, explaining who I was and each time was told to take it up with someone else in the office, but no one ever returned my phone calls.

In those first days of the hunger strike I received no end of advice. Total strangers would call me up and give me their free advice. Friends, relatives, casual acquaintances—everyone had advice for me, predictions for me, warnings for me. I received a lot of advice about the hunger strike. For example, I was told that I would go blind in two weeks. I was advised to take an enema every day. My brain cells would die off at an accelerated rate. I would soon be unable to move on my own power.

At first I was too busy and too concerned about Andrei's political health to worry about my own physical health, but as the days passed my body changed. I lost weight very rapidly and slept very little in the beginning. My sleep improved after awhile but getting up was difficult. I was nauseous and dizzy. My arms and legs ached at the joints. After several hours these conditions would clear up and my mind would be as sharp as glass and my energy level very high for about five to six hours, only to fade out rapidly at night.

I was fortunate to find Dr. Sheldon Berger, an excellent doctor who had had experience with prolonged fasting. He gave me confidence simply by dispelling myths. He explained to me that a person can go a long time without food and not inflict permanent damage on their body. There are two concerns. First, the blood pressure drops so low that upon sudden rising or prolonged standing a faster can easily faint. Second, it is necessary to drink a great deal of water in order to keep the ureic acid level in the body down and thus stave off kidney damage.

At my first appointment, a week into the fast, Dr. Berger took a battery of tests. The morning queasiness and aches were attributable to low blood pressure. My ureic acid level was abnormally high and I was to start drinking eight ounces of water every hour, if not more frequently. I had started to menstruate two weeks ahead of my normal cycle—an irregularity I had never before experienced. The doctor checked this and concluded that it was a result of nervous tension and not the fast. In general, the doctor found me to be fit. He said that I had a very efficient metabolism, just made for fasting, that it was operating well on no nutrients. I told him that my years as a junk food addict in college served as training.

The third day of the hunger strike was the worst for me. I was famished; desperate for food. But Dr. Berger and others told me that the third and fourth days were typically the worst; after that, the body's rebellious spirit calms down and the body becomes acclimated to living off of stored fatty tissues and not external food. And true enough, by the end of the week I could stand the hunger strike a lot better.

Doctor Berger said that his main role was to be my "cheerleader," and that he was. We spoke on the phone every day. He asked me how I felt, what I had done, and what progress was made in the case. He asked all these questions with genuine interest and concern. He said that he would get me through the fast as long as possible, but he left me with this general warning:

"Any organism when it loses thirty percent of its protein dies. You are a healthy woman but you are small, so you don't have much of a reserve."

At the end of the first week I was extremely depressed. Andrei's phone was cut off to my calls. I tried to get through day and night. Sometimes we would manage to exchange one or two words and then a ghastly mechanical screech cut the line. The American phone operators were puzzled by this sudden noise and asked, "What was that? How did that happen?" I was too tired to explain it to each of them.

A desperate pattern was emerging. No major religious or public organizations would announce their support of Andrei's and my attempt to be reunited. It was clear that the United States government, in the form of the State Department, did not intend to help us. And, after the initial flash of publicity, reporters went on to other things. It seemed that Andrei and I had had our media fling. Now we would quietly starve to death.

What remained of our cause was a small band of ordinary people who had rallied around me. There were those who knew me, who had witnessed closely my pain over the last year: my parents, Susan, a few friends in the Russian emigre community, and my colleagues at Stanford who organized letter writing campaigns at the university as word reached them. And there were two men I had never met before, Professor D'Amato and Dr. Berger, who soon after meeting me dedicated themselves to seeing me through this ordeal. A seemingly small and inconsequential group to take on the policies of two superpowers.

My parents reacted to the hunger strike with bravery and love and a bit of ethnic humor. When I first told my mother that I was going on a hunger strike in sympathy with Andrei's, she said to me: "If you must fast, you must fast. Just be sure to eat a little something." The passions and determination that Andrei's decision to fast stirred in me frightened my parents, but they swore to help me however they could. They had watched my pain of the last year, and it tortured them. So, as frightening as the hunger strike was for them, the move to action, the frenetic activity that surrounded us, was a relief from the dull and constant ache of the months that preceded. They wanted me to stop the hunger strike but, swept along in my passion, they acceded to my every request.

I received a postcard from Andrei in the middle of the second week of the hunger strike. He had apparently sent it a few days before the strike was set to begin. He asked me to go to a Russian church and place a candle before the icon to Saint Nikolai. Nikolai is the patron saint of travellers, and my husband, having traveled so much, looked to him as his personal benefactor. Before I left Moscow the two of us had gone to a beautiful, brightly colored church not far from Andrei's home. There we placed a candle before the icon to Saint Nikolai and Andrei prayed that we would soon be together in America.

After I received Andrei's postcard I asked my father to drive me to a small Russian Orthodox church on the west side of Chicago. I knew how important this symbolic act was for Andrei. My father is not a religious man, but he dropped everything to take me to this church. He understood that through this act I was demonstrating my faith in Andrei.

The church building was small; it did not appear to be well-off. There was no one inside except for an old caretaker who spoke only Russian. He let us into the hall. My father hung back, bewildered by the ornate splendor of the iconostasis. I quickly recognized Nikolai, lit a candle, and begged him to bring my traveller home to me. My father held me for a moment and then we drove home.

I heard rumors that a forthcoming evening news program would be devoted in part to the Divided Families issue. The program was "Nightline," with Ted Koppel, on ABC national television. I tried all my contacts to get on to the program, but without success. Even the Chicago ABC news people seemed to have no input into the national show originating out of Washington, D.C.

But Susan, Tony and I were trying every possible alternative and out of one of these came my contact to "Nightline." Tony had called Amy Young-Anawaty, an attorney in Washington who ran a human rights activist public interest law firm. Amy mentioned to Tony that a good friend of hers was a producer of "Nightline," and that she would tell her friend about my situation in Chicago. That was Friday, and the program was scheduled for Tuesday night. On Tuesday afternoon word came in that they wanted me on the show. There was not enough time, nor was it practicable, for me to fly to Washington. So I went to the ABC studio in Chicago, and my appearance on "Nightline" was "live" in the sense that I was one of the monitors Ted Koppel looked at. At the time we thought it was a good idea for me to get on as many news programs as possible, but we had no conception of the clout that the "Nightline" show had.

Prior to the show Tony and I discussed strategy. It seemed to us that by criticizing the State Department for its lack of support we might be able to prod the United States government into taking some action on our behalf. But this criticism would have to be done tactfully. Tony asked me to go over again all my conversations with representatives of the State Department, to recount what steps, if any, they said they intended to take. I told him that the Soviet Desk had only tried to convince me to persuade Andrei to go off the hunger strike, and that the Office of Human Rights had not even returned my phone calls.

"That's it!" Tony said. "Simply say *that* if the opportunity arises— that the Office of Human Rights has not returned your phone calls."

"Aren't we going to have more problems if we criticize the U.S. government?" I asked.

"Lois, Andrei's life is in danger. You have to try everything, and so far you have gotten very little out of being kind to the State Department. If sugar doesn't work, try vinegar."

"How can I fit it into the broadcast?"

"I'm not worried. You're a creative person—you'll work it in."

I first became acquainted with the other United States spouses of the Moscow hunger strikers in the few minutes before the show was to begin, via the electronic equipment that hooked up the ABC studios in Chicago with those in Washington. Elena Balovlenkov, a nurse living in Baltimore, had met her husband Iurii over five years before in a Moscow cafe. Soviet foot-dragging stalled their wedding two years. After they were married and Elena returned to the United States she gave birth to a daughter that Iurii had never seen. She had spent a total of eight weeks with her husband.

Edward Lozansky, a physics professor living in Washington, D.C., was born in the Soviet Union. In 1976 his wife's father, a three-star Soviet general, forced Edward and Tatiana to divorce and then used his influence to get Ed an exit visa. His wife had been actively trying to leave Moscow since 1979. Ed had approached the Young Republicans in Washington to undertake his cause. They were now trying to gain further Washington support for the hunger strikers. So far they had not even been able to get a meeting at the State Department.

At the beginning of the "Nightline" program, as ABC reporter Anne Garrels introduced the story, the camera lingered on the view from Andrei's apartment. I recognized it instantly and started to cry involuntarily. The group had gathered in Andrei's room for the first press conference. In that very room where I had fallen in love with the man whose life story and character had been quietly embodied in the furnishings. The walls were now covered with placards about divided families. And here it all was on national television. It again struck me that my husband had thrown down the gauntlet to Soviet power. I felt that only I stood between my husband and that power. I pulled myself together.

The report from Moscow finished and then we spouses each spoke for a moment, introducing ourselves and our cases. Then a man from the State Department was introduced. The government spokesman had a lot of time on the "Nightline" program. He described how difficult these divided family cases were. He said that our cases demonstrated that we could never be too wary about the Russians. He said that we were dealing with a country militarily powerful and arrogant. They do not keep promises, and until they do we cannot begin to renegotiate new promises. It was obvious that he was referring to military promises—to arms limitation negotiations. The State Department was using our opportunity to appeal to public opinion and save our spouses to make the Reagan administration pitch about the need for the arms build-up!

I had a sense then of the insanity of the world. Here was the Soviet Union, a superpower, arbitrarily denying my husband his right to live where he wanted to live. And here was another superpower, the United

States, using that fact to convince the public to support an escalation of the arms race.

After the advertising break, Ted Koppel addressed me and said that he had been watching my reaction on the monitor. He said that by my expression he sensed that I disbelieved the government spokesman when he said that the government was doing everything it could to reunite divided families. Then my face came on the screen, and I had a chance to deliver my simple one-liner that came over loud and clear. I said, "Maybe the government is interested in us, but the Office of Human Rights in the State Department won't even return my phone calls."

Ted Koppel turned to the government spokesman and confronted him with what I had just said. The spokesman sputtered a bit and said, "Well, I think that is inexcusable. I always return *my* phone calls."

I did not know what to think of the "Nightline" show when it was over. I felt that we had been used. A simple human rights issue was turned into propaganda against arms negotiations. And yet I had managed to get in that sentence about the State Department not returning my phone calls. Tony, who was with me and my mother at the ABC studios, said that my remark had broken open the program. It was like driving a truck through a theatrical play. It was unanticipated and effective.

Promptly at 7:00 the next morning my phone rang. It was the Office of Human Rights in the State Department, returning my phone calls. It seemed like quite a few people watched "Nightline." The man on the other end of the phone line did not say anything about not having called earlier nor about last night's broadcast. In fact he had nothing substantive to say at all.

Later in the day the Young Republicans called me. Kathy Royce, the young woman who had been working on behalf of Ed and now on behalf of all the spouses, spoke very excitedly into the phone:

"You've got to come to Washington. We've clinched it. We've got an appointment at the State Department and even the White House looks interested."

She and I made all the arrangements and spoke a bit about strategy. Then I asked, why the turn around? After all, the Young Republicans had been trying to get a State Department meeting on this issue for a long time.

"They were embarrassed by your comment on 'Nightline' about not returning your phone calls," she answered.

I had a meeting with Tony in his office the afternoon following the "Nightline" show. Tony had a colleague of his with him in the office when I arrived, whom he introduced as Professor Steven Lubet. I blurted out Kathy's message—that we would have a meeting at the State Department and maybe at the White House.

"That's terrific, Lois," Tony said. "The meetings may be very useful. How are you feeling? Do you have enough strength to go to Washington?"

"I'm feeling okay. A bit weak. Dr. Berger said I could go but only if my mother went along to watch over me. And she's already arranged to take time off from work."

"Steve," Tony said turning to his colleague, "do you think that we can broach the subject to Lois that we have been talking about?"

"I think we can make a substantial jurisdictional argument," Steve replied.

"What are you talking about?" I interrupted.

"Lois," Tony answered, "Steve and I have been talking about an idea that I had when I couldn't go to sleep last night. It's just an idea, and it's totally up to you whether you want to take any action."

"What action? What *are* you talking about?"

"We think," Tony said measuredly, "that we can work up a jurisdictional argument that would give a federal court in Chicago the power to entertain a legal action by you against the Union of Soviet Socialist Republics for damages. Your damage claim would be the pain and suffering, and loss of consortium, that you have experienced as a result of their violation of their international obligations to let Andrei leave the country."

I was stunned. It slowly sank in. "You mean," I said, "that *I can sue the Soviet Union?*"

"Yes."

"My God! Has it ever been done before?"

"Not in a human rights case."

"What kind of case?"

"A couple of commercial cases," Tony said.

"Did they work?"

"No."

Steve interjected: "But there *was* jurisdiction. What's the chance of claiming that Lois's case is commercial?"

"Slim," Tony said.

"Wait a minute," I said, "let's get this straight. You think that I should sue the Soviet Union?" I paused and added, "For what?"

"For your suffering. And your lack of marital consortium."

"For how much?"

"Let's say fifty million dollars."

"Well, that will be flattering to Andrei. . . . I can't believe this. You say no one has done it before."

"So, there is always a first time."

I admit I was very intrigued. "How can it be done?"

"Steve and I both feel that we can state a legitimate claim to federal court jurisdiction in this case, and certainly that you have suffered as a result of the Soviet refusal to let Andrei out. We also can show that the Soviet Union has violated numerous international commitments in refusing an exit visa for Andrei."

"Might this lawsuit get the Soviets so mad that they will do something terrible to Andrei?"

Tony replied slowly and carefully. "Lois, I am not advising you to sue the Soviet Union, nor am I advising you not to sue them. I just don't know what the repercussions might be. And as a matter of professional ethics, I don't want to be in a position to suggest that you sue anyone."

"Tony, I'm asking you not as a lawyer, but as a friend." I sincerely felt that this man had become my friend, a dear friend in the course of this last week. "What will this lawsuit do for Andrei? Might they get mad and arrest him or put him in a hospital?"

"They can do anything," Tony said. "They can do anything without the lawsuit. No one can predict what any defendant might do once you sue him."

"I guess I haven't made myself clear," I said. "What I want to know is what will probably happen."

"The probabilities, as I see them—and your guess is as good as mine—no, I take that back, your guess is better than mine—is that such a lawsuit will have the same effect as all the publicity you are getting. Namely, it will help to ensure Andrei's safety. I can't imagine that the

Soviets would do anything nasty to Andrei if you sued them, because hardly anything would be so stupid in terms of world opinion. But just because I can't imagine it, doesn't mean that they might not do it."

I liked the idea of the lawsuit very much. I wanted to go ahead but I knew that such a legal action would be very expensive and I had no idea how I could pay for it. Working as a waitress the past year I had managed to save up several thousand dollars that I had intended to use when Andrei finally came to the United States. As it was, a great deal of that money was being spent on the phone calls and airplane flights connected with the hunger strike. I told Tony that I could not pay him much now and that I doubted if my future prospects looked that bright.

Tony told me not to worry, that he would not charge me anything for his time. Steve added that, while his own time was committed to some other cases, he could help a little on this one and certainly he would not charge me anything.

"OK. Let's do it. Let's sue the bastards!"

"You should talk this over with Susan first," Tony said.

"I will," I replied, "But in the meantime you'd better hit those books and start doing the research or whatever you do to file the lawsuit."

And Tony put aside all his other commitments to work on my lawsuit. Steve Lubet helped. Susan helped. Her law firm, Coeffield, Ungaretti, Harris and Slavin, volunteered the use of their copier, docket clerks, and so on. And my Russian friends helped translate the motions into Russian so that we could serve them on the Soviet Embassy.

The basis of the lawsuit turned out to be deceptively simple. Tony carefully omitted from the lawsuit any claim that the Soviets had done anything wrong to Andrei, or hurt Andrei in any way, by denying him an exit visa. He explained to me that any such claim would be thrown out by an American court on the ground that it was a complaint against a foreign government for an act of that government against its own citizen in its own territory. No American court would countenance such a lawsuit, any more than it could countenance a suit by the Soviets against the United States in a Soviet court for a wrongful denial of someone's Social Security benefits. Therefore, to make the case appro-priate to an American court, Tony said that I would have to be the sole plaintiff, and that the harm committed was totally against me. The

Soviet government had harmed me by depriving me of my spouse. The deprivation was wrongful, because prior to our marriage the Soviet Union had signed various treaties that guaranteed to their citizens the right to leave the Soviet Union. Since I was an American residing in Chicago, a local court would have jurisdiction in my case.

However, a government may claim "sovereign immunity" from suit. The point that Steve and Tony had been discussing before I arrived at the office was that the Foreign Sovereign Immunities Act of 1976, in which the United States had liberalized the rules regarding suits against governments, seemed to fit the circumstances of my case. Naturally, the fine points would have to be argued in court. But the point was that there was a sound initial basis for asserting jurisdiction.

Two interesting and significant changes were made in the lawsuit during the day and a half that it took Tony, Steve and Susan to draw up the papers and file them in court. The first was a result of Tony's checking with various friends and colleagues about legal strategy. One of his discussions was with his friend Luis Kutner, a prominent "elder statesman" of human rights in Chicago. Kutner suggested dragging the United States into the lawsuit. Either sue the United States as well as the USSR, Kutner advised, or bring it in as co-plaintiff.

Tony immediately liked the idea. He had been incensed anyway at what he considered the cavalier treatment by the State Department of my case. He felt that they should be called upon in court to explain what, if anything, they had done for me. But it was even better to bring the United States in as co-plaintiff. There were procedures under the applicable federal rules for bringing into a lawsuit "necessary co-plaintiffs," that is, persons who belonged in the lawsuit on the plaintiff's side. The United States belonged on my side because of their international legal obligation to protect their citizens in their dealings with foreign governments.

The second and most important innovation in the case came from Susan. She suggested that, in addition to the lawsuit for fifty million dollars in damages, we might ask the court to issue an injunction against the Soviet Union that would seek to bar all Soviet transactions in wheat and in gold on the Chicago Board of Trade unless and until Andrei was allowed to leave the Soviet Union. We liked this idea as well. No one could possibly know what a federal district court judge in Chicago might do. If there was any chance that he might grant the injunction, then the Soviet Union would be in a major commercial bind. They might not want to risk even a slight chance of such a fiasco just for the sake of keeping Andrei in the Soviet Union.

We held a press conference when the lawsuit was filed. Dr. Berger kindly appeared and recounted the results of his examination of me earlier that morning. He had checked my blood pressure while seated and while standing. Seated, my blood pressure was very low. When I stood up it plunged dramatically; the doctor remarked that he could not find any pressure at all. At the news conference he reported that my weight had dropped from 110 to 98 pounds, and a reporter wrote in the afternoon edition that I looked "pale and wan."

The lawsuit got extensive coverage in the Chicago papers. It went out over the Associated Press wires and on national radio. I now had to rest up for the trip to Washington which would take my last strength. There I would meet in person with Elena and Ed, the other spouses. We spoke on the phone that weekend. They called after hearing of the lawsuit. We were all optimistic about the meeting at the State Department.

My mother and I arrived in Washington on Monday afternoon. I had set up meetings with my Congressional representatives, or their aides, before leaving Chicago. Congressman Sidney Yates met with my mother and me for a moment in between committee meetings. He had already introduced a resolution on behalf of Andrei and me into the Congressional Record and I thanked him.

Next my mother and I met with Senator Charles Percy's aide, Diana Smith. She was very professional and reserved in manner. The week before, she had repeated to me the State Department's stance in opposition to hunger strikes, the need to act quietly, and the fact that there had been nothing in my husband's biography to anger the Soviets, at least not until the hunger strike. Now she attentively listened as I explained the lawsuit and our desire for United States cooperation. She asked what the Senator might do. I requested a Senate resolution on behalf of the binational spouses to demonstrate the backing of Congress to the Soviets and to the State Department. I asked for a phone call to get us into the White House. She promised nothing and said she would look into it.

Our next stop was on a street corner in the business section of Washington, D.C. The Soviet Embassy was located two blocks away. Washington D.C. law prohibits protests with placards close to a foreign embassy. The Young Republicans had rounded up about thirty people. They marched about in a circle carrying placards that denounced the lack of human rights in the USSR. I managed to march around the circle a few times before I had to sit down and rest. A lawn chair appeared from somewhere and I sat in the middle of the circle. My mother took up my placard and continued to walk about in my stead. She also was exerting herself, her health impaired by recent serious illness. When the camera crews came by they asked that I take up the placard and march once more so that they would have some "dramatic" shots.

The protest march left me feeling drained and a bit sad. The people of Washington walked by on their way home from work, barely curious. "Oh no, not another demonstration, what's this one for?" was the reaction, while my mother and I, exhausted from the travel and strain, my joints starting to ache again, carried placards chanting, "Unite Divided Families," "Free Iurii Balovlenkov," "Free Andrei Frolov," and so on.

We spouses then put down our placards and walked over to the Soviet Embassy. The photographers wanted a picture of us in front of the official Soviet mission to the United States. It is a stately Georgian mansion surrounded by a railing and shrubbery, in no way distinguishable from the others on the street. There were no guards, no guard boxes, no plainclothes officers of the United States government whose purpose was to prevent the local populace from entering, as there are Soviet guards for that purpose stationed all about the U.S. Embassy in Moscow. We stood there awhile, pictures were taken. The next day the State Department told us that the Soviet Embassy had filed an official protest against this raucous demonstration on their threshold.

After the protest march the spouses met to prepare for the next day's meeting at the State Department. We had just received word from Renate Kiblitsky, the German wife of Iosif Kiblitsky, that German Foreign Minister Hans Genscher had made a personal appeal to the Soviet Minister of Foreign Affairs Andrei Gromyko. This news buoyed us. It was such intervention by the French Government that earlier had led to the release of Ina Lavrova, who went on a hunger strike in February so as to be with her French husband. We thought we might expect something similar from our own government. We thought that for that reason we had been invited to Washington. We thought that was the point of the State Department meeting.

We spouses prepared a list of suggestions on how the State Department might help our wives and husbands gain release. I was chosen to present our ideas at the meeting the next day.

We met in the morning in the lobby of the State Department. The lobby was grand and bustling, conveying a sense of important activity. Our group was disappointed that the protest march had received so little coverage. Still, someone on the White House staff had told the Young Republicans that the Vice President wanted to meet us. It seemed that calls from Senator Robert Dole's and Senator Percy's offices had done the trick. I mentally thanked the efficient aide of Percy. I was not surprised to find out several days later that Senator Percy had entered a Senate resolution on behalf of Andrei and myself. The Vice President would meet us later in the day.

Our morning meeting was with the Assistant Secretary of State for Human Rights, Elliott Abrams. His was a high post. At the time, Alexander Haig was his immediate boss. We were led into a small conference room. Elena, Ed, myself, Kathy from the Young Republicans, and a young State Department official, the man who had called me at 7:00 A.M., sat at the table, leaving a place at the head for the Assistant Secretary of State. Off to the side were my mother, a woman from the Helsinki Commission (a Congressional watchdog group that monitors the Helsinki Accords), and an older man, a "lifer," a professional State Department official.

The Assistant Secretary of State entered the room. He was in his late 30's, tall, lean, well-groomed, well-dressed and twenty minutes late. He spoke:

"Good morning. I'm sorry you had to come to Washington under such tragic circumstances. Your spouses have chosen a dangerous course. We at the State Department do not condone hunger strikes. Your spouses have challenged the Soviet state. If the Soviets were to release them it would be seen as backing down, therefore, most likely they will not release your spouses. Andrei Sakharov's case was different because protest and public pressure had reached such a high level. Your spouses should go off the strike and wait for the next legal opportunity to seek an exit visa, hoping that the Soviets will forgive their precipitous behavior."

I didn't understand. We had all heard this reasoning before in separate phone conversations. It never made sense to me. If the Soviet Union was concerned about not looking weak, then refusing to let five people go to their husbands and wives in the West would simply point up this weakness, that a superpower should fear five such people. It seemed to me that such reasoning was the tack that the State Department should have taken.

Even if Abrams's advice would have been reasonable at the beginning of the strike, now in the third week of a total fast it seemed anachronistic. Our spouses were not about to come off the strike and now we had come to Washington seeking that same protest and public pressure that had made the Sakharov hunger strike a success.

Abrams was in fact criticizing our spouses for being intemperate. He had not a word of censure for the Soviets for placing them in such a desperate position. Perhaps he simply felt that he had to raise all the problems before starting the real discussion. We politely responded that we understood this line of thought but now that our spouses were past the point of no return, let us see what we could do to help them. It was my job to present our ideas.

"We would like to have medical information on our spouses," I began. "Senator Paul McCloskey of Maryland has wired the U.S. Embassy in Moscow asking them to inform us of the medical condition and of Soviet harassment of our spouses every forty-eight hours. We can't get through to our spouses as their phones have been closed off to our calls. We are very worried."

"I'm sorry, but that will not be possible," Mr. Abrams quickly responded. "The U.S. Embassy doctor is not licensed to practice medicine in the USSR."

"We simply want him to check their medical condition, not administer aid. The French Embassy sent over their doctor to do a check up. Surely the same laws exist for the U.S. Embassy that exist for the French," I asserted.

"I'm sorry, but we cannot send over the United States doctor."

We moved on to the issue of formal protest. Kathy reported to Mr. Abrams that Foreign Minister Genscher had made a protest to Andrei Gromyko and that the European Parliament was taking up the case on behalf of the European spouses. Ideally we would like to see a similar American protest, Secretary of State Haig to Gromyko.

Mr. Abrams shifted in his chair. He did not respond directly and simply asked, "What else?"

"It would be best to work in conjunction with the French and German governments," I said, "especially since they have already begun to protest. That would depoliticize the conflict; it would not become a U.S.–USSR confrontation but would focus on the issue of divided families."

I was getting excited—it seemed he was listening. Ed was also encouraged and began to present his idea to Mr. Abrams:

"Since the Soviets are violating the Helsinki Accords we ought to send cables to the thirty-four governments that have signed the accords asking them to register their protest to the Soviet government concerning the illegal detention of our spouses."

"I'm sorry, but we can't do that," Abrams broke in. "No one would agree to protest."

"How do you know that?" I asked.

"Well, it's not the sort of thing that the Helsinki signatories involve themselves in."

"Why not? This is a violation of both the letter and the spirit of the Accords."

"Yes, but chances are that only a few of the governments would respond and we don't want to make a request if the majority won't respond," he explained. "Most likely the French and the German governments won't cooperate with us. So, that idea is scrapped."

I did not understand. He did not know what the reactions of the other governments might be. He just made assumptions and used them as an excuse for our own government to do nothing. The prompt protest of Genscher belied his assumptions. And the Helsinki Accords. What were the Helsinki Accords for if not to protest the violation of human rights? And the question was not simply one of internal violations; the Soviets were also violating our human rights and we were citizens of three major Western powers.

I blurted these thoughts out to Mr. Abrams. He sat up and repeated the State Department's general stance on hunger strikes. Here Ed and Kathy and I had been gushing on about formal protests and he was not even prepared to listen. "The State Department was opposed to hunger strikes and our spouses should go off."

"We heard this advice repeatedly several weeks ago," I interrupted. At that time I begged my husband to reconsider. He didn't. And now that time has passed. You are a diplomat. You are supposed to flow with the tide of events, read the situation and adapt to it. Our spouses are on the hunger strike to the end, as am I. What are you going to do to support us now?"

Mr. Abrams was taken aback by my outburst. He felt I was presumptuous. "We have not yet decided what measures should be taken."

"When will you decide? The Department has had time to consider. We are in the third week of a total fast. Time is of the essence here."

"We are not sure what steps should be taken, if any. Perhaps the best policy is not to do anything, not to protest and risk angering the Soviets further."

"What is the alternative? To sit quietly by as we die publicly?" I had to say it. I had to remind this official of the gravity of our situation and the intensity of our conviction. I was bewildered by his stony attitude. The State Department was always ranting about the general lack of human rights in the Soviet Union. Here was a case involving several of their own citizens, and the Assistant Secretary of State for Human Rights, the division of the State Department in charge of such concerns, did not want to support us because he was worried about angering the Soviets.

At this point my mother broke in, as mothers are apt to do.

"Excuse me, perhaps I shouldn't interrupt but I feel I must," she stammered. I knew her and I knew it was for effect. Having secured his attention she continued. "Mr. Abrams, sir," she now spoke clearly, staring directly at him. "Can you honestly say that you have done all that you personally could do to help these unfortunate people?"

It was a mother's question. She simply cut through all the formal bullshit and admonished him for his poor sense of morality.

It did the trick. His adam's apple bobbled. He did not answer her.

"Look," he said, "I had this meeting with you to find out more about your cases."

"Fine," I broke in. "Do you have any questions for us?"

"Well, no," he uttered. The farce was drawing to an end. "We will get in touch with you in twenty-four hours to tell you what, if anything, we will do. I know the press is waiting for you downstairs. It would be best if you held off commenting until we got back to you."

He got up and left the room. We filed out. In the hall Elena, Ed, Kathy, my mother and I commiserated with one another. The young staffer again requested that we withhold our comments in dealing with the press. Then the older man came up to me.

"Congratulations," he said.

"For what?!" I answered. "That meeting was a fiasco. You won't do anything for us. What is there to congratulate me for?"

"For being a good wife."

We went downstairs. Honoring Mr. Abrams's request we did not comment about the content of the meeting. After finishing with us the journalists interviewed Mr. Abrams. We found out later via television that he was not at all as judicious as he admonished us to be. The group headed over to the Senate Office Building and there we deposited ourselves in a small room in Senator Dole's office to await the phone call from the White House. Kathy's mother had worked for Senator Dole for many years. While everyone waited I met with an aide of Illinois Senator Alan Dixon. He was polite but as a new senator there was little that Senator Dixon could do except continue to write letters to Ambassador Dobrynin.

I returned to Senator Dole's office. Still no call. The Senator came in, introduced himself and offered his moral support. I was tired. My joints began to ache in a way that felt different from the usual morning pains. I lay down on the floor and instantly fell asleep. When I awoke about a half hour later my mother told me that we would not be going to the White House to talk with the Vice President. The State Department had still not called and given their approval for such a meeting.

Ed, Elena and I were angered by this latest delay. In order to calm us an official at the National Security Council, Paula Dobriansky, in charge of Eastern European affairs, agreed to meet with us. Elena recounted to her our experiences at the State Department and the overall minimal amount of support that our cases had received over the years. Ms. Dobriansky was disturbed that so little had been done, especially when she heard that there were no more that twenty cases of husbands and wives that were forced to live apart. We felt that her concern was in part evoked by a political rivalry between the State Department and the National Security Council. Nevertheless, she said that she would look into it and try to convince the Vice President to get involved.

My mother tried to cheer me up on the flight back to Chicago that night, but what was there to say? She had followed me about for two days, trying to keep me calm and see that I rested. She would not let me carry a thing and I had so many papers with me, copies of the lawsuit that I passed out to various Washington officials. She was not in the best health herself to be carrying files about, but she was dedicated to me and to my cause. She understood why I felt I had to put myself on the line and she never tried to dissuade me.

My mother is a light sleeper and on Saturday nights when I called Andrei she would often awake as I dialed and redialed, and spoke to one operator after another. After I spoke to Andrei she would wait for a few minutes and then get out of bed and sit down beside me. She would ask how he was, what he had done this past week, how his health was. She spoke about him as if she knew him, as if he were her son-in-law away on a business trip. But she did not know him, had never met him, and because of the language barrier could not speak with him or read his letters. She accepted it all in stride and did not lose faith.

That flight home her faith was beginning to crack. She had put even more hope in the State Department meeting than I had. On the flight to Washington she was excited and said that we had clinched it—we had been invited to Washington because the government now intended to do something to help Andrei. Flying back to Chicago she was bitter. She had realized that we could not depend on the government to do a thing. She tried to conceal her disillusionment. She said all the standard things about everything looking the darkest before the dawn, but I knew that my mother, who was always an optimistic person even in the midst of her own illness, was now in the throes of black pessimism.

We arrived home late. My father met us and excitedly asked about what had happened in D.C. He also had expected too much. We managed to tell him briefly about the events of the last two days before the "Nightline" program began its broadcast. The show began with shots of the Falklands War and then a shot of me, sitting on the curb outside of the State Department, my head between my hands, completely broken and exhausted.

Mr. Abrams came on next. Asked to comment on our case he said:

"The actions of the hunger strikers are counterproductive. By making a direct challenge to the Soviets these people have made their own situation worse. There is not much reason for optimism."

That was it.

To say this to a small group of people in a conference room in the State Department is one thing, but to say it on national television, which the Soviets were undoubtedly watching, is quite another. Now the Soviets would truly feel as if they would be backing down to a direct challenge if they released our spouses. The Assistant Secretary of State had presented it this way to the American public. He had complicated our situation immeasurably and further endangered our spouses. He was doing the Soviets' work for them, providing them with a public rationale for not releasing my husband. Mr. Abrams, the Assistant Secretary of State for Human Rights and Humanitarian Affairs, said nothing about human rights.

My heart and my head pounded all night. As soon as the working day began in Washington I made my phone calls: Percy's office, the National Security Council, Young Republicans, and the office of the Assistant Secretary of State for Human Rights. I wanted to speak directly to Elliott Abrams but my calls were not put through, nor did he phone back. I spoke to Mr. George Lister, the older man who had sat in on the meeting and said those kind words to me. He was shocked when I told him what Mr. Abrams had said on national television.

"Why did Abrams say that?" I asked "Why is it the State Department's policy to make getting my husband out of the Soviet Union as difficult as possible?"

He regained his official tone and said that he would find out what had happened. I went to Dr. Berger's for an examination. As usual, he asked me to tell him everything that had happened in Washington. My words came out in a jumble; my head was in a fog and I had trouble catching my breath. The strain of the last two days had worn heavily on me. Dr. Berger said that the new aches in the joints of my arms and legs were signs that my body protein was starting to break down. He said that I had to rest and that I had to gain control over my emotions—they were doing me in.

I then went to Tony's office. While appalled by what Abrams had said on "Nightline," he was not surprised.

"You're accomplishing more in Chicago than anyone could accomplish in Washington. They just use you over there. Here you've got the press and TV on your side all the way. When I was litigating the Vietnam cases I spent some time in Washington with Senators and Congressmen and their aides. I had one single impression when I left Washington: that a whole lot of people there are thoroughgoing hypocrites."

"But will they notice what I do if I confine myself to Chicago?"

"Why shouldn't they? This is a very important state in any national election. If you get grass roots support here, they will have to notice you in Washington."

We continued along that line and I was encouraged. Toward the end of the day I received word that the Vice President wanted to see the binational spouses. I called Tony, who surprised me by saying that he was opposed to my going.

"You're weak and you could have a physical setback. You're on a hunger strike and yet you want to run a marathon. Do you really need to see Bush? By going there you will be doing more for him than he will do for you."

"But, Tony," I argued, "it doesn't do me any good to sit around here. Besides, seeing Bush will escalate the story. He's the Vice President! It may put pressure on him to do something. After the spouses meet with him, if he doesn't do something people will consider him to be powerless."

"The very definition of a vice president!"

The next call I received was from my self-appointed friend at the State Department, Mr. Lister. His tone was entirely different now from his astonishment that morning about what Mr. Abrams had said.

"The next few weeks will be painful and tragic at best, Lois. You must be careful not to let personal anger rub off on those not responsible. Don't ever forget that the Soviets are the enemy here. It is they who are committing the evil."

"Fine. Then why didn't Elliott Abrams say that last night? Instead, he explained why it was good tactics for the Soviets to continue the evil. Who's paying his salary?"

"Please, Lois, you've got to control your anger. The Vice President wants to see you. You ought to go."

"Why? It's just a publicity stunt for him. Does he have the power to override the State Department on my case?"

"No." Lister paused. "But go. You may be sorry later that you missed this opportunity.'

I made the travel arrangements for the next morning. Our appointment was for 11:00 A.M. Washington time. I had to catch the 7:00 A.M. flight out of Chicago. The day did not begin auspiciously.

Before leaving for the airport I tried to get in touch with Andrei. Unable to get through to his apartment I called Iurii's mother (Elena had given me the number). Iurii's mother answered the phone and said that Andrei was expected to stop by later in the day. She was very worried because she had not seen her son in two days, in fact, no one had.

A thunderstorm blew up on my way to the airport. I made it there on time only to find out that there would be no flights out to Washington until the weather cleared up. While waiting at the airport I again tried to call Andrei at Iurii's home. A man answered the phone whose voice I did not recognize. He brusquely said, "There's no one here," and hung up.

The electrical storm continued. The minutes ticked away. It became clear that I was not going to make the 11:00 appointment. I made several phone calls to Washington on the outside chance that the Vice President would reschedule our appointment. To my surprise, he postponed the meeting until the afternoon so that I could participate. I was relieved and flattered. Once I had decided to go back to Washington I threw myself into the prospect. Surely the Vice President could do something if he really wanted to, I kept reassuring myself.

When I got to Washington I again tried calling Moscow, but there was no answer. I called the *Chicago Tribune* correspondent in Moscow, and he said that no one had seen Andrei or Iurii for two days. Elena had also been trying to find Iurii but with no success. We sat in Young Republican headquarters, awaiting the meeting with Bush, but thinking of our husbands. Every ten minutes we called the number in Moscow. It was getting close to our appointment when Elena's call finally went through. Her mother-in-law answered the phone. She did not speak into the receiver but to people in her apartment:

"It's his wife, let him speak to her."

Iurii came to the phone. Breathlessly he said, "Elena, the police are here. The police are here."

The line went dead. We tried to call back, but the phone did not even ring.

Perhaps this was it. The Soviet authorities had finally tired of all the bad publicity our spouses had been attracting. They were rounding them up, accusing them of some crime—anti-Soviet activity, most likely.

Elena was close to hysterics. She called the State Department thinking that they might be able to do something. I myself was at the lowest point of depression. I offered to call my contacts in Moscow to find out more. I called a journalist and then someone on the Embassy staff. It appeared that no one knew where Iurii was, but Andrei had been into the Embassy that afternoon. He had been called into OVIR. There they told him that if he cared to complete a new application form his case would be immediately reviewed.

I felt as if I were on a rollercoaster. A sudden high. I was faint. It could be meaningless. It could be a trick.

I tried to suppress my confused emotions when we met with the Vice President. There was a gaggle of reporters who snapped photos and then left. The Vice President asked each spouse to tell his or her story, though it was obvious that he had been well briefed and already knew the details. It was encouraging. He listened attentively. After promising us his support, Mr. Bush left the room and a representative from the State Department that we had not met before made some promises. He said that a written protest would be made the next day to the Soviet Embassy, and a high-level oral protest would follow. After all the proper procedures had been taken the Vice President himself might get involved.

As things turned out, the written protest was not made the next day; it was made twelve days later. The oral protest was not made at a high level, but was made at the junior attaché level. At the time I was not so concerned with Vice Presidential promises—kept or broken. Andrei was filling out a new application. I jumped on the emotional rollercoaster, this time going up.

I tried to call Andrei's apartment as soon as we got back from the White House. I thought that maybe his phone had been cleared along with the new development with his application. Andrei picked up the receiver. His deep voice said, "Hello. . . ," and then that ghastly mechanical screech. The phone was cut off. I took the rollercoaster down. My husband was thousands of miles from me. I could not even speak to him. It seemed so ironic and yet appropriate that they had asked him to fill out a new application form, the first step in the maze of this incredibly arbitrary and hypocritical procedure. It was all hypocrisy, all these government procedures, there and here.

A F

Back in the beginning of the hunger strike Iosif Kiblitsky suggested that we five conduct a demonstration in which we would demand to exercise our right to leave the country to be with our families. The demonstration was to take place in front of the Ts. K. Building—The Central Committee of the Communist Party of the USSR.

In accordance with the law, which Kiblitsky knew well while the rest of us had only hazy notions, we wrote official notifications of our intentions to the Supreme Soviet of the USSR, to the Central Committee, to the KGB, to the Ministry of Internal Affairs and to the Moscow City Executive Committee. Lozanskaya typed out these notifications on my typewriter, on which I had formerly written my articles and essays. We listed my home as the return address and sent them off to all the designated agencies. The notification contained a list of our names and addresses. We informed them of the date and time of the proposed demonstration and the content of the placards that we intended to carry. The placards bore enlarged photographs of our wives and husbands and children. Balovlenkov, Kiblitsky, and Lozanskaya had children, and the demonstration was set to coincide with the official International Day of the Child.

The demonstration was announced for the first of June. Notification was sent two weeks prior, as required. According to the law, permission from the authorities was not needed. All that was needed was warning of our intentions, and we did not even need an answer to our notifications.

Such demonstrations in front of the Central Committee building or on Red Square, or, more accurately, attempts to carry out such demonstrations, can be counted on one's fingers. Kiblitsky cited a very large figure, several hundred, but he included all sorts of demonstrations by artists, demonstrations on side streets which were witnessed by only a few people, and single person demonstrations. He even counted those occasions when someone yelled something out the window in regard to their rights or unfurled a sign. Well known was the fate of one genuine political demonstration on Red Square in support of Czecho-slovakia during its occupation by Soviet troops. The demonstration consisted of several people who held out on Red Square for several minutes. Plainclothes officers of the KGB, carrying briefcases stuffed with rocks and representing the "wrath of the people," beat them off the Square.

However, there were cases where people secured exit from the country through demonstrations. I had heard of demonstrations by ethnic Germans who were then allowed to leave for West Germany. These demonstrations, like ours, were made up of several people, but they took place not in the center of town and not in front of central governmental institutions. By Soviet understanding, to announce our intention to demonstrate in front of the Central Committee building constituted extreme insolence. We ourselves had little hope of being able to carry out our plans but we were sure that the attempt would be noted by foreign journalists. And this proposed attempt, as it turned out, worried the authorities most of all.

A week before the proposed demonstration, during the third week of the hunger strike, signs of the authorities' concern over our actions sprang up. Until then they had not patently reacted to our hunger strike. Balovlenkov was taken out of his home late at night by the police and delivered to his neighborhood division of the KGB. He was read a paper with accusations of anti-government activities and with the warning that if he did not stop his actions then the charge would be turned over to the prosecutor. Such cases call for a closed trial with a pre-arranged verdict. Witness a whole series of closed trials against dissidents in the last few years. Kiblitsky was warned by them in a slightly different manner. He was summoned to the OVIR of the Moscow region. Since he had no legal address in Moscow and lived in Podolsk, a nearby town, he was under the jurisdiction of the Moscow regional office. There, KGB workers verbally accused him of acts of provocation. Tatiana Lozans-kaya received a summons to the police in regards to a violation of the passport regime: she was still harboring the Lithuanian woman in her apartment. And I also received a summons to come to the Moscow City OVIR "for a conversation with the governing body," as it was written on the postcard I received summoning me.

Balovlenkov said that under no circumstances should I show up for this conversation. He said that the KGB waited for me there. I agreed with him that most likely it was the KGB and not OVIR that summoned me, but where the functions of one of these organizations ended and the functions of the other began no one knew. In our case it was all the same, even if the summons had come from the Government itself. But it would be illogical on my part not to show up at OVIR. After all, I, like the rest, was seeking permission from OVIR to leave the country. Balov-lenkov got upset and out of agitation did not let anyone else say any-thing. He tried to convince me that if I went to OVIR on this pretext I was making things worse for myself; I was demonstrating the weakness of my position. I, in turn, advised him not to respond to police sum-mons, to refuse to go to the police unless officially ordered, as I had done. Even so, I was not at all certain of what I should do.

Before the hour of the appointment assigned to me on the summons I was busy with an affair in connection with our hunger strike. I arrived at OVIR forty-five minutes late. I was feeling very weak. It had become too difficult for me to travel on Moscow public transportation, known for its overcrowding. I took a taxi to OVIR. It was difficult for me simply to walk an extra hundred steps. We were all in the same condition.

Appearing at OVIR in response to a summons one must hand over the OVIR postcard to a policeman at the entrance and wait until called. My postcard listed the room where they received everyone who had handed in an application with a request. I was not surprised when the policeman, after stopping in at this room, quickly returned to me and said that I was wanted in a different room altogether.

In this other room an OVIR bureaucrat in the uniform of a police major sat at an empty desk. OVIR workers wear police uniforms since OVIR, like the police, is under the Ministry of Internal Affairs. At a chair set against the wall sat another man with an unassuming though pleas-ant appearance, his hair just beginning to gray. Such people of indeterminate age and appearance, whose occupations are difficult to determine, are often called "young man", but this "young man" probably knew how to wield a weapon and was fluent in the methods of struggle without weapons.

I did not even manage to say "how do you do" when the "young man", paying no attention to the police major, took it upon himself to scold me for coming late. I did not start to argue with him. I simply remarked that I was busy with personal affairs. He did not like my answer. With an irritated expression on his face he got down to business.

"Who are you, respected citizen, to threaten the government?"

"Of what do these threats consist?" I asked.

"You are writing appeals to the government, collective petitions."

"Yes, I wrote them. Really, are appeals to the government already considered threats? Then I also wrote to the Supreme Soviet—do you represent the Supreme Soviet here?"

"I represent the Committee on State Security (KGB), while Major Semenov here," he carelessly nodded his head towards the major, "represents the Ministry of Internal Affairs." His own name he did not give.

"Good. Copies were sent to your organizations. But are acts that are in accordance with the basic law of the state, in accordance with the constitution, truly threats to the Government?"

"In the Constitution it is written that a citizen of the USSR must not bring damage to the state."

"You are talking about general notions, while I am speaking of concrete articles of law, in accordance with which we intend to conduct our demonstration."

We squabbled for about fifteen minutes more about how to interpret the Constitution. From all that he said I understood that he could not counter my references to the law with anything concrete, only with broad demagogic discourses.

"You interpret the constitution too freely," I told him. "You obviously are not familiar with it."

Upon my last words Major Semenov became so disturbed that he shifted positions in his chair repeatedly, failing to find a comfortable posture. For him, this "young man" was the highest law in the land, the highest power and justice. Throughout our conversation he did not utter a word.

"You should make your applications to OVIR and not to the Government."

"I handed in applications to OVIR, twice."

"You can hand one in again."

"I know. I can apply to OVIR my whole life until the day of my death and for the next hundred years after that!"

"You are bitter."

"You're right. You can't play with people's fates the way you do."

"You can fill out a new application."

"And how long will it take for this application to be considered?"

"I can't say—perhaps a week."

Usually such applications to OVIR are examined for two months or more.

"Fine. I'll fill out a new application today."

It occurred to me that with the promise to examine a new application they wanted to hold me back from participating in the demonstration. The answer to the new application would be the usual refusal, and they would take their time considering the application before refusing it. I left the office saying that my participation in the demonstration was my inalienable constitutional right. I emphasized that I did not trust them.

A week later I was called to the telephone and a familiar voice said that this was the same man with whom I had conversed several days ago at OVIR. Again he failed to name himself. He asked why I had not come to OVIR to find out the official response to my application. I answered that OVIR never acted that quickly. He then said that my request had been decided affirmatively; I was permitted to leave for the United States. I myself could come and make certain of it. I told him that I would come in the next day.

While I spoke on the phone, one of the correspondents, Balovlenkov and both Tatianas were in my room. The women immediately congratulated and kissed me. But I was suspicious; I thought that this was a KGB maneuver. Balovlenkov supported my suspicions but Azure called me a pessimist.

Satisfaction and joy I nevertheless experienced. Who knew what would happen next, but it appeared that the authorities had made a concession. The fear of being deceived was, however, quite strong. It was decided that I would continue to fast until I had something concrete in hand.

The first of June, the International Day of the Child, was the day for our demonstration in front of the Central Committee building. Upon leaving my apartment for the demonstration I was met on the stairs by two men who blocked my way. They told me that I was to stay at home. They were quite polite but one of them stood in my path very determin-edly. To argue with them about the legality of their actions was useless; they were only executing orders, and blocking my way did not require much effort. They could have lightly shoved me and I would have fallen. It was the twentieth day of my hunger strike. Just in case, I poked my nose into my back stairs. There were other people there. My escape hatch was known to them.

That day we were all under house arrest. The foreign correspon-dents went to the Central Committee building for nothing. But our adversaries were taking no chances. According to an Associated Press report that my wife later showed me, there were upwards of one hundred police and plainclothes officers milling about the site of the proposed demonstration.

With nowhere to go—guards at my door—I lay on the divan in my room. My chest was drawn, my shoulders bent. My voice had changed, often breaking in mid-sentence; I had difficulty breathing. Now and again my thoughts became confused.

Why was it necessary to do all this? Why was it necessary to risk my health? Why was it necessary to forfeit all that I had achieved in a life of fifty years? All because I—no longer a young man, of little value to the state, and without close relatives in the USSR—wanted to go to another country to be with my legal wife! It is absurd, fantastic, and probably unfathomable for the American reader. Why was the govern-ment's money, that is, the people's money, spent on KGB agents who earned their pay following me? There was not simply one man on the payroll: someone followed me, someone else read letters, someone else compiled all this information and made reports to a superior. Either I had lost all reason and no longer understood anything, or they had lost all human, common sense. More likely, they never had it to begin with.

For sixty-five years they have spiritually enslaved people in the name of some sort of "shining future" which had been devised at a drawing board. How did it happen that they were allowed to play games with the souls of hundreds of millions of people? Why have they not yet been bound in straightjackets?

Recollections sprang up in my exhausted brain. Now it appeared to me that my abilities and energies had been wasted on stupidities. As in a hall of curved mirrors, normal life became a misshapen distortion. Now my entire being, all the cells of my body were concentrated on one point: this last mass of energy that had not yet been spent, in anticipation of what seemed to me to be the last effort of will, the last absurdity which would crown my life.

I recalled my mother. She feared everything, especially the police. She could not dismiss her childhood memories when the Cheka, the KGB in the first years of Soviet power, made their arrests. Her father, Sergei Ivanovich Shcherbatov, was a relatively rich man. They lived in Nizhnii Novgorod, now Gorky. When the revolution came my grandfather moved his family to Moscow where they were less well-known. My grandfather on my father's side, Peter Ivanovich Frolov, lived in Tver, now Kalinin. He worked as an accountant at the Morozov factory. It belonged to Savve Morozov who was famous because of his support of the revolution. My grandmother on my father's side was Alexandra Adrianovna Belsky before she married my grandfather. I don't know what kind of relationship she had to the famous aristocratic family Belsky. Under the Soviets many people hid their background and their names. They say that after the revolution people were often shot because they bore famous aristocratic names, even though these people might not have been aristocrats by blood. My father's older brother graduated from an officer's school before the revolution and fought in the First World War. Under the Soviets he hid his officer's rank and lived as a simple worker in a factory in Leningrad. At the time of the revolution my father was a student at the Imperial Technical Institute in Moscow, now the Bauman Institute. He graduated from the Institute under the Soviets and worked as an engineer in Moscow.

My father suffered for the straightforwardness of his character. He often said what he thought about the life that surrounded him, which always frightened my mother. He did not respect Soviet power. My mother was especially frightened that I might inherit this side of my father's character and that only failure awaited me in life.

My father worked in one organization and lived in Moscow at the same address almost his whole life. He designed electric power stations. As far as I remember he always held the position of group engineer, chief specialist, or chief engineer of a project. These are not the highest positions for an engineer in the Soviet Union. He had been awarded two honors: the Order of the Red Banners and the Order of Lenin, considered the two highest honors in the Soviet Union. They testify to the professional quality of my father's work, especially if one takes into account that he never was a member of the Communist Party.

My mother had no education besides the gymnasium, high school, that is. She painted a bit, semiprofessionally, and it enabled her to work in an architectural studio as something similar to a designer, by the American understanding. I had no brothers or sisters.

My parents possessed a minimum of creature comforts. They lived together in a single room in a communal apartment. Books, a small summer home and a motor bike were the sum total of their possessions. Towards the end of his life my father built the small summer house outside of town with his own hands. I helped. There he and my mother spent the summers cultivating fruit trees.

After my father's death my mother was left with five thousand rubles, and the summer home was sold for two thousand rubles. This money was all she had besides a small pension. She continued to live in that room in the communal apartment. I traveled about the Soviet Union, lived at various addresses, spent several months a year in Moscow, and after my mother's death I continued to live alone in our room.

During the war our family had been evacuated to the Ural Mountains where my father worked on the construction of an electric power station. The war years remain in my memory as hungry years.

The postwar years, my last years at high school and first years at the Institute, were years of hope for my generation. No one knew what kind of life the future would bring. Everyone thought seriously about their future professions. But disillusionment followed at our heels, destroying one hope after another. The strongest disappointments awaited those who devoted their lives to the humanities.

Since childhood I was drawn to literature but my father continually impressed upon me the need to be an engineer. He felt that people in the humanities were deprived of the possibility to act according to their own principles and convictions in their work. People in technical professions were in turn deprived of initiative but it was much easier for them to live, easier for them to preserve their convictions unscathed. In general, those in technical professions were more respected than representatives of the humanities who, in one way or another, were obliged to support the official morality and ideology in their work.

While studying in the engineering department of a technological institute I read a great deal of fiction. I probably spent more time on my personal reading than on my professional training as an engineer. I especially read Western authors. It was a natural interest; I loved literature. But also at work here was a spirit of contrariness. I had a natural thirst for that which was "not recommended."

I suppose this spirit was a result of my battles with my father. I agreed with my father's world view but not necessarily with his individual decisions. He wanted me to act according to his plan for my life. Out of this conflict, made more acute by the closeness of Soviet life, by the fact that I lived together with my parents, was born this spirit of contradiction. It first became evident when I insisted upon reading what I wanted to read while studying at the Institute.

In Stalin's era, Western authors were kept to a minimum in school programs. Stalin was battling with Western influences and the schools taught only Goethe's *Faust* and Schiller's *The Robbers*. Of course, each of us had books of the classic Western authors in our homes. Many of my schoolmates' homes had excellent libraries and there were enough Western books in public libraries, but the study of Western authors was not encouraged at school. At the Technological Institute I started to take out a large number of books by Western authors and the library staff took note of this habit. I received rebukes from them and was advised to read author-laureates of the Stalin Prize in Literature. I thanked them for their advice and continued to read Western authors. Every time I checked out the next book I saw a silent reproach in the eyes of the librarian; she sincerely considered my interests unpatriotic.

Those were the last years of Stalin's life, or, as they were later called, the epoch of Stalinist senility. In practically every student examination there was a special question dedicated to the inventiveness of Russian scientists. No matter what the science, a student had to be able to prove that Russian and Soviet scientists were the first to think of everything. The joke that went around Moscow was: "Russia—the birthplace of elephants." It testified to the fact that the Russian people had not lost its sense of humor and had managed to preserve the independence of its thinking. There was another joke on this theme. It claimed that X-rays were discovered not by Roentgen but by an illiterate Russian blacksmith living in the age of Peter the Great who came home late one night very drunk. Suspecting his wife of infidelity he told her that he knew what she was thinking and what she was doing—"that he saw right through her."

In those years I first became disillusioned with much of what I saw in Soviet life. I recall very well how in my student years the notices of Komsomol and Party meetings were posted in the halls. The last point to be discussed at this or that meeting was inevitably someone's personal affairs. On the minutes it was even printed: "The personal affair of so-and-so," with their full name listed. They would discuss, for instance, how someone cheated on his wife or drank too much or was not a good friend or parent. One time the subject of such a discussion was the personal life of the dean of our department. It turned out that the dean had lovers. The wife of the dean was an instructor at the institute who taught us higher math. The public examination of her husband's sexual life took place in her presence. Since she was a Party member she was obligated to be there. Also present were some of her students who were Party members and therefore also obligated to attend. She could not bear to sit through the entire meeting and left in tears.

One day rumors flew at the Institute about how one student in a class on Marxism-Leninism, obligatory for all departments, began to discuss his personal understanding of the theory. The teacher was a young woman who was distinguished by the narrowness and primitiveness of her opinions. As if in corroboration of her very narrow views she wore glasses with thick lenses. It seemed as if she were always looking in only one spot.

The teacher did not interrupt the student, who probably just could not bear her vapidness any longer. I also endured her with great pains. There were other teachers who at least contrived to show Marxism-Leninism in an interesting manner. This teacher nodded her head to his words, encouraging him to speak. When the student stopped she said, "Continue, continue. I'm listening carefully." I can picture the icy tone she used. Encouraged by her words the simple-hearted student (he was from the provinces) continued to speak. He spoke for almost the whole academic hour, practically forty-five minutes.

Those who were present at this class later told me that he had said nothing that contradicted Marxism-Leninism in principle—the most he did was try to step beyond the bounds of the textbook. Several days later he disappeared without a trace. The teachers recommended that we not take an interest in his fate. Some spoke with sorrow in their voices, others with severity. The open discussion of Marxism-Leninism was evidently a dangerous precedent in the eyes of the authorities.

We could only hope that the poor student was merely thrown out of the Institute and out of Moscow back to his permanent place of residence. But something worse might have happened to him. It depended on how he conducted himself at his interrogation. If he said something inappropriate he might have said goodbye to his freedom. Along with their freedom many lost their lives; not everyone could survive Stalin's camps.

Other rumors passed about another student in his final year who was to become an engineer. They said that he had been drinking in company he was unfamiliar with. He said something improper and disappeared. Three other students were accused of discussing political topics while getting drunk in their own room at the dormitory. What exactly they said was not mentioned at the meeting in which their personal conduct was discussed. They were simply accused of "being drunk and talking about politics."

Life in the Institute taught me to be very careful when I spoke. A thoughtless word could bring grave consequences.

I was studying at the Institute when Stalin died. I remember his burial in Moscow very well. An enormous crowd of people rushed into the center of the city where the body of the leader had been placed for general viewing. Because of this mourning many people say that the Russian is in principle a slave; that he revered his tyrant Stalin most of all. I must say in response that it is characteristic of people in general to revere their tyrants. It is enough to recall the recent history of the German people. These feelings of reverence have by-passed the American people because of the shortness of their history.

As far as the funeral of Stalin is concerned, I think people were attracted most of all by the extraordinary nature of the spectacle. Not all of us had managed to see Stalin alive. The prospect of seeing him dead was more than most could pass up.

A part of the population truly did get caught up in the mass hysterics which the government did its best to provoke, using every means of mass media. I remember very well how the most adroit of my contemporaries clambered on rooftops and described with great excitement the miracles they had seen those days. They saw sidewalks break up under the feet of the crowds, they saw street lights topple over from the pressure of the mass movement. It resembled a natural disaster. There were too many impressions, more than the psyche of the average man could bear.

Afterwards, while the burial of Stalin was still fresh in people's minds, Lavrenti Beria, the head of the MGB at the time, was overthrown (MGB was the current name for the State Security Department, now the KGB). Everywhere people started to talk openly about Stalin's crimes. Khrushchev's thaw had begun. Though not of long duration, it gave people of my generation much hope, hope that was to be unfulfilled.

I fervently took to my work as an engineer-mechanic, hoping to invent many new things and achieve success in life. At that time the backwardness of Soviet techniques and technology was subjected to open criticism. I went to work at the Moscow Carburetor Factory, a subsidiary of the Likhachev Automobile Factory. It was then the largest automobile factory in the USSR. Wishing to gain experience in all ranks of production, I began in the shop working with my hands as an equipment adjuster. Many of my suggestions were introduced into production and I was transferred with honors to the position of engineer-designer.

The director of the factory had played on the factory soccer team when he was younger. He was an extremely energetic and outstanding personality. Likhachev, the first director of the plant, and after whom it had been named, was a great fan of soccer, and the factory team was a professional soccer team in the full sense of the word. Likhachev promoted players into managerial positions, though not all of them, and in accordance to their abilities.

Our director had gone on a business trip to the United States with the purpose of studying American practices in the automobile industry. He brought back ideas about the organization of production. He often called meetings of the engineers and explained these new ideas to us but, alas, not all of them could be implemented.

The director regarded me with great favor and secretly granted me the status of "thinking engineer". I did not have any concrete obligations; I could walk about the various departments the whole day, examine production, and then set forth my considerations on improvements. This set-up was not bad for me. Many of my colleagues were green with envy but they did not attempt to bother me in any way. I was under the protection of the director himself and he was a stern man, who dealt summarily with people in accordance with the Western model of a director that he so admired. He could quickly fire anyone who opposed his program.

I often worked closely with the head designer, who earlier had worked as a chauffeur for someone high-up in the Government. For some reason he resigned from that job. Sometimes when a member of the Government dies his chauffeurs are transferred to different work. They do not remain in the Government garage. The next stage of his career was the position of head designer. He received an engineering diploma at night school. As far as I'm concerned he was not a bad person; he tried to be fair and he understood people well. His appearance was striking. He was tall, with large handsome features and a silver head of hair. By his appearance he could have been the President of the Academy of Sciences, but this very impressive looking man did not understand a thing about engineering. Once in my presence he was discussing a technical problem with his subordinates and he could not analyze on paper the forces acting on a machine part. A student of the first year would have been able to solve such a simple problem. But I cannot very well criticize him for that without acknowledging that he had a nose for sniffing out the abilities of others, and this ability is probably the main characteristic necessary for management.

He and the director were irreconcilable enemies. When the director yelled at his "generals" in his office he used the foulest language of the street or soccer field. All to whom these chastisements were related were to stand up and listen standing. The head designer alone dared to sit on the windowsill when he was being rebuked. The director could not bring himself to forgive the independence of his behavior. I related to both with a sufficient measure of respect; it was interesting to work with them, and they both spoke with me in a respectful tone. A Soviet director can spew curses at his head designer but he cannot do the same thing with a rank engineer or worker.

This was a happy time in my life, but along with the recognition of my abilities, I wanted money. An engineer-designer, which I was by official title, could not receive money for his ideas. People in other positions at the factory could, but not an engineer-designer because ideas were considered his specialty. I received a monthly paycheck which hardly supplied me with food and was not enough for clothes. I had to have my father's old suits resewn to fit me. Practically all of my friends were in the same position, except those who sought out illegal means of acquiring money. Very many people in the Soviet Union toss aside their professions because they feel that society rewards them too little for their labors. They then take any job available including un-skilled labor, preferring unskilled labor to injustice. Such people number in the several millions according to unofficial statistics that are passed around by Soviet scientists and high level economic planners.

I decided to leave the factory. I suppose my spirit of contradiction was again at fault, but I found it demeaning to have to continually ask for that which I had earned, like a child asking his parents for an allowance. Leaving the factory was a step that most would consider foolhardy. It would look bad on my records and could hurt my career. But I no longer valued such a career. Moreover, such a step was easy for me. I had no family, no responsibility other than to myself.

The administration could have refused to release me. By the laws that existed then willful resignation was threatened with court action. When the director of the factory found out about my desire to quit he went into a rage. He had considered me his disciple. The desire on my part to have a little money was seen as a manifestation of evil inclina-tions. The head designer was sincerely upset when he said goodbye to me. He said that I was being too hasty, that in the course of several years he could set me up with decent pay. In the USSR all earthly comforts take years to attain.

Leaving the factory, I decided to change professions and I surren-dered to my literary passions. I enrolled in the evening division of the

Institute of Cinematography in the screenwriting department and, upon graduating, worked as an editor at the Central Television Network in Moscow. I was one of many editors in the amalgamation "The Screen," which produced films for television. This was the era of the emergence of dissidence as a movement in the country and correspondingly the era of the authorities' battle against it. Under the momentum of the dissident movement new things were happening at various publishing houses, at film studios and on TV. Interesting films and books appeared. Formerly unknown foreign authors were translated into Russian. Of American authors we learned of Faulkner, interest in whom soon replaced our interest in Hemingway, whom we had discovered in the Khrushchev years.

But the Jubilee approached—the one hundred year anniversary of the birth of Lenin. This anniversary drew near like the clouds before a strong rain, swelling larger and larger, taking on threatening proportions. In any year, walking along the corridors of the television studios, one usually saw titles on Lenin themes posted on several doors in a row. Behind these doors sat the people who worked to bring these Lenin projects to the screen. But now there emerged special editorial offices which worked only on Lenin. Among ourselves we editors spoke of what a depressing year awaited us. Many of us were invited to transfer to the special Lenin editorial staffs, with an increase in pay. I was one of those invited. I quit television, preferring not to await the arrival of that depressing year. It all reminded me too much of the Stalin era when the name of the great leader who had brought happiness to humanity was shouted out from every wall, every page and every screen.

A few years later I heard that the Chairman of the Committee on Radio and Television, whose post was comparable to that of a Minister though actually higher since ideological work in the USSR stands above all, was fired for the clumsy execution of the Lenin campaign. The government held him partly responsible for the flood of jokes about Lenin that appeared as a reaction to the campaign. I can easily believe this story; there were so many jokes. The whole country went crazy from the multitudinous images of Lenin and from the sound of his name which was heard everywhere day and night.

I remember one Lenin Jubilee story I heard from my uncle. It was not a joke but a real life story that gave birth to many jokes. My uncle was an engineer, a specialist in rubber production. At the time he was the head engineer of a large plant in Moscow. He told me about another factory in the Moscow area where the basic item of production was prophylactics. In connection with the approaching Lenin Jubilee, the chief of the factory decided to distinguish himself and do his own bit for the anniversary. The factory issued a children's balloon with the image of Lenin printed on it. Unfortunately, when these thin elongated balloons were inflated they often burst in the hands of their frightened young owners. The director of the factory was almost fired for this foul-up. Under Stalin he could have lost his life.

When I left television during the Lenin Jubilee, I drove jeeps on various expeditions for three years, mostly for entertainment. I traveled about the North, Siberia, the Far East, Central Asia. When I was a schoolboy my favorite writer was Jack London. I read everything of his from cover to cover. Now a fully grown man, I finally satisfied my passion for travel in the spirit of Jack London, many years after the passion first arose in me. My friends laughed and said that I had traveled more than Jack London, that I should have become the Russian Jack London long ago. That is how Soviet life is: everything in it takes place way behind time. Having waited for an apartment ten, fifteen years of his life, a Soviet moves into a new apartment without any feeling of satisfaction. It is impossible to wait so long for everything.

After my travels and after the Lenin Jubilee, I returned to work in my former position at the television network and at "The Screen." Television had changed greatly during the three years of my absence. It was the beginning of the 1970's. The director of the creative organization "The Screen" was a tall brisk man who threw quick, thorough glances at people, rapidly sizing them up. He was one of a new type of Soviet bureaucrat on the ideological front. People said that besides being director he held a title of general in the KGB. I do not know if this rumor was true, but the official who stood above him, also tall and very gloomy, who used to drink cognac alone in his office, sometimes sleep-walking late at night through the offices of the organization with the movements of a ghost, was openly and directly from the Committee on State Security (KGB). The films that were subject to his acceptance he viewed in solitude, like an executioner.

We editors used to joke amongst ourselves that the majority of our bosses were either ex-military people or people from the KGB. The Soviet authorities place service at the head of television and the other mass media on an equal footing with service in State Security. Incidentally, both the mass media and the KGB are shortened in service jargon to "the organs," probably implying that they are the most important organs in the governing body. It was a depressing fact of life that our superiors were so closely tied to state security, but at the same time we editors enjoyed watching them scramble about in their own maze. Because of their high positions they were much more dependent on the system than we, and as a result they often found themselves in bizarre and compromising situations.

These bureaucrats of the new type did not bother with any discussion. They would occasionally say to a small circle of editors, "Discussion is not your business. Your duty is to execute commands. We represent the Party and its Central Committee."

I heard something very similar once from the mouth of the head editor of "The Screen." She was a woman with a very stern face and a low voice. She would occasionally listen to the opinions of others. However, when she couldn't think of an objection or a good argument she put forth the same line of reasoning as her superiors used, almost word for word. Her husband worked in the Central Committee. He was not a member but he held a post there and was an employee of the Government. I think that her husband's position in no small way accounted for the stunning self-confidence of the head editor. She knew TRUTH.

The director of "The Screen" had been a correspondent for the newspaper *Komsomolskaya Pravda* in his youth. He also knew the TRUTH, as do many Soviet journalists who work for the central newspapers. When a newly completed film was shown in the viewing hall the director sat in front of everyone, his tall figure obstructing the view. Alongside him usually sat the self-confident head editor, and alongside them someone else might sit, of a rank like assistant director but nothing lower. Behind them sat the heads of the different departments. Way in the back sat the ordinary editors. The director often spoke very loudly on extraneous topics with those seated next to him. Sometimes he would make loud comments about what he saw on the screen. His tastes were well known by all. He was wild about sentimental love stories and whenever he saw something on the screen that nibbled at his heart he expressed his approval. The head editor sitting alongside him answered through her teeth in a most unsatisfied tone: "What is this? It's full of sweetened cranberries!"

The director and the head editor often disagreed with one another. It was comic to watch as they contested over whose knowledge ought to carry the day—who knew better just what sort of TV films the Soviet people needed.

At the end of the screening the director would jump up and turn to the rest of us in the hall and inform us of his opinion of the film. If he said, "The film is good!", then everyone who spoke after him was to find justifications for his opinion, to speak at length as to why the film was good.

One time after a screening, after everyone had left the hall and was walking down the corridor, still in order of rank—the director and head editor in front, behind them the department heads and in the back we ordinary editors—I, in the seeming safety of the back position and amidst the general clatter of conversation, permitted myself to make a comment: "The film is crap, not worth a kind word." In the front row the director somehow overheard what I had said. He must have had his ear especially cocked to pick up our conversation, for in no way could he have simply overheard. He shot a quick glance back. He had to have a hold on the situation. "Who said that? What's his name?"

After this incident he never left me in peace. The pride of the bureaucrat invested with power had been hurt. He separated me out from the rest. Flames of revenge burned in his eyes. He would ask me my opinion of each film we saw in the screening room. He listened attentively to my words, examining them to see what politically suspect thoughts I harbored. Sometimes he would repeat my words aloud as if searching for their hidden meaning and disguised irony. The tiny angry flames smouldered in his eyes, lying in wait. In my eyes he saw disdain for the ruler of the destiny of art on television. From the moment I had spoken out I was continually being told that he would place my name on the list of those to be fired.

My immediate supervisors kept me on the staff with great difficulty. They repeatedly referred to my professional qualities. And, quite natu-rally, due to her own contests with the director, the head editor was opposed to my dismissal. Moreover, she liked to talk to me about business. In her low, husky voice, lighting up one cigarette after another, settling back in her easy chair, she told me one day that it was impossible to show a large number of churches, icons or crosses in the sequences of a film even if they corresponded to the content. The average viewer would accept this portrayal of religious objects as an urging to religious faith. Or she would say that a screen adaptation of Pushkin's famous tale "Dubrovsky" was not plausible because we could not portray a rebel on the screen; it might evoke undesirable associations among the viewers. She did not say undesirable associations with the present. I was supposed to understand that and I did. About the adaptation of the stories of the Canadian writer Ernest Seton-Thompson she very painstakingly explained to me that his *Stories about Animals* had to be transferred to Soviet ground. I felt that such a transfer would be completely inappropriate. I raised the point that his stories contained people with American national traits, that there was national coloring in everything, even in the descriptions of nature, and that all of this national flavor was necessary in order to bring the vision of the author to the screen. Moreover, he was in his own way a classic; it would be impossible to treat his work so liberally. I managed to uphold my point of view in the conversation about Seton-Thompson, and the Canadian writer was brought to the Soviet screen in an unviolated form. In the discussion about religion I did not even attempt to make a comment. The head editor obviously had instructions from above, directly from the Government, and there was no room for discussion, either by her or by anyone else.

Often short movie-novellas made by young cinematographers in Soviet Georgia passed through my hands. Among these there were some truly talented works. How unsparingly these films were shredded by the hand of the head editor, as if the artistic taste which she, unlike the director, did possess, was given to her in order to see and destroy art under the pretext that it would not be understood by the ordinary viewer. It is a general occurrence in the Soviet Union that high placed bureaucrats "know" what kind of spiritual food the people should consume and what kind they should not, even if the subject at hand has no relation to ideology.

Among my colleagues, the ordinary editors, two women stood out. One of them was known as "an agreeable woman in all ways," using

Gogol's expression. This woman always successfully pushed through the scenarios of her lovers and acquaintances. She knew all the gossip in the world of film and literature. She knew a great deal about the bosses of every rank and how to approach them. She was the most influential person in our department, more influential than the head of the department. We were all frightened to argue with her. The authors who were under her patronage were by no means talented—on the contrary they were quite drab—but they were endowed with the instinct of divining trends and moods and therefore they were always successful.

Another woman in our department was known as Crazy Clara. Either she was the illegitimate daughter of Stalin or she concocted this idea and spread the rumor about herself. Her mother had once worked as a typist in the Government. Clara was beyond forty years old and had always been single, but she was constantly reminiscing about this or that husband that she had divorced. Clara had obvious symptoms of alcoholism. In the evening alone by herself at home she would get smashed and call up her various bosses in order to "clarify" relations with them. They all forgave her her drunken pranks.

At one time she had graduated from a higher party school with a specialization in ideological work. She was then sent to television where she should have occupied at least a position of head of a department, but she worked as a simple editor. The Party bureaucrats evidently could not entrust her with more. At the discussion of films and scenarios she always spoke a great deal, a great deal of nonsense and a great deal about her personal thoughts and feelings. Everyone openly amused themselves during her "performances" and at her expense. Sometimes she was simply told to keep quiet because she was holding up work. Clara was offended. She would address us all and say that she was a very kind person. She was not a mean person, but she often made dark allusions to the fact that she was an employee of the KGB and, if she desired, could ruin the official position of many of us. No one believed her. Apparently for the sake of convincing us, Clara often struck up conversations of "provocation," making remarks critical of the government in the areas of film and television. No one supported these conversations and they served as another source of laughter at Clara's expense. Poor Clara bore this general mockery with great difficulty.

One night she got drunk at an office party. She yelled out in the presence of all her colleagues that she held the post of major in the KGB. I don't know why but everyone took this drunken admission seriously. After this party everyone made wide circles around Crazy Clara, no one wanted even to laugh at her. Now completely alone, Clara started to drink even more and once turned up at the police for drunkenness. But this in no way reflected on her career. The head of the department tried to fire her several times on the grounds of her being totally useless. Her supervisors invariably kept her on the list of active workers in our department.

In the office next to ours worked a recent graduate of the Institute of Cinematography—Igor Gritzkov. He stood out because he always contradicted the bosses even when it was clearly useless. In his absence the bosses called him schizoid. However, all of Gritzkov's reasoning was notable for its clarity of thought, strict logic and knowledge of the business. He loved to show the bosses that they were wrong or simply insufficiently professional. Gritzkov wrote plays in which all the characters were ancient heroes. The relations of the heroes of antiquity in Gritzkov's plays were meant to represent relations in Soviet society. Gritzkov indiscriminately passed out his plays to everyone to read. Copies made their way to the Party bureau and to the first department of the television network—the department of the KGB.

One time Igor wrote a letter in defense of Vladimir Bukovsky, the famous dissident who was then in prison. The year was approximately 1974. Gritzkov made many copies and distributed them on the desks of our department early in the morning. One of our editors was the first to come to work. He had always been considered a good comrade. He loved to drink and he loved to sing. He had a pleasant baritone voice and he preferred Russian ballads. He loved free-thinking conversations, dissident conversations. And he wore a beard. At the time our bosses were opposed to beards and sometimes bearded colleagues were not allowed to enter the premises under the pretext that the photographs on their IDs did not coincide with their appearance. So this bearded lover of song, free-thinking conversation and beer was the first to arrive at work. He gathered up the letters on the desks and took them to the Party bureau at work. Unfortunately he was a member of the Party. His former colleagues later discussed his behavior in great detail. The general opinion was that Gritzkov's letter would have wound up in the KGB's hands one way or another. However, the bearded one could have just as easily turned around and left the office.

The letter hardly could have helped Bukovsky. But who knows—what if we had all written letters?

Gritzkov was a man with a tortured conscience. He was oppressed by his duties at the network. For all of us our jobs were more like those of censors than editors. Gritzkov was fired for "amoral behavior." Perhaps for him this letter was an attempt at moral purification. The authorities understood morals in their own way. Gritzkov soon found himself in a psychiatric hospital.

Several years later, after I had quit television and was a free-lance journalist, I accidentally ran into Gritzkov. He was perpetually grinning and his head shook slightly. His hair had grayed considerably. They had tried to make him genuinely crazy—it was too difficult to make Gritzkov renounce his own views. He now worked loading freight.

I myself did not work long in television, all together only two and a half years. I got so sick of hearing that they were planning to fire me. I became a free-lance journalist. Again in the spirit of Jack London I traveled all about the Soviet Union, but now with assignment certification from the magazine *Around the World,* which is somewhat similar to the American magazine *National Geographic.*

My travels took me again to the North, beyond the Polar Circle to the Arctic, to Siberia, to the Far East, all the way to Chukotka, opposite from Alaska. I wrote about all sorts of adventures experienced by people in struggle with nature. My heroes were geologists, sailors, polar pilots, drivers on distant roads, hunters in the Siberian taiga. I had to portray their lives to be more romantic than they were in fact. Moreover, my heroes always had to come out of dangerous situations victoriously. There was no other option. No one ever told me these rules; I was supposed to have understood them myself if I wanted my essays to be printed. I sold these essays for radio broadcasts and for scenarios for short films.

Besides this work, I went out on assignment for the magazine *Village Youth* twice a year. I wrote so-called "critical material" for this magazine: essays containing criticism of the existing situation in agriculture and the position of the youth in the countryside. At the time "the struggle against the failings in agriculture" was being conducted in the country, but of course this struggle came into existence under the strict control of the Party. It was possible to write about certain failings but impossible to broach the reasons that engendered them, reasons that lay in the foundations of the socialist system. This unsuccessful "struggle" has been going on already for decades. Perhaps the fuss about it in the media calms some and gives some hope. The condition of people working in the countryside has truly changed and the press has played some part in this change, but the overall effectiveness of agriculture in the USSR has not improved. The production of food for the country remains, as before, insufficient.

The profession of journalist in the USSR is a very prestigious one. Journalists who are permanent correspondents of the central newspapers are allowed to intervene in many spheres of life. In many cases, though only if it corresponds to the interests of the government, a journalist can demand adherence to the laws and the restoration of justice where it has been violated.

In my travels for *Around the World* I was not a staff writer but only one of its correspondents. People were glad to receive me everywhere. Some people even tried to register complaints with me and I was forced to explain that I did not possess the authority of a *Pravda* correspondent. I was often told that like all journalists I probably wrote a lot of lies and colored the truth. Even so, an awful lot of people wanted to fall into that world of brightly embroidered lies.

I did not trade in lies but I had to search for heroism where there was none or where there was and should not have been—where normal work should have been without risks and adventures. The editorial staff's demand for heroism placed me in the position of a fool. The people to whom I came often understood my position and sympathized with me. Sometimes they were cynical and themselves tried to feed me all sorts of cock and bull stories. But whatever the approach, I was always looked upon as a person in a special position who could do a lot if only I wanted to.

I recall one curious episode from a trip. I was in Kolym on the edge of the country alongside Chukotka, opposite from Alaska. I made it to a small settlement late at night in the midst of a cruel frost. There the builders of a future hydroelectric station lived and worked. All around us was a frozen white world in which all living energies were directed towards battling the cold. The air seemed palpable, like a fog. The dwellings, the trees, the rocks on the mountains—everything was covered with white frost. The operating machines emitted enormous clouds of white steam. People sat behind the panes of small windows of shelters that reminded me of wartime dugouts, refuges from which it would be dangerous to show oneself for more than a few minutes.

I found a small wooden hotel, two stories high. I told the administrator who lived there on the first floor that I was a journalist. The hotel administrators in such settlements are directly subordinate to the boss of the construction site. As far as they are concerned it does not matter who comes to stay in their hotels; they will treat them as their boss commands.

This administrator said that she would put me up temporarily and then see what her boss said. On the wall facing the street in the room to which I was assigned there was a noticeable layer of white frost. On one bed there was a pile of four blankets that had been gathered up from the four beds that stood in the room. Under the pile of blankets lay a half-dressed man. On the table stood an open bottle of vodka. The man was pleased with my arrival. He got up from under the blankets, sat at the table and invited me to have a drink. He said that it was impossible to fall asleep without vodka—it was that cold. Indeed our breath hung in the room. We chatted. I asked him who he was. He was an electrical mechanic who came here to assemble a new generator for the electric station that provided the people of the settlement with electricity. The old one had broken down. Whether or not there would be light or heat in certain homes and buildings of the settlement depended on this man. Then my new acquaintance asked me who I was. I answered that I was a journalist.

"You lie," he answered calmly and in complete certainty.

I wasn't the least bit offended but I was curious as to why he did not believe me.

"Because," he answered, "I have seen how correspondents live. They're given special rooms with all the conveniences, sometimes even saunas. Correspondents are given special food which has been prepared for the bosses and they're treated to free cognac, vodka and wine."

He exaggerated a bit, but only a little bit. Correspondents from the central newspapers might live in such conditions.

The next morning I presented myself to the head of the construction project. He was very pleased to have a correspondent of such a popular magazine bestowed upon him and his project. When he asked about how I had settled in I told him about the conditions in the hotel. He immediately called the hotel and ordered them to move my things to a different room. When I returned to the hotel the administrator was bustling about with sheets. My things had been moved to a room on the other side of the staircase. I stepped into the room and was amazed. It was tropically warm, as if on another planet and not just across the landing. There were rugs on the floor and soft furniture. The kitchen cupboard held an assortment of dishes. There was a television, a radio and a record player. All together there were three rooms assigned to me alone.

Tentatively stepping behind me, like a serf who has been allowed to gaze on the lord's comfort, my former roommate entered my new lodgings. He examined everything and then went into raptures. He was filled with pride for me, his bottle-mate of the night before.

"Now I believe that you are a correspondent," he said.

The administrator started to push him back to his own room. It didn't even disturb her that this man was my acquaintance. All my attempts to have him moved into my room ended in nothing. The administrator and the boss of the project told me that this room was for special assignment only. The Party bureaucrats from town stayed here.

After a while one of the Party bureaucrats showed up. He was from the regional Komsomol and had come to check on how the local propagandists were working, to see how well they had explained the most recent successes of Soviet power to the workers on the construction project. His brains were not so inclined as to appreciate the irony of the situation. Having drunk a bit, this young man, no more than twenty-five years old, started to brag to me about the kinds of rooms that had been set aside for the "management" in other places, at other construction sites, some with "entertainment" and saunas. These privileges he also undoubtedly attributed to the latest successes of Soviet power.

I imagined what this young man, a person of the most elementary nature, still only a member of the Komsomol, would become later as a Party official. How he would rise up the ladder of his career, how he would try to get into the central ruling body, how he would hold his career dear. How completely sincerely he would suggest that all of these "special" things—special stores, special hotel rooms, special hospitals, special health resorts—deservedly belonged to the ruling comrades, and himself with them, as people who had earned a special place in society. It never occurred to him that because of these special things the people lacked the basic necessities.

I recall another construction site on the Trans-Siberian Baikal-Amur railroad. I was there during the first year of its construction. I witnessed the most horrible lack of order, which in Stalin's time would have been pronounced sabotage. Under Stalin, whenever there were construction failures they would search for people in the industrial production end who had deliberately caused the failure, that is, saboteurs. But as time passed the disorder and mistakes continued, as they always do, proving by their existence that they are an integral part of the system and not concocted by individual, ill-intentioned people.

On a high mountain pass covered in deep snow several meters high the equipment for the construction of the future railroad tunnel sat out against the elements of nature. This equipment might be called for in two, three years at the soonest. In the meantime the preparatory work had just gotten underway. They had only just begun to lay the road that led to the site of the future tunnel. Special vehicles with specially adjusted motors broke into the deep snowbound valleys, overtaxed as they dragged along the sharp gradients. I went up to a young engineer as he slipped down from the cabin of one of these special vehicles.

"What are you doing here?" I asked him.

"We are building communism!" he answered in Soviet jargon, irritation in his voice.

Speaking with me in greater detail he asked:

"Are you really going to portray all this confusion as the heroism of the workers?"

The workers truly had displayed heroism in such difficult and at times dangerous conditions. The machinery often fell through the ice on the mountain rivers. Avalanches rained down from the mountain slopes. They were not at fault because someone from management wanted to report back to his superiors in the Government that the equipment had been brought to the pass ahead of schedule, even if it made no sense at all.

Newspapers, radio and television were actually saturated with such bulletins about this construction project which the government had attached so much importance to. Everything was being completed ahead of plan. In two, three years this project would be a horrible site. A picture of incredible amounts of equipment, construction materials and human effort ruined for nothing. It was simply throwing the people's money away, racking up losses numbering in the billions. In many places along the construction site managers were fired, but the new managers in the same old harness continued on as before. More money was wasted and the deadline for finishing the project was pushed further and further back, but the newspapers did not stop writing that the plan was being overfulfilled.

Such lies are created everywhere in Soviet life, and in the end become self-delusions. I felt myself an indirect participant in these big lies even though I calmed myself with the fact that I worked for a magazine that was almost geographic in nature.

I often sensed a suppressed, though poorly hidden, exasperation in the workers at construction projects about the way work was organized. They clearly understood how unproductive and ineffective their labor was, how their occasionally heroic efforts in the final analysis went for naught. One time some workers told me that they were going to write a letter in defense of Solzhenitsyn. At that time a campaign was going on in the press with the goal of discrediting this selfless man who has told the truth about the Soviet Union. My conversation with these workers took place in the wild taiga. There were ten of us in a small van. For two weeks we ate only canned fish. As usual no one in authority concerned themselves with how these men were to live, figuring that they would manage somehow. These workers in the wild Siberian taiga, far from the bosses, far from any civilization at all, had not read any-thing that Solzhenitsyn wrote. They simply knew that he had been accused of slandering the Soviet system. People long ago learned to understand everything backwards. If a person is accused of slandering the Soviet system that means that he is an honest person who speaks and writes the truth. For them Solzhenitsyn was the personification of protest against the system and they wanted to express their support in a collective letter, fully aware of how dangerous such a letter would be for them. They were tired of keeping silent.

One summer I made a very interesting journey across practically the entire Soviet Union. I traveled with experimental drivers in three cars from the Riga automobile factory. We started out in Liepaia, a city in Latvia on the shores of the Baltic Sea, and went across the country to Vladivostok on the shores of the Pacific Ocean.

When we made this trip, the Government was preparing to make public the new constitution. It was to replace the old constitution granted by Stalin. The new constitution, as far as I knew, differed little from the Stalinist constitution. In it, however, were guarantees of the privacy of postal correspondence and telephone conversations. The new constitution, like its predecessor, affirmed the formal rights of citizens to political freedoms, including demonstrations. I need hardly repeat how well all of these promises were translated into practice after the new constitution was enacted. True, the authorities sometimes expend a little effort to create the appearancce of adherence to the statutes of the constitution, but very often they do not even bother with appearances.

When I traveled through the country with the experimental drivers, everywhere an enormous stage production was in preparation. There were general meetings at factories, at plants, at all large organizations, for the purpose of preparing in advance the warm approval of the constitution which the Communist Party intended to "give" to the people, and which no one as yet had seen. In every town that we passed through, large or small, there already hung enormous signs with the slogans: "We Approve of the New Constitution!" or "We Warmly Approve of the New Constitution!" or "We Unanimously Approve of the New Constitution!" The new constitution had not yet been officially published anywhere but its unanimous approval had already been organized and proclaimed.

The population accepted these slogans calmly, even indifferently, as it had long been accustomed to reacting to every lie printed in large white letters on enormous red banners. Again, my consolation was that I worked for a semi-geographical magazine and was not obligated to write about the "general fever" in connection with the new constitution. On this particular assignment I wrote about how great the country through which we traveled was. How beautiful the grandeur of its nature and about the good people we met along the way. And these observations were all true.

The head editor of the magazine with whom I continuously had business was considered a liberal. Previously he had been the head editor of the entire publishing firm which put out our magazine. In that capacity he tried to put into practice some of his own ideas. His career went downhill. At the magazine he had a reputation as a kind person. He always tried to help authors, especially those like myself who did not have a permanent source of income. He offered me assignments, paid me well, and established my reputation as one of the best writers at the magazine. I tried to justify his high opinion of me, and now and then took on assignments in the most difficult conditions where "normal" writers would not agree to go.

The head editor had an assistant who had formerly worked in the Komsomol. Behind his back he was called the "Gray Consul" because he tried to make everything dry and withered, to castrate everyone's writing. I do not think that the Gray Consul was personally to blame— rather it was the official politics, the official orders to the editorship of the magazine. He was only executing orders. Such a person sits on every Soviet editorial board. Sometimes it is the assistant to the head editor, sometimes it is the secretary-in-chief, sometimes it is the head editor himself. The distinctions in position do not change the essence of the job which is to see to the orders of the Party and its Central Committee for Press and Literature. The exent to which Gray Consuls have strength-ened the restrictions on literature over the years can be judged by looking at the editions of magazines that were issued several years ago. The articles, essays and stories used to be more interesting. They were even written in a more interesting language.

One of the first types of censorship in the Soviet Union is aesthetic censorship. Not too long ago the government tried to control the styles of clothes worn by Soviet people. Now clothing is beginning to escape the control of the government since so many foreign clothes have found their way into the country, especially into the capital.

For fifteen years the government battled with tight pants, a fashion from America. Under Khrushchev young men who wore tight pants and other Western fashions were called *stiliagi*, from the word "style." They were harrassed for the use of foreign styles. The police used to nab *stiliagi* and rip their tight pants along the the seams. If they did not like their haircuts, which were also seen as a challenge to Soviet style, they would cut their hair extremely short to the point that these young men looked like Soviet prison convicts. The struggle against tight pants ended only when loose pants came back into fashion in the West. After the tight pants, the struggle with beards began, and then with long hair. Now the government no longer battles against the fashions of trousers, or beards or long hair. As before, they criticize these fads but there are no "struggles."

The government has opted for a very clever maneuver. American cigarettes, manufactured in the USSR according to American license, have shown up on sale in government stores. In cafes visited by young people American music is heard from all sides, though of course it lags a few years behind. And people say that eventually American blue jeans will be produced in the USSR. Smoking American cigarettes, listening to American music, strolling about in American jeans, a substantial part of Soviet youth does not feel itself so unlucky, unhappy and deprived. In this way the government manages to head off dissatisfaction among part of the youth. Such tactics of internal politics are undertaken in full seriousness. Soviet life very often seems a parody of genuine, normal life.

My work as a free-lance journalist coincided with the campaign on language. Party directives called for every editorial board to try to bring the Russian literary language into uniformity, into a form that pleased the Party bureaucrats at the Ministry of Culture.

The materials that I brought to the magazine were edited by one woman, the head of the department. My first impression of her was of a person who was easily frightened. For some reason she was frightened when she first saw me standing in the offices of the magazine. Perhaps it was because I wore a beard. After a few minutes, feeling a bit more at ease, she sincerely smiled as she offered me a cigarette. She seemed a well-intentioned person but when she took to editing my text that initial fear again appeared on her face. As the Gray Consul probably demanded of her, or as she herself understood her task, she tried to make the text even, smooth, gray, of no character at all. Once she removed from my text references to two characters—one, that he had red hair, and the other, that he had no hair at all. When I attempted to explain to her that the one really was red-headed and the other bald, it did not help at all. She saw in these descriptions an exception to the norm and would not agree to leave them in the text.

The desire to bring all the variety of nature to one color—to gray, all tastes to one taste—the taste of distilled water, and all signs and numbers to one common denominator, is all very characteristic of Soviet reality. The system strives to take from people their individuality, to turn them into a faceless uniform mass. It is especially difficult for the creative intelligentsia in such a society.

In certain instances the authorities support individuality, but only in order to export it. The Theater on Taganka is a very clear example of such "art for export." It is significantly better known in the West than in its own homeland. Muscovites cannot buy tickets to this theater; only a few dozen tickets are allotted to open sale each day. The rest are sold to foreigners and distributed among high bureaucrats for the members of their families and their friends.

The Soviet Union is a country of deceased human hopes, unfulfilled desires, of human capabilities squandered and buried alive. It is a country covered with innumerable graves of people murdered in the literal, physical sense, and by an even greater number of graves of people doomed to a spiritual death while their physical life continues. Will these dead ever arise from their graves? There are so many of them—an entire nation, a nation that had the greatest hopes.

I sifted through my recollections as if I were totaling up all that had happened to me in my fifty-year life. I had always refused to play the games of the Soviet authorities according to their rules; I left for the sidelines. But now I was sick of even that passive stance. I did not want to lie down in that grave prepared for me in the Soviet cemetery. The final moment was here. I understood clearly that if I did not resist now my life would end.

I had finally followed their rules—all my actions were completely legal. I was legally married to an American. I had satisfied their conditions of play. But they changed the rules at whim. I could stand it no longer. It was a question of human dignity.

As I came to this conclusion I became tense. Out of anger my hands involuntarily formed fists. But I had to control myself. I had to be calm. I read in the medical instructions for fasting that during a long fast a person should avoid all stress. As far as calm surroundings and stress were concerned . . . well, the KGB did all that it could so that now, in the fourth week of a total fast, we still had to think about how to keep from going insane. But the thought itself that my mental insanity would make a lovely present for them—that they would watch with ecstatic pleasure as their ever obedient doctors committed me to a mental institution—this thought forced me to gather my last drops of energy and will.

PART III

CHAPTER 8

THE LAST ROUND

A F

I told the foreign correspondents who visited me that I would continue my fast until that moment when I had in my hand a Soviet foreign passport. Under conditions where hard rules do not exist, where laws are not observed, it is very easy for Soviet government employees to engage in deception, and I would need whatever leverage the strike afforded until I was sure that I had won.

I went to OVIR to make certain that in fact I had been granted permission at last to emigrate. They truly did confirm to me in words that "my question had been decided affirmatively." I asked them to give me an official notification on paper. They answered that not all the necessary formalities had been concluded. With this news I left OVIR.

Balovlenkov kept repeating that it could be a trick, more likely than not it was. He listed similar cases of refuseniks, some of whom I knew personally. There was one family I knew of that had been waiting almost seven years for an exit visa. They handed in their applications twice a year; every time they were refused, and every time they were told that their next application would pass through. But it never did. They were not alone—such cases abound. The authorities might very well reason that the deceived person calms down for a while and stops whatever activity he is engaged in in expectation of the improvement of his situation. When the deception becomes clear he is like a bicyclist who has lost his momentum and falls. He is no longer capable of continuing his struggle. He has to wait for the next appropriate moment.

I waited for the official written notification from OVIR. Finally a postcard came, but all that was written on it was that I should call OVIR. I called and they said that I should come in; they needed to clarify something in my affair. This news hit me like a cold shower. After the "clarification" they would no doubt change their "affirmative decision."

At OVIR I was told that they needed some sort of supplementary certificates and that I had to complete the application forms again. I asserted that a year had not passed since I first filled out the application forms, and according to OVIR rules, application forms and all the documents handed in with them are valid for one year. This stipulation was an internal rule of OVIR and not a law. If the Soviet authorities use and abuse laws at their own discretion, they behave even more callously with rules. I had to gather up the blank forms and go home.

I had constructed for myself the most gloomy prospect. I thought that after OVIR received my new forms they would tell me that these new papers required examination and the minimum time for consideration was two months. I would be forced to call off the hunger strike to await their answer. When the answer finally came two months later, the foreign correspondents would have forgotten me. The story could not possibly continue endlessly with unabated interest. In two months our group of five would no longer exist. Each of us through one means or another would be knocked off the track, through promises and tricks. Could we all gather together again? Would each of us have the emotional and physical strength? Would the West take an interest in us again? During this time the authorities could spread rumors that we had not fasted at all. They could spread rumors to compromise each of us in something. We were enemies to them and where enemies are concerned any method of struggle is allowed, even the dirtiest.

The foreign correspondents who came to visit me said that the diplomats believed that the Soviet authorities had decided to trick me, and after me all the others. The journalists and I felt that the single correct line of behavior was to announce to the Western press that I had received permission to leave, that all that remained were some insignificant formalities and that I would soon be flying out of the country. At the same time the Western press reports expressed concern that the Soviet authorities were not averse to deception at the very last moment, that a trick could be expected at any time.

The last round of the struggle began. I felt that OVIR's stalling truly was a maneuver on the part of the authorities that would wind up in subsequent treachery. The enormous staff of KGB employees receiving wages on assignment to this case had to earn their pay somehow, that is, think up new ways of smothering the story. The demand for new application forms and new certificates was obvious evidence of the proposed treachery. But this fight was carried on openly and they were used to acting in secret. In an open fight before the whole world we were stronger. This conclusive round was perhaps the most dangerous for me and consequently for the whole group, since now I, and no longer Balovlenkov, was considered the leader, according to the foreign correspondents and diplomats. This change probably came about because the press conferences were held in my room, and because of the attention my wife was attracting in the United States. The Soviet authorities' usual tactic was to pick out the leader and first settle accounts with him. It would then be easier to deal with the rest.

Interest in our story continued. Everyone wanted to know who would be the victor in this final contest. At this time it became known in Moscow that my wife had filed suit in Chicago against the Soviet government in which, along with material claims concerning my detention, there stood the question of cessation of the grain trade with the Soviet Union in Illinois. Such an action was unprecedented and no one could predict the results. Even when material losses are involved the Soviet authorities will sometimes act counter to their own best interests for the sake of world prestige and perceived strength.

LBF

At 8:00 A.M., May 31, I got a call from Andrei. He was standing in an open booth at the Central Telephone and Telegraph Office on Gorky Street in Moscow. I knew the building well. The digital clock on its facade had often reminded Andrei and me to hurry on our way lest we be late for the theater. That day Andrei had gone there to order and wait for a call to America. He had only a few minutes on the phone but that was enough to tell me what I had waited a year to hear.

"OVIR summoned me and said that I will receive an exit visa."

I was numb. Could it really be true? I asked Andrei if he had written confirmation and he said no. He told me that he had not broken the fast. I said that I would not break the fast until he did and that we must have written confirmation. He expected a post card from OVIR by Friday; he would call me then. I said, "I love—" Our time had run out.

In a couple of hours my parents' apartment was a zoo. Howard Tyner of the *Chicago Tribune* was the first to call. Howard had served in Moscow as a foreign correspondent and he understood the Soviet sys· tem. He and Jim Gallagher in Moscow offered all the help they could within the bounds of professional journalism. When Howard called to read me the *New York Times* Wire Service story out of Moscow he was doing so as much as a friend as a journalist. He also suspected a trick and he advised me to publicize the OVIR promise of release as much as possible. He advised me not to relent in anything but to force the Soviets either to keep their promise or to break their word publicly.

The decision about publicity was not really up to me. Our phone did not stop ringing. Some journalists tired of trying to get through and simply came over. Television, newspaper, radio. They asked me if I had gone off the hunger strike. I told them that, of course, I had not. We wanted proof, written confirmation. I believed that my husband would not be a free man until he stood on Western soil.

Susan and Tony believed that it was an unlikely time for the Soviets to be playing games. It seemed to them that the promise of an exit visa was the Soviets' response to the lawsuit and all the publicity. The first hearing for the lawsuit was scheduled for the day after the Soviets had announced to Andrei that he would receive an exit visa. By signalling us in this manner that Andei might be released, they undercut the potential problem that our lawsuit for an injunction presented to them.

The day after Andrei called, my mother and I took the bus down· town and all around us people were reading the newspaper with my picture right at the top. The headline read: "Soviets say hunger striker can go." We were met by more reporters in the lobby of the Federal Court Building. Tony hung back in the corner, an impish grin on his face.

The Soviets did not show up in United States District Court in Chicago, nor did they appoint a lawyer. At the last moment a woman from the United States Attorney General's office flew in. She asked that the U.S. Government be released from the case; that they not be forced to stand as co-plaintiff. She made some excuse about our not comply-ing with procedural technicalities in notifying the United States of its involvement.

"What exactly are these technicalities?" Tony asked standing before the judge. "Do you have a list with you?"

"Well, no," she replied.

"Well, your honor, I don't know what the Attorney General's office is complaining of when they speak of 'procedural difficulties.' Moreover, the United States is hardly responding in the spirit of the case."

Tony then asked the judge for a two week continuance on the ground that there might be a positive signal from Moscow regarding Andrei's exit visa. Judge Stanley J. Roszkowski turned out to be intimate-ly familiar with the case from reading all the newspaper accounts, and he set the date for the hearing on the preliminary injunction back two weeks.

That night a woman called me from Spokane, Washington. She was also married to a Soviet citizen who was not allowed to leave. She and her husband had been waiting for three years. He was not on the hunger strike. She called to tell me what Mr. Goodman at the Soviet Desk at the State Department had to say about Andrei's promised release. All the spouses knew this man fairly well since we all spoke to him so often. He told her that, according to his reasoned and experienced opinion, all of our activities, the hunger strikes, the publicity, the lawsuit, did not make the Soviets change their mind about Andrei. They would have released him in a couple of months anyhow.

I marvelled at his omniscient knowledge. How is it that the same man who always told me how unpredictable Soviet behavior was in such cases now was ready to predict that the Soviets had intended to release my husband in a couple of months? I marvelled at his arithmetic. By any calculation the very soonest that my husband could have expected permission from the Soviet authorities by quietly going along the OVIR maze was in eight months.

Mr. Goodman also told the woman in Spokane that our affair was at a very critical stage and that I ought to be extremely careful and drop everything antithetical to Soviet interests. This last comment did not jibe with his earlier statement that the Soviets were intending to release my husband in any case. More importantly, I did not understand why he was passing along this "critical advice" to a woman in Spokane, Washington, and not to me directly.

I tried to call Andrei's apartment every day hoping that they would lift the ban on my calls now that Andrei had been promised a visa. The first time I got through was at 11:30 Thursday night, early Friday morning in Moscow. I was thrilled to have gotten through, but the news was not good. Andrei had received a post card from OVIR but, instead of confirmation of his impending departure, it simply asked that he call OVIR.

I felt that they were continuing to play games with us. My alarm communicated itself to Andrei. Afterwards I felt guilty that I had not borne up better and given him more confidence. Andrei said that he would find out more about this last delay as soon as the OVIR office opened. I should call him back in two hours.

When I called back two hours later, no one answered the phone for a long time. Finally someone picked up the receiver and that deafening screech came through. The line was again cut off.

I was now certain that we had been tricked. Why not? We had been deceived all along, running after certificates and visas and work, like two mice in a wheel. So why not one more deception? My heart pounded. I could not sleep. I could not sit. I could not stand. I was too weak to pace.

That morning Andrei called. He told me not to worry anymore; he had received confirmation. He said that I was to begin to eat—that I should be very careful and call the doctor first. He said he loved me.

I could hardly catch my breath. Later in the day I calmed down, but a vague anxiety remained with me. I was not relieved, thinking that we still had a long way to go. In the days to come I received only spotty news from Moscow. Andrei's phone remained closed to my calls. Howard Tyner and Jim Gallagher tried to keep me informed but their involvement at this time was guarded. They did not want their concern to jeopardize Andrei and me, or compromise themselves. They, and the State Department, told me about the various dead ends and new demands that Andrei was facing. He had to collect numerous certificates from offices all over Moscow and I was concerned that he did not have the strength to do so. Most seriously, Andrei would not be issued an

American entry visa until he received a medical examination. Without this visa, the Soviet authorities would not sell him a plane ticket. It appeared that the Soviet medical administration refused to give Andrei this examination and the U.S. Embassy was not allowed to give him their own. I kept asking them to step in, but they were hesitant to bend the rules.

I could not relax. I had been living on the edge emotionally and physically. Despite all the attention in the press I felt that at any moment the Soviets would pull the rug out from under us. It did not make any sense for them to renege publicly but I still felt it was a possibility. The last minute delays and hassles they were creating for Andrei convinced me all the more.

My Russian friends said not to worry. The Soviets would let Andrei out, they just wanted to make the two of us sweat. It sounded so silly. Why should a superpower take an interest in traumatizing two people? How is it profitable? The best answer to this question was given to me by Mr. Lister, the State Department official who had appointed himself my friend. When asked why they were coming up with new excuses, why they were dragging this out, he answered:

"Because in addition to being bad, they're stupid."

A F

I brought the newly completed application forms to OVIR. The inspector took them from me and began to get nervous. She bustled about but did not check through the papers.

They had demanded from me certificates from all the organizations where I could have earned money as a writer, certificates stating that I did not owe anyone anything. In Moscow there are several hundred magazine editorships, publishing firms and movie studios where I could have earned money—that is, before I was blacklisted. To go to each in order to get certificates was senseless and absurd. These organizations would have refused to give me such certificates in any case. I immediately sensed that this OVIR request was a repetition of the story with the certificates from my ex-wives and I did not go running for them this time. I was correct. As it turned out, these certificates were not necessary—the inspector did not even ask for them. It would appear that this tactic was standard operating procedure at OVIR.

I was finally given the official notification on a post card bearing OVIR's stamp. It included a list of the procedures and documents necessary for acquiring a foreign passport. For instance, I had to be cleared and officially released from my Moscow apartment, and I had to pay 201 rubles of government tax. These procedures required a great deal of paperwork which was normal in the course of receiving a foreign passport in order to leave the country for permanent residence elsewhere. But in order to gather these last documents—certificates from the housing, electricity, telephone, television antenna and radio cable administrations, etc., saying that I was paid in full—I would have to go to at least eight different organizations. I feared that I did not have the strength to run around to all these places, so I announced the end of my hunger strike to the Western press and told my wife to go off the fast. It had lasted twenty-six days.

The last scandal with my neighbor began. Before leaving I was required to make general repairs in my room and some other repairs in the communal areas of the apartment. My neighbor started to yell at me that she did not need any repairs. But I was concerned with the housing administration and not with my neighbor's whims. I was obligated to see to the completion of this work regardless of her protests. I paid for the repairs to be done. When the workers brought in the paints and brushes my neighbor raised such a cry that they were forced to beat a hasty retreat.

"Misery and dirt is all I'll see from your blessed repairs," she kept repeating.

I came to terms with the technical inspector at the housing administration office. I paid him for all the repairs and they would be undertaken after my departure or not at all—it made no difference to me. But my neighbor could not calm down. She said that I owed her twelve kopecks for some sort of common expenses in the apartment, or perhaps it was twenty kopecks, she was not sure. In order to put a stop to these ridiculous claims I placed a ten ruble bill on the window sill of the apartment's kitchen. The screams became stronger. Now she insisted at the top of her voice that she was a person of principle and that she did not need my money, she had her own. The ten ruble note continued to sit on the window sill until she finally scooped it up and the argument of principles which had gone on for more than a decade was over. I did not have to speak with her again.

When I put my last signature on the certificate from my place of residence I overheard the women sitting in the passport section of the housing administration discuss my case after I had left their office. The door was open and I stood in the corridor putting all my papers back into my briefcase. They told one another about a certain resident of Kropotkin Street who was leaving for America.

"Good fellow!" one of them said. There was not a trace of irony in her voice.

These women in the passport section had continuous dealings with the police but this did not stop them from expressing their approval of my actions, though only after I had exited the office and they were left to themselves.

I went in to see the head of the housing administration office. His official post meant that he also had to be a member of the Communist Party. He took another document from me and watched as I signed it. He winked at me and wished me "Bon Voyage!"

I was left with obtaining a medical examination required by American law for an American visa. According to Soviet law, the medical institution with jurisdiction over my place of residence should have given me the examination and the accompanying certificate.

At the registration office of the medical polyclinic where I had been on the files since childhood they did not know what to do with the instructions from the consular section of the American Embassy. They sent me to the head doctor of the clinic. He told me that he would not give me an examination until he had received official instructions from a Soviet institution. To my question of which institution, he answered:

"A higher one."

Such an answer was a completely natural one for a Soviet bureaucrat, doctor or not. The higher organization was the regional medical administration. To my question of whether the regional administration was authorized to give such orders, he answered:

"They would not be."

"That means the Ministry of Health?" I queried. "But then the Ministry of Health would have to receive instructions from the Ministry of Foreign Affairs!?"

The head doctor was satisfied with my comprehension of the situation. Such orders would take at least two weeks, if not more. I wanted to leave as soon as possible, before the KGB workers who were in charge of my affair thought up anything new.

I asked the American Embassy to let their doctor give me the medical examination but they said that would be impossible. Apparently the rule that the doctor could not render aid to Soviet citizens still applied to me. When I told the American officials that the Soviet medical organizations refused to accept me, a Soviet employee of the consular division of the Embassy assured the head of the division that I must be mistaken. She said that no Soviet clinic would refuse to give me a medical examination and that I should go to a Soviet clinic for foreigners in Moscow. But there they refused to accept me because I was not a foreigner. I was advised to go to a clinic where the patients pay for services. There they refused to take me because I had no address in my passport. I now had a foreign passport and I was already struck off the housing list at my apartment although I continued to live there.

All the while that I ran about to the clinics I was frightened that something might happen to me on the street. I was afraid that I might lose consciousness. I did not have the strength to jump these hurdles set up by the authorities, much less deal with the ordinary, daily tribulations of life in Moscow administrative organizations. In short, this medical exam was killing me. I was just beginning to come out of a state of starvation after twenty-six days of a total fast. In the meantime my only food was fruit juice and I continued to lose weight.

I called the U.S. Embassy and told the Consul about my last failure at the clinic. In response he asked me to somehow, somewhere get just a chest X-ray—that all the rest would be done at the embassy in violation of the rule against treating Soviet citizens. The Consul, Wayne Leininger, had been sympathetic to us from the beginning. He always seemed truly concerned about the divided family cases and word had it that it was due to his efforts that the Ambassador arranged to meet us at the reception in his home.

In a paid clinic on Arbat Street I made a deal with a radiologist who gave me an X-ray and wrote down in the patients' log that I had been sent there by the organization "USSR Foreign Trade." After several days of constant chasing about from clinic to clinic I was finally invited into the office of the Consul to receive my United States visa.

Now I only had to buy a plane ticket.

The diplomats and correspondents asked me all the time on which airline I intended to fly. I answered that I could only fly on the Soviet airline Aeroflot, and that I wanted to fly to Montreal. From Montreal I would somehow make it to Chicago. My wife and I still could not communicate and I did not know what sort of plans she had made. There were no direct flights to the United States since President Reagan cancelled them as part of the sanctions against martial law in Poland. Everyone shook their head in response to my words and said that I ought to fly out with any Western air company to any Western capital, but not on a Soviet airplane.

I did not ascribe any special significance to these words, assuming they were the prejudice of foreigners to things Soviet. But then Soviet people began to tell me about instances when the authorities brought back people they had released on the very airplanes they had flown out on. A Soviet airplane is considered Soviet territory wherever it may be. And the power of the Soviet government is law on board.

The authorities really could make it look as if they were releasing me. They had given me a foreign passport, even sold me a ticket on an airplane to the West, but while in the air on the twelve hour flight to Montreal, something additional, "new circumstances," would come up in my case. For example, they might discover that I had done something they considered illegal and they would have to hold me even on the ladder of the plane as I made my way to foreign ground. At the same time this announcement would have compromised our whole story and the concern about it in the West. Such logic was undoubtedly in the foul minds of the KGB workers. Such an organization as the KGB cannot in principle act with honest, open methods, or its power would have ended long ago.

My safe departure from the USSR to the United States as the first member of the "Divided Families Group" amazed everyone and still continues to do so. Perhaps the KGB had prepared for me some last "unpleasantry". Perhaps they would have seized me and sent me back to Moscow just as I stepped out on the ladder of the airplane as it touched down on free soil. But the cards were reshuffled. I changed the course. The experience of the last months convinced me that the KGB was such a bureaucratic organization, like all Soviet organizations, that it needed time to change its plan of action.

When the Aeroflot clerk at the counter for tickets abroad sees a passport that is stamped "Permanent residence in the United States," his or her face changes and the tone of voice becomes icy cold. Even today the words "emigrant" and "traitor" stand side by side in the official morality of the Soviet Union. People going abroad are addressed "citizen" and not the customary and more polite "comrade." At the Aeroflot ticket counter Soviets who go abroad on official government business trips are addressed "comrade." "Citizen" is used for prisoners and people under criminal investigation who are suspected of some crime though it has not yet been proven. KGB workers strictly observe this rule of dividing the population into "comrades" and "citizens."

The woman clerk had this cold expression on her face when she took my passport. She went into a small room behind her booth. When she returned she said that I could fly to the United States only via Montreal and only on Aeroflot. I insisted that I wanted to buy a ticket to Frankfurt where I would transfer to the next flight to Chicago. Lois had arranged for a ticket from Frankfurt to Chicago and had passed this message on to me through the Consul at the U.S. Embassy. To get on the flight to Montreal I had to wait three weeks, but there were open seats on the flight to Frankfurt the next day. In order to make the flight to Chicago I would have to be in the airport at Frankfurt for all of two hours. The German government required no transit visa and they knew this at the Moscow office of Aeroflot. The clerk finally flared up at me and said that I had to fly to where I was sold a ticket and not to where I wanted. She announced to me that Aeroflot would not sell me a ticket to Frankfurt. I demanded an explanation. I was told it was because I needed a visa to the Federal Republic of Germany. This was a lie, but she kept to her story. Aeroflot would not sell me a ticket unless I had a visa.

I left the Aeroflot office and called the American Embassy. I informed the Consul of my problem. I told him that I could not stay in Moscow another three weeks to await the Montreal flight. He asked me to telephone him again in a half hour. When I called back, he told me that he had talked to the Consul of West Germany and that he would issue me a visa to West Germany not in a week, as it usually takes, but immediately, that day. It was the prerogative of the West German Embassy to waive the usual waiting period.

Two hours later I was again standing in front of the clerk at the Aeroflot office with the West German visa in my passport. I had a ten-day transit visa to West Germany. When she saw the German visa my friendly clerk's face darkened with dissatisfaciton. She said:

"Nevertheless, we cannot sell you a ticket to Frankfurt."

"Why not?" I insisted.

"Well, uhm, I must consult with my boss. He must take part in this transaction."

"I don't need a boss. I need a ticket to Frankfurt. Sell me a ticket on tomorrow's flight to Frankfurt."

She again disappeared into the little room. When she returned she confidently said:

"We will not sell you a ticket to Frankfurt. You must fly where you are sent!"

I remained cool. "Fine," I said. "Then I'll just call the West German Embassy right now and tell them that the visa of the First Consul is not being honored by Aeroflot."

The next day, along with a group of German tourists on their way home from a lovely trip to the Soviet Union, I safely left the territory of the USSR. In an hour and a half I was in Frankfurt, on German soil, and by the end of the day in the airport in Chicago.

I was met by journalists, by police, by photographers and cameramen. And my wife. My little wife who had turned out to be so strong, to have carried on the struggle for me with the governments of the two superpowers. Her whole body nestled in mine, this close and dear being. I was stifled by tears.

Chicago, America, which I was now seeing for the first time, for some reason did not surprise me or seem alien. There was something mystical in this, as if I had seen all of it before, long, long ago. To the questions of the journalists the next day I answered that the city was splendid, but to Lois I simply said that this town suited me.

L B F

On Thursday, June 17, I spoke with Wayne Leininger, the U.S. Embassy Consul in Moscow. Through him I finalized the travel plans with Andrei.

I had bought a ticket from Frankfurt to Chicago and it would be waiting for Andrei at the Frankfurt airport. I had arranged for Lufthansa to escort him from the Soviet plane to the flight to Chicago. I relied on Wayne to convey these directions to Andrei—and waited.

Midnight, Saturday, June 19, I phoned Lufthansa in New York to find out if Andrei was on board the flight out of Frankfurt. The clerk checked the manifest and reported that he was. Andrei was free. It took only an instant for the news to sink in.

Everything I had experienced in the last six weeks had had an extraordinary sense of immediacy and urgency, but hearing that Andrei was free I felt as if I had been sleeping my whole life and only now suddenly woke up. No—it was more like a sudden plunge into an ice bath; I had an overwhelming sense of the reality of the moment.

I ran to tell my parents. They too had awaited the thrill of this moment and we three revelled in it. We were exultant. We laughed about several episodes of the hunger strike, most of all about the gloomy predictions of the pundits Abrams and Goodman of the State Department.

I called Susan and Tony. They had been right in their reasoned certainty about the Soviets' intentions of releasing Andrei. I joyfully would have given them the opportunity to say "I told you so," but that was not their reaction to the news that Andrei was out. Both individually heaved a sigh of relief. Andrei's struggle for freedom had become their struggle, too, and they were thrilled by the news.

In the meantime, we had received some word on the fates of the other hunger strikers, although their cases were not resolved finally for quite some time, and in one instance not resolved at all. Three days after the Soviet authorities announced that they would release Andrei, they announced that they would release Tatiana Azure. As in the earlier case of Ina Lavrova, who had gone on a hunger strike in February and was then allowed to go to her husband in Paris, the French government had been very supportive of its citizens kept apart from their spouses by Soviet arbitrariness. Under the pressure of French involvement, even Valery Volobuyev, a biologist in the Siberian city of Novosibirsk who had announced by phone his participation in the Divided Families hunger strike only to drop out a week later, was also released to go to his French fiancee. He and Tatiana Azure left for Paris one month after Andrei came to Chicago.

Iosif Kiblitsky's health began to fail. The French doctor warned him that his body was beginning to suffer irreparable damage. He lay sick in bed when the West German Ambassador came to visit him. No one knows what was said at their meeting but the next morning, after having eaten nothing for thirty-seven days, Iosif Kiblitsky broke his fast. There was speculation in the press releases out of Moscow that the German government had secured a promise of Iosif's release from the Soviet authorities, and the Ambassador conveyed this agreement to Iosif saying that he would be allowed to emigrate if he quietly ended his fast. It would appear that German Foreign Minister Hans Genscher's personal appeal to Soviet Foreign Minister Andrei Gromyko had been effective. Iosif left Moscow two months after Andrei.

Tatiana Lozanskaya and her father were reconciled. Her father, the three-star Soviet general, relented to his daughter's wishes to be reunited with her husband in America. He promised her his support, and it was rumored in diplomatic and journalist circles that he used his influence to put his daughter's departure up for the approval of the Central Committee of the Communist Party. Once again in her parents' good graces, Tatiana stayed on in Moscow and did not leave until the end of the year.

And what of Iurii Balovlenkov? Iurii was called into OVIR the day before Andrei was to leave Moscow. There he was told by an official that his application to emigrate "had been acted on favorably." It was the forty-third day of a total fast. He emerged from the office and said to reporters: "I should be happy, but I feel so awful physically. I know they are not deceiving me, but I just cannot believe it."

The timing of the news about Iurii's release was excellent from the Soviet point of view. His was the last case of the original hunger strikers. Now Andrei was released and a new promise of freedom had been granted to Iurii. How magnanimous the Soviet authorities are! The timing of the news also blunted the answer to the question of why Andrei was the first and, at that time, the only one released. It took the spotlight off the legal action we had taken in Chicago and the important precedent it had set.

So Iurii went off his fast and waited to recover before starting the final chase for the exit visa and accompanying documents. He entered a hospital where he was given liquid nourishment for two weeks. Feeling better, he left the hospital and went to the OVIR office to get his first certificate—the postcard—that he would need in order to collect all the other documents. The official he spoke with looked surprised to see him and said that there had been no action on his case; Iurii must be mistaken. The official claimed that no one from OVIR had ever spoken with Iurii.

Iurii announced another hunger strike. Elena was beside herself; she wanted to go to Iurii to convince him to stop before his health was too far gone, but the Soviets did not want to issue her a visa. Under the pressure of publicity she was given an interview with an official at the Soviet Embassy in Washington. She stated her case and seeing that she was sincere about trying to stop Iurii's fast, the Soviets agreed to give her and her daughter a visa. They flew to Moscow and begged Iurii to reconsider. It was the first time Iurii had seen his daughter and he gave in to their pleas. Being a nurse, Elena herself brought Iurii back to health.

Iurii still lives in Moscow and Elena and their daughter Katya live in Baltimore. Iurii was told that they might release him in 1985.

Why was Andrei released while Iurii still languishes in Moscow and Elena still calls the State Department for "advice?" Tatiana Azure and Iosif Kiblitsky were released because their governments took an active stance in support of the hunger strikers. Albeit this was a minor concern in the course of international relations, but it was a violation of the human rights of citizens of the Soviet Union and of the West. The French and West German governments took the only moral position. Tatiana Lozanskaya was released due to the influence her father has within the Soviet Union.

And Andrei? Why was Andrei released? He had no influence. He had only his bravery and instinct to guide him. I had no influence and, perhaps consequently, little or no support from public agencies and the executive branch of the government.

I was greatly disappointed and disillusioned by the United States Government's failure to support us—by the State Department's seeming indecision, stalling and habit of cloaking everything in secrecy. My family and I felt as if we had been strung along. The U.S. Government was not at fault for my husband's and my situation, but the State Department did not support the interest of its citizens in a human rights violation by a foreign government.

It was baffling. Our case seemed to offer the possibility of scoring a real human rights victory against the Soviet Union. The State Department might have translated all their anti-Soviet ranting into moral action if they had actively sought the release of my husband, especially if they related to our case as a pure and simple issue of human rights, independent of geopolitical and military considerations. But perhaps that was the point. A tragic and unsuccessful resolution of our case would have scored them more points in the propaganda war between the two military superpowers than Andrei's release would have. Mr. Goodman's disclosure to me, prior to the Haig-Gromyko Spring 1982 talks, that divided family cases are always good from a propaganda point of view, kept haunting me.

In the course of one year and during the hunger strike we were led to believe that the State Department intended to take some actions, but very little materialized. The State Department's advice to us spouses was veiled in vague statements of what the Soviets might or might not do. They spoke of their own actions in the same way—what they might or might not do. All with the purpose of having us sit quietly. The most often-heard sentence was: "We're not sure what would be the best move at this time." Such a sentence, said with the proper inflection, can sound reasonable. Like a grandmaster weighing alternative chess moves. But, it seemed that the State Department was not only not sure what would be the best move, they were not even sure of the alternatives. Their system was no system. Ignore the problem and it goes away.

In its methods the State Department seemed like a mirror image of OVIR: stall and blunder along until someone decides, preferably someone outside of the department. However, in the Soviet system a decision by OVIR is final; there is no genuine recourse. Instead, the full, cruel weight of the oppressive Soviet system is brought to bear on the citizen. My husband was left with the alternative of risking his life in a desperate attempt to attract world attention to his plight. Within the American system we had recourse to the State Department's decision not to support us—recourse through the press and through the courts.

I realize fully that in terms of the difficulty and seriousness of United States relations with the Soviets my struggle to free my husband was of very little significance, but it was distressing to view the State Department's incompetence and inaction in dealing with such a small, though clear-cut case. What does the State Department's handling of our small case say for the general conduct of our relations with the Soviets?

I was indeed fortunate to be surrounded by concerned and capable people throughout the hunger strike, most of all my parents, Susan and Tony. We fought with every weapon at our disposal against the arbitrary and unreasonable actions of the Soviet government. We won using those elements of the American system that provide us with freedoms so alien to the Soviet system—the free press and the independent judiciary. This was a victory of ordinary people up against enormous odds—the sweetest victory of them all.

When I heard that Andrei was on the flight to Chicago I knew that it was over. The fear of the last year, the pain of the last year, was now gone. I had finally gotten what I wanted—the opportunity to build a new life together with Andrei. The pain of waiting had made my feelings for Andrei even stronger and my doubts about our relationship were calmed. I saw what suffering and risk Andrei had undergone in order to come to America and to me. I too had invested much and I was just as dedicated to making our marriage a success as I had been to getting him out of the Soviet Union. I knew that the adjustment would be extremely difficult for us and that Andrei would find many more problems here than he had anticipated. Still, as I fell asleep that night after hearing the news of Andrei's release, my head was filled with dreams of the joys of discovery that lay ahead. Most of all, I hoped that here Andrei could find the peace and contentment that he was looking for.

THE PSYCHOLOGY
OF AN EMIGRE

A F

Towards morning I had a horrible dream. My back was damp with perspiration. There occur such dreams which by the distinctness and precision of their details appear to be a continuation of real life. They follow on a person's heels, do not give him any peace, and leave him to wake up early in the morning still more tired and worn out than when he fell asleep the night before.

I dreamt that I had been called into the Moscow OVIR. A very polite, carefully dressed middle-aged man, with streaks of gray in his short cut hair, spoke to me in a quiet, almost friendly voice. He told me that my departure from the Soviet Union to be with my wife in Chicago was impossible because it was not in the interest of the government.

"Why?" I asked with external calm, while inside I was seething. It was as if he and I were standing on a balancing board and his even tone placed me on the same level of calm.

In the beginning of our conversation he had informed me in this same quiet and polite tone, all the while examining me with a fixed stare, that he was a representative of the KGB. However, he probably had tired of carrying the burden of its power and I was tired of experiencing its continuous, incessant, every hour, every minute pressure on my life. I had reached the end. I was ready to spit in the face of this power, and I was ready now. He sensed this exasperation, my interlocutor, beyond any doubt he sensed it, just like two wolves meeting in the forest sense each other's mood. But this forest was the Soviet jungle in which he had fangs and I was in a muzzle and chains, on a short leash, bound by my collar. In this jungle the basic laws of nature in the struggle for survival had been violated. He had complete power over me, I was no threat for him. He did not even have to bare his fangs. I could flash my teeth as much as I pleased, not frightening him in the least.

"New circumstances have been discovered in your case," he said to me sternly and secretively.

"What new circumstances?" restraining myself even more. "Since I handed in my request for permission to leave you have ceased printing my work in the magazines and for films. You tape my phone conversations, friends are frightened to call me."

He couldn't hide the satisfaction on his face. It was as if he wanted to say, "Yes, this has all gone according to plan. This is exactly what we needed."

"You read my letters," I continued, "and listen to my conversations not only on the phone but in my room too. You follow me on the street! You forget that the constitution of this country provides me protection from the government's meddling in my personal life!"

He tenderly smiled at me, as one smiles at a child, saying nothing.

"You don't even intend to deny all this. Sometimes you do your shadowing openly. Your goal is to frighten me, to frighten my friends, to isolate me from the whole world, to make me alone and helpless, completely under your control. What kind of new circumstances can there be, besides circumstances created by you yourself? Your car circles and every day produces new circumstances. And all this is done on the people's money, I hasten to add, on my own as well."

He looked not at me but to the side as if he were contemplating something.

I continued. "Not long ago I openly said to your two *stukachi* 'Who are you? What sort are you?' Is this the new circumstance—that I recognized your valued co-workers? I warned other people that they were *stukachi*, while you wanted me to work for you, pass along other people's conversations, steal their address books. Are these the new circumstances? You want one out of every two people in this country to be your co-worker, so that people fear one another and are obedient to you!"

My interlocutor looked at me as at a man doomed, he almost even pitied me. I hated him more and more. At last he spoke.

"What have you come to? You, a Soviet journalist. You married a foreigner. An American. You were warned that marriage with foreigners creates problems. And now look at how you are behaving yourself. What is written in the constitution? There it is written that a citizen of the USSR should in every possible way, with all his might, strengthen the socialist system. But what are you doing?"

I no longer could hold on to my external calm. The unsteady board on which we two were balanced overturned.

"You even turn the constitution into a code of behavior written by the KGB. You want to know everything about me—what I do, what I say, even what I think. You want to choose my wife, my place of residence." I grabbed him by the lapels of his jacket, a jacket that bore the look of being fresh from the store, and began to shake him and spit in his face:

"I no longer will live as you would like me to. . . "

It was as if he expected my prank. He calmly tried to free himself, pushing aside my arms.

"I'd sooner die of this fast I've been on for two weeks now than agree to be obedient to you. If I'm arrested I will die in a prison cell. If I'm dragged to the mental hospital, I will die in the ward. I am going to demonstrate in front of the Ts.K. Building. And if nothing works then I will set myself aflame on Red Square or in front of your monument to the Iron Felix!"

I woke up from the dream. From the windows of the room in which I had fallen asleep, from the height of the flight of a bird, one could see the shore of Lake Michigan, the green trees of Lincoln Park, the steely blue of the lake on the horizon where it meets with the sky. To the side stood the tall buildings of the city, unaccustomedly tall for me, set against the clouds. Beyond the window the wind howled like in the riggings of a ship. The endless stream of cars flowed along the highway that ran by the shore of the lake, and this stream whirred like a waterfall. From the direction of the city, black clouds and lightning flashes drew near. This world which I saw upon awakening seemed to me more unreal than that which I saw in my dream. But both were reality; one had just passed while the other arose around me like a fairytale.

In the distant dreams of my youth I wanted to live in a city, large, enormous, teeming with activity like an anthill, but directly alongside the elements of nature, alongside the wind, the clouds, the waves, the green grass and trees. I wanted this city to be unlike any other city that I had ever seen. Had my dreams really come true? Does it ever happen that everything is as distinctly clear in a dream as it is in reality? I felt that my soul had torn itself away from earthly existence. Perhaps I was no longer living. Had I sunk into an eternal dream?

I again opened my eyes and looked about the room. Alongside of me slept my wife. I felt her warmth, so close to me. It struck me how much she was forced to endure these past months. She had to suffer alongside me through my nightmares. These nightmares were my birth-right in a country with a horrible history. God granted her to under-stand all this and experience it together with me. She suffered and worried far more that I did, for I, after all, was used to such suffering. Several of my comrades had received a fate far crueler than mine. My parents died also never having seen normal life. But she, my wife, this little warm bundle of a human body, resembling a child's, loving me selflessly and devotedly—why did such ordeals fall to her lot? She was born in a free country.

Not far from me lay books that I could not read in my own country, books the reading of which was sometimes threatened with jail. These books were silently passed from hand to hand, for it was impossible to speak about them except on the street, suspiciously peering about to spy any curious ears that happened by. Could I really read and speak about these books freely now?

Recently an American newspaper printed an article that I wrote. When I wrote it, for the first time in my life I did not think about what could be printed and what could not, about what the rank and file editor would cross out, about what the head of the department would elimi-nate or order me to do over, about what parts the head editor would mark with his red pencil, or whether the entire piece would be deemed inadmissible. In the Soviet Union, after an article had gone up and down the appointed ranks several times, pushed on like a stone in a stream, made completely round, smooth and perfect, like millions of other articles, in no way conspicuous from the general mass either in shape or in color—after all this molding and shaping the article would then be read by the censor, who sometimes picked at particular words in which he saw some sorts of allusions which I never intended and yet which would be perceived in a "criminal light" by all those who read the article.

In my entire life I never saw a live censor. It sufficed that he sat within me, stood behind me, guided my pen on the paper, and reminded me every minute that if I wanted to earn a living with my pen, if I wanted to live expressing my impressions and thoughts on paper, then I should always remember what would pass and what would not pass. And if there was too much of that which would not pass, then in the eyes of all those people who read my articles before they were published I would be a poor professional who took up too much of their time. After all, they often felt and thought just as I did but, unlike me, they far better sensed the bounds within which it was necessary to hold oneself. When something I had written finally appeared on the printed page I often did not recognize my own text. It had lost its content. It had been castrated. Could I really write freely now?

Was the nightmare truly behind me, never to return? Would this city out the window that I saw through the ghostly fog suddenly disappear? When would I finally awaken?

... A year has passed... This year went by for me as it would for a person born anew. I examine the life around me with wonder. I am learning to speak, I am learning to walk and travel about the city and the country. I am learning to associate with people. I am learning to work. Everything here looks different from my homeland, and at the same time there is much that is familiar—things I had once read, seen in American movies and heard on American radio broadcasts directed to the Soviet Union. Moreover, behind the externally unfamiliar characteristics of America I see something that I recognize. It is surprising—human nature is the same everywhere. In principle an American is in no way different from a Russian. An American differs most of all from a Russian in that he lives in better conditions with a large degree of independence from the government.

I never in my life saw so many smiling people as I have in America. Average Americans always smile and always answer when greeted: "Fine, thank you." America says "Fine, thank you," from morning to night. America can say "Fine"; for her everything is ready to go and at an affordable price, everything sealed in cellophane. An American can buy anything his heart desires, and whenever possible someone is convincing him to buy more. Sometimes it seems to me that America consists solely of buyers and sellers, and of everything they buy and sell. And people smile, smile and say, "Thank you, thank you."

In the Soviet Union people do not smile as often. They buy things of poor quality from the government, and even these inferior items do not exist in quantities sufficient for normal life. Therefore, people are often in a bad temper, and insult one another with no apparent cause. But, at the Central Market in Moscow, where farmers receive good money for the vegetables and other foods that they have raised on their own private parcels of land, the picture is completely different. These people try to satisfy and please their customers. They are in good moods. They are polite, like in America.

American life staggers the imagination with its abundance. The whole country seems like an enormous supermarket where the shelves are stocked with everything that a person might desire, and in any amount. The country seems crammed full with all sorts of food, clothing and cars. And it is all wrapped so brightly that I want to put on dark glasses to protect my eyes.

Here, in America, I now find that I can have the material things for which I strove my whole life in Moscow, but I relate to these things with more indifference than I expected. I can now understand what I need better than I formerly could. Before, when I envisioned living in America, I expected to be free immediately not only from material needs, but spiritually and politically as well. These freedoms all exist alongside me in America, but I now realize that I cannot yet take advantage of the spiritual and political freedom. I will only be able to enjoy it to the full when I become an American, when I am able to speak and read in English, when I can write in English. This last achievement will remain inaccessible to me until the end of my days.

Is it not enough that no one here will disturb me, neither neighbors, nor the police, nor the KGB? Here I can say whatever I want. But to whom? My friends remain in my homeland. In newspapers and books printed in Russian I read about life in the USSR as if about life in a distant country, now closed to me, just as America had once been. I left the land of my forefathers' graves, of my native language, of my thousand-year history. Can there be spiritual freedom outside one's native language, outside of one's native culture? Can there be freedom for a lone man, freedom in an alien country? In the USSR, all my friends and I dreamed of the day when there would be no censor. Now there is no censor for me, but what and for whom should I try to write? In Moscow we all wrote "for the drawer" in the hope that someday, somehow, our work would be published. In the meantime we showed our manuscripts to friends, perhaps ten, fifteen readers, but still we wrote. Here the desire to write has evaporated. Americans are busy with their own affairs, their life—this strange, inexplicable life. They in turn cannot understand what I think about. I will not be able to see my old friends; I cannot speak or spend time with them. They no longer exist in my life.

I chose to leave the Soviet Union, but I now understand the calculations of the Soviet authorities when they deport a writer to the West. They figure that with this move the writer disappears, ceases to write. Many of these writers derived their meaning in life from the struggle for freedom for their homeland, and to them exile is equivalent to spiritual death. Who am I in their eyes? A man who has attained freedom only for himself. And have I achieved freedom?

Now I recall my life in the Soviet Union, for all its hardships, as a life in which there was a vital nerve—a goal and a striving towards it. Having come to America, it is as if I performed a surgical operation upon myself, removing this nerve, depriving myself of the goal and the striving. I am left with only recollections.

And, to my surprise, I find that there are parts of my former Moscow life that I now recall with nostalgia. Many of the apartments that I have visited in America are so splendid, yet I find myself missing those small Moscow apartments, with their still smaller kitchens, always crowded with friends.

Sometimes I feel like a war veteran who, when meeting an old comrade-in-arms, reminisces about the war years as some of the best in his life. In war, life was genuine—there were genuine friends, genuine enemies, a genuine goal. Peaceful life can seem pitiable and uninteresting. People who have spent long years in prison and in the camps similarly indulge in such recollections. It was necessary to endure a cruel struggle simply to hold on to life and human dignity, and therefore both were so dear.

Now, for Lois and me, our year together in Moscow seems romantic, full of struggle and meaning. We met in the library, went to the theater, strolled about Moscow, traveled to Leningrad. We argued about literature, about history, about politics. And all our misunderstandings ended quickly as soon as we remembered that we had enemies and that we must be together. Otherwise they could do to us whatever they liked. Now in America we are forced to talk and argue about simple and real things. We argue more often and more seriously than we did in Moscow. In the heat of these arguments I sometimes say that I regret having left my homeland. I understand that when I say such things I offend Lois very deeply. My words sound like black ingratitude towards her, the woman who did everything that she could for me and everything that I myself wanted. Then I hold Lois's head to my chest, I stroke her hair as I did in my first days in Chicago, and I beg her forgiveness. I recall her letters which traveled across the ocean to me in Moscow. In each of them were words of love. In such moments I am ready to cry.

I also do not want to be ungrateful to the country which accepted me. I have gained freedom of conscience in this country. I am not required to love that which I do not love, vote for that for which I do not want to vote, and believe in that which I do not believe. I have achieved a measure of human dignity that I formerly did not possess.

I remember very well how a person in my country might have paid with his life for a carelessly uttered word. And now the present Soviet system has replaced the terror of blood with psychological terror. Terror is terror. It is always the highest form of violence against man. Does a person deserve the title of human being if he agrees to endure this violence against himself?